How th

OPERATION
10

OPERATION 10

Hardiman Scott

A Cornelia & Michael Bessie Book

1817

HARPER & ROW, PUBLISHERS, New York

Cambridge, Philadelphia, San Francisco,
London, Mexico City, São Paulo, Sydney

FIRST U.S. EDITION

Library of Congress Cataloging in Publication Data

Scott, Hardiman.
  Operation 10.
  "A Cornelia and Michael Bessie book."
  I. Title.   II. Title: Operation ten.
PR6037.C92506   1982   823'.914   82-47542
ISBN 0-06-039011-5   AACR2

82 83 84 85 86 10 9 8 7 6 5 4 3 2 1

For Anne and John

I

The car was a brown Cortina that had seen better days. Its nearside front wing was dented, and there was rust along the bottom of the doors. Farrell disliked such neglect; a pity it hadn't seen at least a little soap and water. It drew up alongside where he was standing, in the middle of O'Connell Bridge, on the upstream side, in clear sight of the statue of the great Irish patriot, Daniel O'Connell himself.

Farrell had been leaning on the parapet, looking down at the muddy waters of the Liffey. The pale May sunlight did more to illuminate its grubbiness than to flash its magic. Farrell was disappointed. For him it had always been a dream river. Now he moved over to the kerb as the car's driver leaned across inside, opened the passenger door and squinted up at him.

"Would you be knowing the way to Drumcondra?"

Farrell returned his gaze unsmilingly.

"I drove through Drumcondra only yesterday," he said.

"Sure, and was it raining?"

"I like the rain."

That, too, was the pre-arranged reply. The driver laughed.

"Then you've come to the right place, Sergeant Farrell. Hop in now, will you? I've kept you waiting, I know." He thumped the dashboard. "The old lady's had one of her moods on."

Christ, thought Farrell, if that's the way they run things, no wonder Ireland is still divided. It was a symptom of the Paddy factor, as his army mates called it. He got in and slid the seat back to accommodate his long legs. The girls, with old shawls draped round their shoulders, sitting on the pavement with their cardboard begging trays, watched incuriously. He no longer interested them. He'd had the look of a tourist, but he'd answered their pleas with a cold stare. The truth was, he didn't know whether to despise them or feel sorry for them. Could they really be so poor, when everything around them looked so prosperous? Perhaps old habits died hard.

5

Beside him, the driver held out his hand.

"The name's Sean O'Sullivan. All that password hocus-pocus. Sure, I nearly didn't bother. Wouldn't I have known you a mile off, Sergeant, from the description they give me?"

Farrell shook his head.

"I wouldn't have known you, though."

He still didn't. All he knew was what he could see. He wasn't impressed. A cheerful, sandy-haired lad, all brawn and not much brain. Still, if he was only the go-between, then—

"You'd best fix your seat belt, Sergeant. It's the law over here, and we wouldn't want to get stopped now."

Farrell was surprised the police didn't stop a car in that condition anyway, but he did as he was told, cursing himself for not remembering. As they drove across the bridge, O'Sullivan handed him a pair of sunglasses. "Orders is you wear these. Load of balls, I say. I mean, Mother of God, you're one of us, aren't you?"

Farrell put the sunglasses on. They had broad side pieces and pads behind the lenses. He couldn't see a thing. Still, it was a sensible precaution.

"Need to know," he said shortly.

There was a pause. "What was that, Sergeant?"

Farrell frowned.

"Nothing. It doesn't matter."

The phrase was the basis of proper security in any undercover organization: to be told only what you needed to know. If O'Sullivan hadn't heard of it that was the Army Council's problem, not his. He wasn't there to tell them their business.

"Please yourself, Sergeant. Sure, but aren't you the chatty one?"

Farrell saw he was being baited, but refused to rise. His companion whistled briefly through his teeth.

"And to think," he said, "I might've got the girl to fetch. And her a redhead too. That's the story of me life, so it is . . ." He laughed ironically. "So off we go then. We'll be there in fifteen, maybe twenty, minutes."

Farrell settled himself into the seat without comment and closed his eyes, largely because there was no point in leaving them open. But the blindness worried him. He didn't like being so dependent upon someone else. And he didn't like the sensation of disorientation. So he tried to keep trace of their progress, noting the turns, but it was impossible. Hell, what was fifteen or twenty minutes when he'd already waited so long?

Sergeant Patrick Farrell, Royal Corps of Signals, was stationed at Colchester, England. He was thirty years old, six foot two in his socks, and an Irishman. It didn't matter what was on his birth certificate. It didn't matter that he had been born and brought up in Birmingham, and spoke pure Brum, flat and aggressively unmusical. It didn't matter that he'd never been to Ireland until the British Army sent him there three years ago, and then it was to the North, to Belfast. But he was Irish all right. His parents, indeed his whole family, were Irish, and he was proud of his knowledge of Irish history. His grandfather, after whom he was named, had been one of the men with Patrick Pearse, James Connolly and Michael Collins in the Easter Rising of 1916.

As a boy, in a dismal terraced house in Yardley, he'd listened to his grandfather's stories, and had thrilled to the sheer poetry of their heroism. Granda had been with Pearse and the others throughout the whole siege of the General Post Office, and had stood with him in front of the building on that famous Easter Monday morning for the historic proclamation of the Irish Republic:

"Irishmen and Irishwomen: In the name of God and of the dead generations from which she receives her old tradition of nationhood, Ireland, through us, summons her children to her flag and strikes for her freedom." Farrell knew the words by heart. "We declare the right of the people of Ireland to the ownership of Ireland, and to the unfettered control of Irish destinies, to be sovereign and indefeasible . . ."

Farrell cherished the richness and nobility of the words. He knew too how things had gone wrong and the whole rising had been bungled, and British troops, in sheer vengeance, had gone about the streets of Dublin shooting and killing indiscriminately. It had only been out of common humanity, to stop the terrible bloodshed, that the patriots in the Post Office had surrendered. It had been a nurse who had brought out the message of surrender; but if the battle had been conceded, they hadn't lost the war. That war, to rid Irish soil of the British invader, continued. Its techniques might have changed, but not its purpose: "the unfettered control of Irish destinies, to be sovereign and indefeasible".

Young Patrick Farrell had gone into the British Army. What else was there for a Yardley kid just out of secondary modern with

7

scarcely a CSE to his name and the dole queues getting longer every day? Besides, his parents approved. They were folk of little spirit, as lapsed in their patriotism as they were in their religion, and they had been worried by the inflammatory stuff Patrick's grandfather had been feeding him. Granda approved, too, but for different reasons. In a marvellous atmosphere of secrecy, in the back kitchen over tumblers of whiskey after the others had gone to bed, the old man had told him: "One of our own, in the heart of the enemy camp, boy. You'll be useful to us yet, see if you're not." So, down the years, he had been. Only in small ways, like passing information to none other than Brian Kennan when, as Director of Operations, he had come to Britain to organize a bombing campaign, and then, on his tour of duty in Northern Ireland, he'd got information to the Provisional Army Council about "Claribel"—the network of portable radar sets that could not only trace the line of a bullet but could tell where it came from. But he'd never done anything big, not until now.

On the whole, the British Army had been good to Patrick Farrell. It had trained him well, taught him some electronics, and promoted him sergeant while he was in the Six Counties. Ironic, he thought, but at any rate proof that his work for the IRA during that time was never suspected. He had an anonymous contact, a telephone number supplied by his grandfather. The old man had been out of active IRA work for years, and Patrick never asked him how he came by the number. He simply used it. On the last occasion, he was briskly cut off, and then when walking alone in civvies off duty, he was snatched from the pavement, hauled into the back of a car, hooded, and driven to a house in one of the estates off the Falls Road. It was on that occasion that he was able to give details of a new ultra-high frequency waveband which the security services were using for internal communications. He was told never to use the telephone contact number again.

On his return to England, Sergeant Patrick Farrell was rewarded with a cushy number. He was appointed Permanent Staff Instructor, attached to the 95th Colchester Communications Squadron, Territorial Army, teaching radio operations and electronics to part-time soldiers. He knew the Army meant it as a reward for good service; it was a job which only a real trustie would be given, because a PSI was left to get on with things on his own, merely reporting to his CO from time to time what he was doing. He could even organize his own time off, and most blokes would have envied him. But for Farrell it was an anti-climax. He felt he was neglected. The work was futureless, boring, repetitive, so that to his basic anti-British feeling there came gradually to be added a more specific resentment. He felt himself discarded, pensioned off before his time. The Army, he concluded, had decided that he was sergeant material and no more; he'd reached his peak, and he was ambitious enough to resent it.

At the same time the IRA did not seem to want him either. He knew there was a Colchester cell, but he had no way of reaching it. For once his grandfather was no help, and his Belfast contact had refused to tell him. He must be patient, he was told, sleep quietly. His time would come, and when it did, it would be something big.

Frankly he hadn't believed that soft Irish voice. That was just the sort of crap they sold you when they wanted you out of their hair. But he had believed all right when he was told with the same quiet earnestness never to use that number again, or measures would have to be taken. As a soldier in Belfast he'd had to tidy up now and then after such "measures", men with their kneecaps shattered, screaming in the gutter.

So they were signing him off. Well, sod them. Two could play at that game. He dug in at the Sergeants' Mess instead, organized his life for his own comfort, got himself a steady bint out in the town, and made a couple of "business" contacts round the place, where he could flog off such army stores as wouldn't be missed. But it wasn't the sort of life he would have chosen and his disposition, never sunny, grew more and more sour as the months dragged by.

Then, suddenly, everything changed. He was coming out of Williams and Griffin's store in the High Street one windy March afternoon when he felt a touch on his arm. As he turned, a young man in tweed coat and flannels pressed a folded piece of paper into his hand. "You dropped this by the cash desk," the young man said, and before Farrell could thank him he had disappeared into the crowd.

The paper looked unfamiliar. Farrell unfolded it. The message, written in block capitals, read: PATRICK—I'LL BE AT THE CASTLE IN TEN MINUTES.

If he had any doubt about the note's origin the use of his name—symbol of every Irishman—would have convinced him. He glanced round. In the busy street the brief interchange had gone completely unnoticed. Methodically, he tore the scrap of paper into tiny pieces and dropped them in a litter bin as he made his way to the bottom of the High Street. At the corner of Museum Street he saw the youth again and followed him through the iron gates into the castle grounds, past the memorial plaque to the Cowdrays beneath two huge chestnut trees, and along the path to the left side of the great walls of the Norman keep. The young man led him round the back of the keep and paused in front of a grey stone obelisk. Farrell stood a foot or so behind him, leaning into the wind, and read the inscription about the shooting of two Royalist captains in 1648. On such a bitter afternoon, there was no one else in sight. The young man glanced at him.

"The obelisk's your mark," he said curtly. Then he turned and walked in a straight line back along the path and across the thin wintry grass to a corner between the main wall of the keep and a massive buttress. The walls were rough with large clay-coloured stones and boulders, bits of flint and, higher up, lines of Roman brick. The young man stood on two lichen-covered stones about a foot from the ground and pointed up to his right. Just within reach was a narrow crevice running between two blocks of stone.

"When everything's ready you'll get a letter through the post saying your Aunt Mary's died. Five days after the letter's date, your instructions will be here. Is that clear?"

Farrell nodded. There were a hundred questions he wanted to ask, but this was neither the time nor the place.

The young man stepped down and walked swiftly away, leaving Farrell alone on the grass, his pulse racing. So it hadn't all been crap. There really was something—and something big. A moment later an Indian girl, sheepskin coat over her yellow sari, came round the corner of the keep, camera in hand. Farrell gave her a friendly smile as she walked down to read the inscription on the obelisk, and then he went back along the path.

He never saw the young man in the tweed coat and flannels again. But it all happened precisely as the youth had said. A few weeks later the letter arrived, apparently from his father. Farrell went to the drop at the castle on the day appointed, and his instructions were waiting for him, neatly typed, in a waterproof plastic envelope. He was given a date to be in Dublin ten weeks later. He was to wait in the middle of O'Connell Bridge, on the upstream side, at three in the afternoon. A car would pick him up, identification procedures were set out, and he would receive further orders at a secret meeting place.

When he left the castle grounds Farrell was exultant. Something big, it had to be. Something involving his position in the British

Army, otherwise they would never have given him so much notice, plenty of time in which to arrange leave without arousing suspicion. With his training and background, he might even be commanding an important operation. But what was the point in speculating? He'd find out soon enough.

He went to see his commanding officer the following day. There was no problem in fixing a whole week off early in May. It would be his first visit to the Republic, and he meant to make the most of it. He felt he was at long last going home—his true country. And Ireland, apart from the grubby Liffey and the beggar girls, had more than lived up to his expectations.

At Dublin airport he hired a car from the Murray desk and drove slowly into the city, passing indeed through Drumcondra. But he turned off so that he could drive along the shore of Dublin Bay. It sparkled in the sunlight. There was a different blue to the sea, a different green to the fields. A brilliance, a purity, a freedom. This is what it's all about, he told himself, breathing the salty tang of the sea air into his lungs.

For the next few days he travelled the country widely. But it was Dublin that meant most to him, with the statues of its many heroes, and the places, the holy places, known to him only as names in his grandfather's stories. Ah, there was history around him in every stone, evidence of an unquenchable courage, and still the dream had not been realized, still there was a part of Ireland not of the Republic, not independent and free.

He had waited a long time for this moment, and now it had come he would not fail. He would not fail his Granda. He would not fail himself. He would not fail Ireland.

"We're nearly there now, Sergeant. And how is it you're feelin' behind them goggles?"

Farrell shifted in his seat and turned his head towards his companion.

"Fine, thanks. Fine . . ."

Perhaps he'd been too quick in judging O'Sullivan, too harsh. The man was active in the Cause, and clearly trusted.

"Do you do a lot of this sort of thing?" he asked, trying now to be friendly.

"Now and then. Now and then . . . I've done me training, mind, but I've not been in action yet, more's the pity. And I wouldn't be knowin' what the Army Council has in mind for us now, so it's no use you asking."

Farrell smiled. "And if you had, you wouldn't tell me."

"Right." O'Sullivan laughed, and slapped the steering wheel. "Right, boyo."

A moment later the car turned up what had to be a side road, because they left the sound of traffic behind. Another couple of minutes, a sharp swing to the left, and they crunched on the gravel of a driveway and stopped.

"Journey's end," O'Sullivan announced. "And by the look of things we're the last ones in. Orders is you're to keep the glasses on till you're inside and seated. That's the way it is. I'm sorry."

Farrell approved. If this was a safe house then they wanted to keep it that way. And what he didn't know he couldn't let slip. He opened the car door and waited for O'Sullivan to come round and help him out. They crossed the drive and went up a short path. He climbed four shallow stone steps, feeling each one with his toe. The door ahead of them must have been already open, for they went straight in. There was a strong smell of institutional floor polish. They walked down a long hallway, paused as if waiting to be directed and then, still in silence, turned left and went on.

Farrell felt they were in a room now; the floor was still bare but their footsteps no longer echoed. O'Sullivan stopped, a door closed behind them, and a hard wooden chair was pushed against Farrell's calves. He sat down. There were small sounds of movement about him, the shifting of papers, a cleared throat.

"You can take your glasses off now, Sergeant Farrell."

He did as he was told. The voice, that of an educated Irishman, clearly came from the lean man hunched forward over the plain deal table in front of him. There were three men on each side of him. So this was the Army Council, Farrell thought, or at least part of it. And this man was their leader, their Chief of Staff. His clothes were nondescript, even ill-fitting, but his authority was so obvious he might have been in uniform. He didn't look much older than Farrell himself, and had long but well-trimmed hair. Perhaps that unmistakable authority was in his eyes that stared darkly bright behind pale-rimmed spectacles with a peculiarly unyielding intensity. Farrell met their gaze, and held it, knowing he was being judged. The silence lengthened.

"You kept us waiting, Sergeant." And still the gaze didn't falter. Farrell licked his lips.

"I'm very sorry, sir."

He had been in the ranks long enough to know that officers hated excuses, attempts to shift the blame. Beside him, O'Sullivan burst anxiously into a babble of explanations: an accident blocking the road, the Garda out in force, a five-mile detour, none of it with any vestige of truth in it.

The Chief of Staff spoke through him, as if unaware of his existence.

"I'm sorry about the precautions," he said briskly. "They make punctuality difficult. But I'm sure you understand our reasons."

Farrell nodded. He essayed a little dry humour.

"I'd have been worried, sir, if you'd sent me a postcard with this address on it."

The Chief of Staff remained unsmiling. But he relaxed his gaze at last. Beside him on the table a lighted cigarette rested in a black plastic ashtray, a thin column of smoke rising from it, completely straight in the still air. He lifted it to his mouth, drew on it fiercely.

"Except for O'Sullivan, your companions have come here in a similar manner. You will leave the same way. The man on your left is Liam Grady."

Such was the Chief of Staff's hypnotic power, that for the first time Farrell realized that he and O'Sullivan were not alone on their chairs in front of the watchful men at the table. The room, too, came into focus: large and bare with a blank notice board on one wall, a desk with typewriter, and a filing cabinet, the long central table and a number of hard wooden chairs. Outside the window he could see, through the trees, something that looked like the corner of a playing field. Were they in a school? he wondered.

The Chief of Staff let cigarette smoke trickle slowly up over his top lip.

"Grady is fresh from the North," he said. "He's one of our best men. You don't need to know any more—at least until he chooses to tell you."

Farrell turned. Liam Grady nodded coolly, his grey eyes observing and assessing. He was a small man, his frame hard and sinewy, and there was a tension in him that crackled like electricity.

"The fourth member of the team is Maura Lynch. Until two years ago she was a nurse. Her skills will be particularly useful."

Farrell began to turn again, checked. "Fourth member?" he asked uneasily. "Who's the third?"

"You'll be needing a driver. O'Sullivan's he."

Farrell frowned. He had feared as much, and only hoped the Council knew what it was doing. He faced the girl on his right.

"Good afternoon, Miss Lynch."

"And good afternoon to you too, Sergeant Farrell."

Her smile was faintly mocking. She was a strange one to be in the Army, he thought: wide blue eyes, long auburn hair, her voice as beautiful as her face and figure, rich and well rounded.

The Chief of Staff drew on his last inch of cigarette, then stubbed it out.

"Patrick Farrell here is a sergeant in the British Army. He's helped us before, and we trust him."

Now that the introductions were over there was a general shifting in the room, an easing of cramped muscles. Farrell glanced along the line of men behind the table. They were surprisingly ill-assorted, from a range of different walks of life, men who worked with their hands and men who worked with their heads. But they were all of them Irishmen, united in the Cause, and he was proud to be of their number.

One of them, a foxy individual with the look of a bookmaker, caught Farrell's eye and winked at him. The sergeant lowered his gaze hastily.

The Chief of Staff removed his spectacles and polished them on a spotless white handkerchief.

"I won't waste your time," he said. "You'll have guessed there's something big in the wind. In fact it's probably the biggest single operation any active service unit of the Irish Republican Army has been asked to do in recent years." He paused. "And if you wonder why you four in particular have been chosen, the answer's simple. Apart from your skills, which we take for granted, what you four have in common is that you're totally unknown to the British security forces. Your names are on no lists, your work up to now has been undiscovered. You can enter Britain openly and go about your business without fear of surveillance. And that ability is central to what must be done. Your stay in Britain will be lengthy. During some of the time you'll be hunted by just about the biggest British police operation ever. And there must be no leads, no leads whatsoever."

His tone was undramatic, his voice quiet. He replaced his spectacles, and leaned forward across the table.

"Three of you—and another—will be living perhaps for six

weeks or more in cramped quarters, under extremely difficult conditions. The fourth member of your team will be your only contact with the outside world. You will be in daily danger of discovery, and quite powerless. Not everyone can face that kind of thing—the isolation, the tension. If any of you feel you can't, now's the time to say so. Far better to back out now. I don't want any false pride endangering the entire operation."

A hush descended on the room. The Chief of Staff looked slowly at each of them. Farrell met his eyes squarely. Sounds like a kidnapping, he thought. And me the outside man. So who's worrying?

The Chief of Staff's gaze lingered, and then moved on. Finally he sat back, took a cigarette from a gold box, tapped its end thoughtfully on his thumbnail, then lit it.

"What," he said, "do you imagine is the object of this operation—of all Irish Republican Army operations for that matter?"

Farrell opened his mouth to speak, but Liam Grady, on his left, got in first.

"To get the bloody Brits out of the North," he said fiercely, chopping the air dramatically with one hand. "A united Ireland."

The Chief of Staff nodded.

"Exactly. And what's happened? Two thousand and more dead in the province, the mainland repeatedly bombed, Mountbatten, Warrenpoint—and we're still no nearer getting the British out than we ever were. Sure, there's some would say that for God knows how many years we've been wasting time and money and good Irish lives."

There was a movement on either side of him, fingers drummed, frowns, the shaking of heads. Farrell saw Grady, his lean body suddenly rigid, come near to protesting openly. Clearly this was an uncomfortable thought, and one not universally shared.

"Be that as it may," the Chief of Staff went on, "be that as it may, the time has come for what the politicians call a 'new initiative'." He allowed himself a thin smile. "Only in their case that means a lot more talk, and in our case it means action. But a new kind of action—one they haven't faced before. Action," he repeated firmly, "that will get the British army of occupation off Irish soil by Christmas."

He broke off, contemplated for a moment the glowing tip of his cigarette. When he continued his voice was hardly more than a whisper.

"Always assuming, my friends, that they want to get their bloody Prime Minister back safely in one piece, and in as much of her right mind as she'll ever be."

2

There was an immediate silence, almost as though the atmosphere itself had gasped. Then Farrell felt like laughing aloud. So that was it. He'd been right—a kidnapping. But he'd never, in a thousand years, have guessed the victim. It made good sense, though. Margaret Thatcher—since the deaths of the hunger strikers—was the woman most hated by every Irishman. And even if those stories about dissension in her Cabinet were true, was there one of them who'd stick to his guns and let her die? Principles were all very well—international commitments to resist terrorist demands—but which minister, which Tory Cabinet, would stand by and let Margaret Thatcher be killed? Not a chance of it. The British Army out by Christmas? Christ, they'd be pulling out long before then.

The Chief of Staff smiled again.

"I see by your faces that the idea appeals to you. But I must emphasize this whole operation calls for the greatest skill, dedication and determination, and perfect planning. Move against a head of state or, in this case, a prime minister, and you've got the whole of the so-called civilized world against you. Remember what happened when that madman tried his luck on Reagan. Suddenly the American President was everyone's hero. The same will happen when we snatch the Iron Lady."

His use of the nickname caused a ripple of amusement. He quelled it by staring intently at the four in front of him.

"It's an important thing, but a dangerous thing we're asking of you. It could fail. The chances of that are very small. But if it does fail, then you must be prepared to kill—not in the heat of action, but coldly, secretly—to kill not only what the world will see as the British Prime Minister, but a helpless woman. For that's what she'll be: a helpless woman."

On Farrell's left Liam Grady leaned forward.

"Bobby Sands was helpless," he said savagely. "And she killed him, and the brave boys who followed him without a thought."

There was a long silence. Grady's words, emotionally loaded as they were, had obviously struck a powerful chord of sympathy in the room. Farrell hunched his shoulders. Such talk made him uncomfortable. Oh, he'd work for the Cause all right, and die for it if necessary. And he'd kill in cold blood if he had to. But he couldn't see the deaths of the hunger strikers in such simple terms. He wondered uneasily if that made him any less of an Irishman.

The Chief of Staff missed nothing. "Something bothering you, Sergeant?"

"No, sir." Farrell hesitated. "Justifications, maybe. I don't think a soldier needs them. They clutter his mind."

The Chief of Staff's gaze sharpened. "Everyone's different, Sergeant Farrell. You'd best remember that."

"Yes, sir."

The reproof was fair, and he accepted it. But now he was wondering, if the four of them were going in as a team, who would be the leader? He had assumed he would be. That's why they'd brought him out of hiding—to command the big one. Now he began to have doubts.

The Chief of Staff sat back. He seemed satisfied.

"The operation is to be code-named '10'. Its strength lies in its simplicity. We take the British Prime Minister hostage, and we don't release her until we get a guarantee that all British troops will be withdrawn from the North, and positive steps have been made towards reuniting our divided country. Plans already exist for proper elections and the necessary constitutional changes." He paused, drew on his cigarette, then stubbed it out. "If the British Government wants to retain any degree of international respect, it will be quite impossible for it to go back on such moves at a later date. Sure the Proddies won't like it, but if they cause any trouble, the responsibility will be theirs, and theirs alone."

There was a general murmur of agreement from behind the table. The Chief of Staff reached for his packet of Benson and Hedges.

"I've talked enough," he said, turning to the bulky, blue-chinned man on his right. "I'll hand over to the Operations Officer. He's dealt with Operation 10's detailed plans."

The senior officer moved the green loose-leafed folder that had

17

been lying on the table at his elbow, and opened it. He was an abruptly-spoken man, businesslike, with dark, sleeked-back hair and a gold ballpoint pen which he had the habit of clicking repeatedly open and shut as he talked. Farrell noticed that not once during the whole of the briefing did he refer to the folder in front of him.

"We see this operation taking place in the autumn," he began, "after those party conferences and when the British Parliament has, returned from its summer recess. You'll need all that time to survey the ground, make your preparations. There must be no mistakes. Grady goes over first, early next week, sets up a base in London. He's the team leader. From today on all orders come through him. OK?"

The question seemed general, scarcely more than a matter of form, but the Operations Officer's gaze settled pointedly on Farrell. The sergeant had felt a sudden spasm of disappointment, but now he thought about it. Liam Grady wouldn't be an easy man to work with. He was clearly a fanatic, and fanatics could be dangerous. But he was also the man most experienced at this sort of work. And anyway, the Army Council wasn't exactly asking for Farrell's advice: they were demanding his obedience. He gave a token, almost imperceptible nod.

"Grady is the overall leader," the Operations Officer continued, "because he will be the one constantly in touch with the main situation. You, Sergeant Farrell, on the other hand, will work largely on your own, organizing transport, the hostage's quarters, provisions and so on. Although ultimately responsible to Grady, you will be required to exercise initiative of a high order."

Farrell smiled inwardly. He's offering me a sop, he thought. He recognizes I'm the senior man and he's trying to make things right. Well, let's just see. Let's just wait and see what all this initiative is going to amount to.

The officer clicked his pen.

"As soon as Grady has found secure accommodation he'll send for Lynch. O'Sullivan will follow as soon as he can get away. You won't contact any of the lads in Britain, and you won't mix with the Irish community. The Brits have undercover men everywhere. Don't underestimate their Special Branch. Sergeant Farrell, of course, remains in Colchester, and carries on completely as normal. You'll have to work out between yourselves a safe way of communicating. There should be plenty of time — three to four months — for detailed on-the-ground planning and organization.

"The pick-up will be made in Whitehall, at the entrance to Downing Street. At 3.15 on Tuesdays and Thursdays, when the House is sitting, the Prime Minister answers questions in the Commons. She is driven across from Number 10. This is an invariable rule and follows a set routine. The subject travels in a black Rover coupé of the older 3.5 type. She is accompanied by a single detective who sits, conveniently for us, in the front alongside the driver. The car has armour protection—beneath and at the sides. The doors are locked. The glass may be bullet-proof—we're not sure of that—but it can be broken with a reasonably-sized sledge-hammer."

He had been rattling off this basic information. Now he took a deep breath and spoke more slowly, making every word tell.

"You will kill the detective and the driver. And anyone else who gets in the way. You must be prepared to be completely ruthless. Such deaths are necessary. That way the British Government is left in no doubt that the Prime Minister risks the same fate. There must never be the slightest doubt in anyone's mind that if our demands are not met within a reasonable time the Prime Minister will be executed. If she resists during the pick-up, use violence, but as little as necessary. She's not to be seriously harmed, and remember your medical facilities afterwards will be strictly limited. Once the subject is in the pick-up vehicle Lynch will administer an injection. This will keep the subject quiet for five or six hours, sufficient time in which to get safely out of London and away."

He relaxed slightly. "So far so good. Any questions?"

Farrell waited. When nobody else spoke he cleared his throat.

"Am I to provide the weapons?" It wouldn't be easy, but it could be managed.

The Operations Officer shook his head.

"Grady will collect the weapons from the Iraqi Embassy in Queen's Gate. You will be provided with hand-guns and two automatic rifles, probably Kalashnikovs, together with ammunition and smoke grenades. Grady and Farrell will be responsible for the shooting. O'Sullivan will drive, and Lynch will deal with the subject."

"A pleasure, sir, and that's the truth."

Maura Lynch laughed softly, her tone bitterly ironic. The Operations Officer ignored her.

"Any further questions?"

19

"This pick-up vehicle, sir." Grady was quicker this time, eager to establish his leadership. "Do I understand that's the sergeant's responsibility?"

"No. He'll be supplying transport for the final journey out of London. You'll be switching to that in a private underground garage about two and a half miles from Whitehall. As to the pick-up vehicle, we're leaving that to you. Just make sure it can't be traced back to any member of the team. As the COS said, at the moment you're all unknown. We want it to stay that way. Nothing makes the Brits more edgy than not knowing who they're looking for."

"And communications, sir?"

"None. You'll be given an Irish number to call, but if you use it that'll mean you're blown. If you succeed, we'll hear it soon enough from the media. You'll simply hide up with the subject, say nothing, do nothing. All contacts with the British Government will be handled from this end. And all statements and press releases will be made by us."

"And we'll have the field to ourselves, sir—nothing else going on?"

Grady spoke tensely and sharply, again asserting his new authority.

"Ah now," said the Operations Officer, "we're planning just one or two—to show them that we're serious. But they'll be done as special operations, not by any of the lads over there, because the police will be picking up every suspicious Irishman in sight."

"And the Garda will be looking for you, too," said Grady.

"They will too. You can leave that problem to us."

There was the merest hint of a self-congratulatory smile.

"When the time comes either for the subject's release, or for her execution, there will be a coded message in the deaths column of *The Times*. We'll go into that later. If she's being released, then a safe conduct to Ireland for the lot of you will be part of the deal. In the remote likelihood of her execution, you'll have to make your own arrangements. Take that into account right from the beginning. Remember, always leave a way out." He paused, his pen clicking in the silence. "As to the final transport, Sergeant, we'll be needing an army vehicle, and an excuse for you to be driving it to London. Our information is that this should present little difficulty. Is that correct?"

Farrell thought quickly. "Quite correct, sir."

Wherever their information came from it was bloody good. As a PSI to the Terriers, he had a couple of Land Rovers allocated to him. It wouldn't be difficult for him to find a reason to take one of them to London—perhaps with some surplus communications equipment for the barracks in Albany Street.

"May we know where we'll be taking the . . . the subject?" he asked.

The Operations Officer smiled.

"I wondered when somebody was going to ask that. You'll be taking her to Colchester Barracks."

If he had been hoping for a reaction, he got it.

"Holy Mary, Mother of God . . ."

These heartfelt words were the first O'Sullivan had uttered since the briefing began. Maura Lynch's hand went up, startled, to her mouth. Grady shrugged, studiedly calm, and crossed his legs. Farrell wrinkled his brow. Obviously the Army knew its business. London and Colchester cells between them had done a good job. But as to hiding-up actually in the barracks—it sounded crazy. What did they know that he didn't? He racked his brains.

"Which is why, of course," the Operations Officer was saying, "we need an army vehicle for the final stage of the journey. Not to mention getting through the inevitable road blocks. That'll be far easier if—"

Suddenly Sergeant Farrell slapped his forehead.

"Abbey Field!" he cried. "All those old married quarters . . ." He checked himself, realizing that the Operations Officer had stopped talking and everyone was looking at him. "I'm sorry, sir, but I've only just seen it. And it's brilliant—the last place, the last place on earth anybody'd ever think of looking!"

"I hope you're right, Sergeant." The gold pen was still at last. "And now that you've worked it out for yourself perhaps, as someone who knows the area, you'd care to describe it for us."

Farrell hesitated, then stood up and moved to one side of the room where he could see both the other three team members and the men behind the table.

"Colchester," he said, "is a major military garrison—has been for two thousand years. Recently there's been a lot of relocation of personnel." He slipped easily into the jargon. "They've been given new accommodation. Then again army numbers are down. Among the 9,000 people in the garrison buildings no more than 4,000 are troops. So there are plenty of derelict or semi-derelict buildings."

He paused. He was quite enjoying himself. He'd been an instructor long enough to do this sort of thing easily and well. He decided to go into some detail.

"The garrison buildings, housing the 7 Field Force, are dispersed widely. There are, for instance, cavalry barracks, with whole blocks that are empty. They're in quite decent condition too. But they do get used occasionally, often without much warning. You can never be sure. They're used during the Colchester Tattoo, and sometimes as a transit camp. We might be lucky, but I'd say it's not worth risking."

He folded his arms.

"Abbey Field, though, is a different matter. It's mostly a big sports area, but there's one section that's totally neglected. No one ever goes there. It's a group of two-storey blocks that used to be married quarters. Everyone was moved out back in May '78. A local councillor tried to get the Army to convert them into council housing, but nothing came of that. They're due for demolition but nothing will happen for at least another year, maybe more. Occasionally kids play around there, but not often now they've broken all the windows, and many of the buildings are well boarded-up. The perfect place, I'd say. And no problems about access. There's a public road not a hundred yards away, and a piece of wasteland between it and an unused side road that goes across the entrance to Abbey Field. Keep out of sight and we could stay there for ever. There'll be no electricity, of course, and the only real snag is that there won't be any water either."

He looked at the Operations Officer, stiffened briefly to attention, and then returned to his seat. Grady avoided his eye, but O'Sullivan smiled at him and Maura Lynch clapped silently.

The IRA officer waited till he was settled.

"Thank you, Sergeant. Your information matches exactly what our man on the spot has provided. As for water, I understand there's a mains cock in what used to be the drying area. It should be possible to get that turned on for you. Otherwise, you'll have to rely on outside supplies, as you will for all your provisions, bottled gas for lighting and heating, newspapers and so on. Boredom will be a serious factor. Incidentally, once the Colchester cell has done what it can about the water, they're being pulled out. Any unnecessary risk is one too many. You'll be on your own—the three of you in Abbey Field with the subject, and Sergeant Farrell on the outside to provide whatever back-up may be necessary. Understood?"

Grady shifted his chair.

"We'll be there some time? A week or two?"

"At least." Now the Chief of Staff took over again. He gestured sharply with nicotine-stained fingers. "It's no use pretending that what we are demanding can be arranged overnight. We'll set several preliminary deadlines, of course, but we must be prepared to give it six weeks or more if we have to."

Grady frowned. "I'll want that much food in ahead of time, sir. And blankets, mattresses, that sort of thing."

"You'll get them. I'm sure Sergeant Farrell can arrange it."

This was hardly a question, but Farrell chose to treat it as such.

"No trouble there, sir. Once I know which flat I can start stocking it up at night." He considered. "I can win quite a bit from the Army, sir, but there'll be things I'll have to buy. Will that be . . . ?"

The Chief of Staff's eyes were cold behind his pale-rimmed lenses.

"This isn't a shoestring operation, Sergeant. It's far too important for that. Naturally you'll receive proper funding." His expression softened. "I appreciate your concern, however. It's true the American support fell off rather badly—what with mealy-mouthed Sean Donlon in Washington and Kennedy busy selling us short with one eye on the Presidency next time round. But it's picked up no end since the hunger strikers—flooding in it is. And we have other sources, too, of course." He offered one of his rare smiles. "The banks have been having things pretty easy of late. We could always call on them for a contribution or two."

Farrell smiled also. He knew what that meant: contributions at the point of a gun. Well, the banks were rich—they could afford it.

"Anyway," the Chief of Staff continued, "we'll be concentrating all we have on you. Apart from a bomb or two to underline our seriousness, other operations in Britain can wait. After all, if you're successful, they won't be needed. Remember, your job, first of all, is to have the right equipment, everything that's necessary, at the right time and in the right place. Secondly, you need to know exactly what to do, and you need to do it—without fail. There'll be no second chances. Bungle this one, and we'll never get within a mile of the Iron Lady again. Oh, she'll boast that she won't be restricted—they all do. But there'll be security men coming out of the woodwork six-deep around her."

He stood up, and everyone else in the room with him.

"Right then, I believe that's everything. There's a place down the corridor where the four of you can get together now and sort out details. You'll leave here as you came, and you won't meet again until Grady sends for you in London. Just remember, the hopes of all Ireland go with you. On that day in October you can alter the whole course of Anglo-Irish history."

As the four of them reached the door, the Chief of Staff called after them.

"Grady—stay a moment, will you?"

They went out, leaving Grady behind. O'Sullivan, who knew his way about, took them into a small room at the end of the corridor. Farrell, ever watchful, saw that he had been right to guess that they were in a school. The corridor was scuffed with children's feet and the room they went into had "Bursar" printed on the door. But its window looked out on a blank wall. A school it might be, but where it was he'd never know. He was relieved. Security was good. The Army knew its business, and that was reassuring.

O'Sullivan went straight to the desk, flung himself into the chair, and put his feet up.

"Mother of God, and isn't this the big one!" He scratched his chin. "D'you reckon we can do it?"

Farrell, standing by the window, didn't bother to answer. It was action, and going into action, you didn't ask if you could do it. You did it.

The girl perched on the edge of the desk.

"We can do it," she said evenly.

"You speak for yourself, darlin'." O'Sullivan ruffled his sandy hair. "Picking Grady I can understand—and you too. With that hard-faced bitch to deal with they'll need a woman. But why they chose me is past all knowing. And me that's only done me three months' basic."

Farrell swung round. The other man was too much the stage Irishman. It irritated him.

"You can drive, can't you?"

"Sure, but you know I can. Didn't I just—?"

"Then that's why you're here. We need a driver. You're it."

His tone indicated that in his book drivers were the lowest possible form of human life. O'Sullivan's affable manner changed. His feet remained up on the desk but his fists clenched and there was a sudden tightly-strung alertness that suggested a temper only barely held in check. Pointedly Farrell turned his back.

Maura yawned, as if unaware of the tension.

"What a pair of dummies you two are—don't you ever listen? Didn't the Chief make it plain enough? The reason we've *all* been picked is that the Brits have nothing on us—and there can't be many Provos that's true of. So the fact is, we're a job lot."

She had spoken humorously, but Farrell knew what she was doing. They were supposed to be a team and already, right at the beginning of the operation, he had come near to provoking a quarrel. Sure, so he was a professional and they were only amateurs. But that made the responsibility all the more his to see that things worked out properly. He changed the subject.

"I wonder what she's like?" he said. "Mrs Thatcher, I mean."

"The Iron Lady?" Maura's voice hardened. "I don't care what she's bloody like."

"You'll be stuck with her, though, for quite some time."

He looked at her. The girl seemed oddly overwrought. She jerked her head savagely.

"But they're all the same, you know. It doesn't matter what they're like to begin with—they're all the same once you've got them where you want them."

Farrell frowned. "You've lost me," he said.

She laughed harshly. "I'm not surprised—you've never seen it." Suddenly her eyes were over-bright, the tendons in her neck standing out like ropes. "But I have. Oh, I've never done it. It was never my department, thank God. But I've watched others, and I know how."

"Never done it?" He felt an unreasonable chill. "Never done what?"

Maura checked. She seemed slowly to come to herself. She relaxed, put one finger up to the side of her nose, smiled round it.

"Ah now," she said softly, "and wouldn't that be telling?"

It was no answer but O'Sullivan, clearly bewildered, guffawed loudly at what he took to be a double meaning.

"Done it? I'm surprised at you, Sergeant. Our Maura's a good Catholic girl, so she is."

Farrell left it. Up to that moment he'd been wondering how it was a pretty, easy-going girl like Maura Lynch had got herself involved in something like this. Now she had given him at least an inkling of an answer.

Behind them the door opened and Liam Grady hurried in.

"Right, friends. And now to business." He glared at O'Sullivan, still sprawled at the desk. "Up," he ordered. "You're in my place."

In another part of the building the Chief of Staff and his colleagues had officially adjourned their meeting and were in the headmaster's study, watching a taped re-play of the previous night's British television news. Nowadays a video-cassette recorder was a regular part of their decision-making process.

What they saw seemed little different from countless news bulletins. Unemployment had increased again, and the Labour Opposition had attacked the government for turning Britain into an industrial waste-land. The Prime Minister had replied that inflation was down and that long-term signs were encouraging, but that unemployment would continue to rise if workers insisted on pricing themselves out of jobs with unrealistic wage claims. An aircraft had crashed in mountains in Italy, and it was feared there were no survivors. Then the Northern Ireland Secretary, Mr James Prior, appeared on the screen. He had been having talks with the Social Democratic and Labour Parties, and now he was being interviewed by the BBC's political correspondent.

The Army Council members had been bored, talking quietly among themselves. Now there was total silence in the room.

". . . Of course there are difficulties," Mr Prior was saying. "But I'm encouraged by our talks. I do believe it's possible for the parties in Northern Ireland and the people of Northern Ireland to agree to some form of meaningful devolved administration."

"But Mr Paisley has already said he's not prepared to accept these proposals as they stand. What is your answer to him?"

The Secretary did not hesitate. "People frequently, for one reason or another, take up positions," he said with quiet reasonableness. "That has often been the case in Northern Ireland, and I can understand why. And I certainly don't suggest that our proposals are the only possible proposals. I'm sure Mr Paisley knows that. So let's not assume failure before we have taken the talks any further. Having said that, I must make it clear that, for myself, I believe the framework devised by the government should in the long run offer an acceptable solution . . ."

The picture changed, returning to the newscaster. He shuffled his papers.

"And now to Gatwick airport, where the strike of luggage handlers is into its third week—"

The Operations Officer leaned forward and switched off the machine.

"'An acceptable solution'," he echoed sarcastically. "They're pissing into the wind, so they are."

There was general laughter.

"And God bless Mr sainted Paisley, I say," he went on. "Thanks to him, and the way things stand, whatever happens to the Iron Lady, we can't lose."

3

Grady was not a man given to self-congratulation. If you knew what you wanted, and set out to get it with sufficient determination, it came your way. Determination was what counted, and he'd always had plenty of that. So there'd never been any doubt in his mind that once he got to London he'd find the flat they needed without too much difficulty. Short leases on furnished accommodation at extortionate rents were plentiful. Grease the right sort of palms with the right sort of money and they'd be in—and no questions asked.

All the same, that Tuesday afternoon, ten days later, as he stood by the bedroom window of the flat in north London, looking thoughtfully down at the narrow drive between high brick walls that led to the secluded lock-up garage that went with the place, he knew he'd been very lucky. He'd needed a flat with some very special features: a landlord who didn't want a banker's reference, their own private entrance, a garage, separate bedrooms for the three of them, and an area of London where their Irishness would neither be particularly noticeable nor lead them to get drawn into any strong local Irish community. And he didn't want a dump either. He'd lived in enough dumps down the years. It was time now for a little style. So he'd been prepared, in fact, to spend several weeks finding just the right place. Yet here he was, after only four days. A handful of small ads ringed in the evening paper, half a dozen phone calls, a quick dash in a taxi, and his search was over. The former tenant had had to leave unexpectedly. He could move in at once.

The deposit was high, of course: that and the first two months' rent in advance had set him back close on a thousand pounds. But the landlord, who'd shown him round, had been only too happy to accept cash. Cash and a strictly six-month tenancy. He was a shifty type in a Montague Burton suit, with crinkly blond hair and a flash briefcase, and Grady had disliked him on sight. Once the agreement had been signed on the leather-topped coffee table in the big front room overlooking Colney Hatch Lane, he'd confided to Grady that it was the cash that had swung the deal. In his opinion cheques weren't worth the paper they were printed on. Guys gave cheques just to hold a place while they tried to raise the necessary. And like as not they never did. And there you were, three, four days, maybe a fucking week down the drain. Whereas cash . . .

And the six-month tenancy? Well now, lighting a long thin cigarillo in its own plastic holder, that was the law for you. Six months in a place and then you could go to the Rent Tribunal. And the ideas those guys had as to what was a fair rent in these inflationary days was so much bullshit.

Grady had watched the banknotes disappear into the man's briefcase, thinking coldly of the risks that had been taken to gain them, the violence done, maybe even the deaths incurred. He didn't know and he didn't want to. It didn't matter. The money was doing what it had been intended for, buying them time, respectability, getting them one step closer to the Iron Lady.

Now he turned away from the window. This was the back bedroom he'd chosen for himself. A low double bed under a dusty orange cover, set against a wide teak headboard with glass shelves, a digital clock-cum-radio, a telephone, all of James Michener's novels in fat, well-thumbed paperbacks. And a wall of mirror-fronted wardrobes beside it. He'd chosen the room for its view, though, not for the furnishings. The flat was on the first floor of a converted Victorian end-of-terrace house, and just beneath his bedroom window was the flat roof of a modern kitchen addition. He liked the backs of houses. They made him feel safe. And he particularly liked the access this one gave him to the rear alley and the garage. There was no knowing when that mightn't come in useful. Always leave a way out, the Chief had said.

He wandered through into the kitchen, put on the kettle for a cup of instant coffee, glanced at the clock. He'd called Dublin the previous night, spoken to his "dear wife" Maura. She was flying over this afternoon, Aer Lingus, Flight EI 164. It was her first time in

England and he must be at Heathrow to meet her. He still had nearly an hour before he need leave. He drummed his fingers on the kettle handle, waiting for it to boil. His dear wife . . . at least she knew there'd be none of *that* involved. Separate rooms for the three of them. And O'Sullivan, when he arrived, would toe the line. He'd bloody have to. They'd be seeing a lot of each other over a long period, and much of it cooped up in some lousy derelict squat. The last thing he wanted was a lot of Godless fornication to complicate matters. They were all good Catholics. They'd have enough on their souls, without that.

The kettle boiled and he made his coffee, strong, with no milk. He took the mug through to the front room, put a record on the stereo. The previous tenant, a John Capstock, had left a stack of old Beatle LPs. He'd left some other odds and ends as well, tins of foreign-type food in the kitchen, sauerkraut and some small dark biscuits that tasted of pepper. There were stacks of leaflets also, from the international engineering firm he presumably worked for. He'd arrived from Europe and had to leave again after only two or three months. There were still pieces of packing case from his last removal, stacked neatly in the downstairs hall.

Grady listened to the record. He'd never thought much of the Beatles—to him Liverpool was hardly more than a suburb of Belfast, full of Irishmen who'd sold out to the British. Suddenly angered, he thumped the stereo cabinet till the pick-up arm bounced across the record, lifted, and the machine switched itself off.

He watched it, cursing himself for a clumsy oaf. That was just the sort of behaviour that disgusted him. Aimless violence. He was on edge, and he knew it. He strode to the window and stood, glowering down. Now the record would be ruined, and all for what? Just so that Liam Grady, who ought to have more self-control, could let off steam. All right, so he was on edge. But, for Christ's sake, everything was going fine, he had no reason.

Below him, down in the street, a white police Rover hurtled by, blasting its siren. He watched it out of sight, its familiar red day-glo stripe and coat of arms, and felt sorry for the poor devils it was after. A thought struck him—maybe a car like that was what they wanted for the snatch. He'd been planning on an official-looking Daimler, with O'Sullivan at the wheel in a neat uniform, but the Rover was higher off the ground, easier to get in and out of in a hurry. And who'd look twice at a police car, cruising up Whitehall?

He shook his head. The idea was lousy and it wouldn't bloody work—it worked in all the stories, but in the stories they always had unlimited facilities, paint-spraying equipment, artists to touch in the details, the right sort of signs and flashers. All he had was that dolt O'Sullivan and a lashed-up garage not much bigger than a henhouse. And he knew damn well why he was edgy. He was going to pick up Maura Lynch from the airport soon, and bring her back here. Even with things straight between them—and he'd seen to that in Dublin, back at their very first meeting—the thought of a woman about the place still made him nervous.

He'd told the Chief as much. They didn't need a woman—it would do the Iron Lady good, being seen to by men. The Chief had smiled at that. Not so much good as Maura Lynch would do her, he'd said. Maura had a way with her, and her own special reasons for hating the Brits ... And besides, they needed her medical training. The snatch apart, they'd be holed-up for a long time—any number of minor health problems might occur. Didn't Grady himself have the gut that might make itself felt if it didn't get the loving care it needed?

Grady had given in then. The Chief knew too much. He'd thought his ulcer was a matter strictly between his doctor and himself. It was an old enemy now, one he'd come to terms with years ago. But Dr Shaunessy, being a good Irishman, had his own loyalties. Grady understood that. Still, the ulcer was an aspect of himself he wasn't exactly proud of. If that Maura started clucking over him he'd just have to put her right. He'd never let anything get in the way of a job, and he wasn't going to start now.

He looked down at his half-empty coffee mug, swore softly to himself, and returned to the kitchen where he threw the coffee down the sink and poured himself milk instead. The clock told him it was time he got started for Heathrow. He'd have to go out round the North Circular, and the traffic on that could be the very devil.

Maura paused in the Terminal One arrivals gateway, rested her single suitcase, looked along the line of people waiting behind the chrome railings at the side. She had a sudden panic that Liam would be there and she wouldn't recognize him. In her head there was no picture of him at all—yet they'd spent enough time together, both at the safe house and afterwards, alone in that coffee bar opposite the National Library of Ireland. And him laying down his rules, cool as you please. She could see his hands, their sharp, cutting movements as he told her over an untouched espresso that his bed was his own and she'd kindly respect it—as if she'd ever planned otherwise, and him the least sexy thing this side of Galway Bay. She could see his hands all right, but of his face she could summon up no impression whatsoever.

Then she saw him. Even if she hadn't recognized him she'd have known it was he because he was the only one in all the crowd who was neither anxious nor smiling. He just stood, looking at her.

She shivered slightly, picked up her case and hurried forward round the end of the barrier. On a job like this the last thing your companions were chosen for would be their sympathetic personalities.

"Darling, what a lovely surprise!" She kissed him warmly. "I was afraid you wouldn't be able to get away."

"I told you I'd be here."

"Isn't this exciting? I can't wait to see the flat."

"It's fine. Fine . . ."

His mouth hadn't responded to hers and his body felt like a lump of wood. But they went through the motions, husband and wife meeting at the airport, on the remote off-chance that someone might be watching.

"How was your flight, my dear?"

"No trouble at all. Hardly up before it was time to be coming down again."

"This way now. The car's just across the road."

"Car, Liam?"

"I told you I'd be getting one. Just a Mini. Three years old, but she's been looked after. There's a million of them on the road."

She took his point. The car needed to be as forgettable as the man. Leaving the terminal building she caught sight of her reflection in the glass door. Wide-apart eyes, long red-brown hair, full mouth, a complexion she was proud of. There was no way they'd get *her* to look forgettable, she thought. And was perversely reassured.

They threaded between the cars and taxis to the short-stay car park and went up in the lift. It had been raining when she left Dublin. Now, in England, the sun was briefly visible between heavy clouds. June, she thought wryly, was busting out all over.

Multi-storey car parks always got her confused. Not so Liam. He got out of the lift at the right floor and led her directly to where he'd left the Mini. The Chief had told them he was reliable. She just hoped he kept his reliability for the things that mattered. She had known only one completely reliable man in her life, her uncle James, and such perfection had driven the rest of them half crazy. She remembered the time when her brother Michael had . . . No. No, there were things it was best not to remember.

The Mini was red, with no extras, totally unremarkable. Liam put her suitcase in the boot, then opened the passenger door for her.

"I bought it privately. Said I was a dealer, and paid cash. There's five months to run on the tax disc. So we don't have to re-license her. The former owner should notify the authorities of the sale, but sure, they hardly ever do. My name's clean enough, but there's no point in getting it on to more files than we need . . . Do you cook?"

The question, tacked on to the rest, with only the merest pause, caught her by surprise. She lowered herself into the car, tucked in her shapely legs, and looked up at him.

"Sure, and doesn't everyone cook?" she said lightly. "It's no great deal. I'll do my share, and gladly." She paused. Liam, she decided, was a man on whom hints were wasted. "But if it's a kitchen slavey you're looking for, then you should call the Chief, and maybe he'll send one over."

Liam grunted, closed the door with surprising care, and went round to the driver's seat.

"We'll manage turn and turn about," he said without rancour. "And when O'Sullivan comes I'll make out a roster."

He backed neatly out of the parking space and drove down to pay at the barrier. She relaxed beside him, feeling she had passed some obscure sort of test.

"And Sean—when are we expecting him?" she asked.

"Saturday. It's better if he finishes out the week where he works. Less noticeable. And fasten your seat belt."

"Seat belt? Isn't this England?"

"Better safe than sorry. By your shoulder, there."

She groped for it. "I didn't know you cared."

"Lot of use you'd be with your head through the bloody windscreen."

"So that's how you drive, Liam Grady." She sighed heavily. "And the honeymoon's over already, I see. Shortest on record."

He didn't even smile, but once they were up on the motorway she was glad of the belt. He drove well, but fast—right at the car's limit.

After suffering in silence for a while, she ventured: "What's the hurry?"

He didn't turn his head. "There's no hurry," he said neutrally.

Even in profile she could see enough of his face to know she shouldn't persist. They drove on at seventy-plus, the tiny car vibrating painfully. She folded her hands in her lap, stared down at them.

"Where exactly are we going?"

"What?"

She raised her voice above the car's noise. "Where are we going?"

"Muswell Hill."

"Where's that?"

"North London."

"Is that good?"

She didn't really want to know, she just wanted to keep her thoughts occupied. They were coming up fast on a juggernaut, and the little car briefly floated sideways in the slipstream.

"Good? It's convenient enough." Liam used the drift to swing out on. "Almost anywhere would have done. Not Kilburn, though."

"And what's Kilburn done?"

"It's done nothing. It's where all the Micks hang out, that's all. We were to keep to ourselves. Remember?"

She hadn't forgotten. But keeping to themselves with this ungiving man would be no picnic. Still, the end was worth the means. And Sean would be joining them on Saturday. The juggernaut was behind them now, and the road ahead clear for a mile or more.

"What do you make of young Sean?" she said.

"O'Sullivan? Met him for the first time the same day I met you. I reckon he knows his job."

She nodded. Of course he knew his job. But that hadn't been her question. She wondered if it was part of Liam's tough act, or if he really saw people solely in terms of their efficiency.

"It's funny really," she said. "We're small enough, in a small country—you'd think we'd have bumped into each other before somewhere."

"That's what the cell system's all about. Nobody knows anybody. But we're not that small. When the chips are down every right-thinking Irishman's one of us. You'll see it every time."

That sort of talk angered her. It was too easy. There were right-thinking Irishmen and right-thinking Irishmen. Her father had been

33

a right-thinking Irishman, but he'd had no truck with the Provos. And a lot of bloody good *that* had done him . . .

"And Farrell? What of Farrell?" she asked. "Is he one of ours?"

"Sure he is. He's well trained, disciplined, tough. And he's been waiting long enough."

"How can you be sure?"

"We have to trust the Chief. And we have to trust each other. Farrell's not the only British Army man we've got. There are others ready and willing. But Farrell's in the right place. What's more, he needs us—needs us to make some sense of his life. The Chief reckons the Army's passed him by. Teaching call-signs to a gang of part-time soldiers—what sort of a job is that for a man?"

"But what about afterwards, when this is all over? He'll be a marked man, Liam. He's no fool—he'll have thought of that. I don't like it."

Grady came up with a line of slower traffic, and swung out into the fast lane again.

"You worry too much. The Provos look after their own. He'll get a new name, a new start somewhere."

"It's all too convenient. He could be a plant."

"He'll not live to tell the tale if he is, Maura. First hint of something not right and I'll take him out. It'll be a pleasure."

Looking sideways at his impassive profile, Maura thought it would be. She hunched her shoulders, changed the subject. For herself, she'd kill if she had to, but there'd be no joy in it.

"This Colchester—sixty miles or so, you said. What are the roads like?"

"Traffic's often thick out of London, but once we're on the A12, it's dual carriageway almost all the way. Anyway, who's going to look twice at an army Land Rover, for Christ's sake?"

At least, she thought, Farrell would be driving. Otherwise, she could just picture them: the Iron Lady in the back, and all of them having a pile-up.

They drove in silence for a while. They were coming into the outskirts of London, endless streets of identical houses below the motorway on either side. So this was England. She'd be glad when the job was over and she could go back home . . . Except that she didn't exactly have a home, not of her own. Since Michael's death she'd taken his place, chucked in her job and gone to live with the old folk. They needed her—Michael had been their whole world. Still, if

Ballybrennan got on top of her there were always the soft green fields of Ireland not more than a minute or two away.

They drove on endlessly, down off the motorway and along wide indistinguishable roads lined with shoddy semi-detached houses. But there were laburnum trees flowering brightly in many of their gardens, and the sight cheered her.

"This place you've found—is there a garden?"

"A garden? Of course not." He thought about it. He really wasn't sure. "There must be a bit of something out the back. And the way in's between high bushes . . . Maybe there *is* a garden. Thinking of growing some shamrock, are you?"

His mockery depressed her. "I could do worse," she said. "We'll be there a month or two at least. I don't imagine we'll spend every hour of every day going over the sainted plan."

He turned to her for the first time. "I shouldn't be too sure of that, my girl. The sainted plan, as you call it—we're going to live it. We're going to have it for breakfast, dinner and tea. And when we go to bed we're going to dream it."

And he wasn't smiling. He really meant it.

Finally they turned right, onto a street where the traffic was thicker and slower, with older houses on either side, and shops. Maura saw street signs pointing to Muswell Hill golf course, and then to Alexandra Palace. She asked Liam about the palace. He said he'd had better things to do than go staring at palaces. Suddenly he swung into a narrow alleyway between two Victorian redbrick houses, stopped the car by stone steps up to a side entrance, and got out.

While he was fetching her suitcase she assessed the flat's situation. For their purposes it could hardly have been better. As he had said, the door was screened by laurels in a dirty strip of garden. It was new, put into an otherwise completely blank wall, presumably when the house had been converted into flats. And behind the house, where the back garden must be, the alleyway continued between high walls to a sheet-asbestos garage, half-hidden beneath an ancient and mossy apple tree. They could come and go as they pleased, totally unobserved. A whole army could. It was the safest safe house she'd ever seen.

He led the way. The stairs, as she'd guessed, were a new addition, and a bit narrow. He paused near the top, reading her thoughts.

"If we go in a hurry," he said, "we go by the back. There's a roof that might have been tailor-made."

The landing had a mirror in a satin-chrome frame, conical spotlights, and red plastic coat hooks. He showed her the airy lounge, teak wall units, black hide suite, huge colour TV, and then the bathroom and the three bedrooms. The bathroom was tiled from floor to ceiling in fishes and water weeds against a dark blue background, and the bedrooms all had big double beds and shaggy carpets. The dusty orange one was his. He took her to the window and pointed out their escape route.

The whole place impressed her enormously. He hadn't asked her which of the other two bedrooms she wanted; he'd simply left her suitcase in the first one they'd come to. It was at the front of the house and noisy, but she didn't complain. It had lacy pink net curtains, and she'd always wanted lacy pink net curtains.

The kitchen was a disappointment, squeezed in beside a dining alcove, almost like an afterthought. Liam had been using it for several days, but the sink and draining board were empty, and there wasn't a single thing lying about on any of its surfaces. She found such tidiness unnerving. If he expected the same of her he was out of luck.

She drummed her knuckles thoughtfully on the formica, aware of him standing in the doorway behind, watching her.

"It's my first night in London," she said. "Why don't we eat out?"

"No. There's a chicken pie in the ice-box. It just needs heating through."

She swung round. "Not straight out of the ice-box, it doesn't. Not unless you want to turn your gut over. I'm not eating junky frozen pie. I'm going out."

He winced inwardly at the coincidence of her mentioning his gut.

"This isn't a holiday camp," he said dourly.

"It's not a prison either."

They glared at each other. He was the leader—she knew that. But he wasn't God. She had to have *some* life that was her own.

He said, "I won't have us living like lords on the Army's money."

Christ! It was the expense that was worrying him.

"I'm not a beggar," she retorted. "I've got my own money. How's that?"

He relaxed slightly. "That's all right then."

His patronizing tone angered her still more. She gestured widely. "And this fancy place—don't you call this living like lords?"

"Certainly I do. But it's necessary. We have to look respectable. The way a lot of us Micks live, it's just asking the Brits to pick us up."

She hesitated. That made sense. Suddenly she felt ashamed.

"I'm sorry, Liam. I didn't think . . ." She lowered her head. "Of course we'll stay in, if you say so."

"You must please yourself. I just wouldn't want you forgetting where all this comes from. Men risked their lives to get it." He turned on his heel, walked away across the landing, paused. "I'll come with you," he said over his shoulder. "We'll go Dutch."

She watched him disappear into his room. He'd had the grace to be embarrassed. Maybe, she thought, he was human after all.

Next morning, Wednesday, Grady took her with him to have their first look at Downing Street. They found a parking space on the Embankment, walked along past the Houses of Parliament and up Whitehall, mingling with the crowds of summer tourists. Grady carried a camera, and took photographs all the time: of the Churchill statue in Parliament Square, of Maura with Big Ben behind her, of the Cenotaph. He wanted a detailed record of the whole area and the roll of film had to seem innocent. He'd be having it processed at a chemist with a twenty-four-hour service, just like any other tourist.

The early June sunshine was weak, casting pale, intermittent shadows beneath the plane trees in Whitehall. Clouds built in untidy mounds behind the Parliament buildings. The forecast had promised rain before lunch. Grady photographed the whole street, taking in the bollarded islands in the middle of the road, each with its bronze lamp standard topped with a crown. There was an island almost opposite the entrance to Downing Street itself, but a car coming out and turning right towards Parliament Square would leave the island well on its left. A car going in, from the direction of Trafalgar Square, however, would need to go round the island.

He and Maura lingered outside the doors of the Privy Council Office and the Cabinet Office just before the entrance to Downing Street. There were uniformed attendants inside each, but no policemen on duty outside. That seemed to be true of every government office down Whitehall.

Grady snapped more pictures. Nobody took a second look at them—a man and a pretty girl seeing the sights. A brown Rover saloon was parked outside the Privy Council Office, a woman in a dark green uniform at its wheel. She'd be one of the official drivers.

He hadn't thought they'd use women. But it didn't matter. Women died no differently from men.

There was a large plane tree set in the pavement not far from the corner of Downing Street and, on the opposite side, by the corner of the Foreign and Commonwealth Office, was a younger and smaller tree. Maura posed by it jauntily and he photographed her. Behind her the barrier railings were drawn partly across the entrance to Downing Street, but were wide enough apart to allow the passage of a single car. A solitary shirt-sleeved policeman stood near the barrier with a personal radio clipped to his top pocket. If he was aware that he'd been photographed he gave no sign.

Grady looked at Maura over the camera. Their eyes met and he smiled ironically. This was too easy. They crossed the road together and allowed themselves to be eased through the barrier along with the other tourists. They were kept to the pavement on the left side, opposite Number 10, and stood near the arched entrance into the Foreign Office courtyard. No policeman guarded the narrow drive-way. A Japanese party was busy with their elaborate photographic equipment, so he changed film reels and joined them. The houses across the narrow roadway had black iron railings close in front of their neat, dark grey brickwork. Number 10 had one window to the left of the doorway and three to the right. The door itself was framed by a wrought-iron arch with a crowned lantern in its centre. A solitary policeman stood outside.

As Grady watched, a tradesman came down the street on foot, carrying a covered basket. Apparently ignoring the policeman, he rang the bell to the right of the doorway. The door was opened instantly by another shirt-sleeved policeman who accepted the basket. Some of the crowd around Grady cheered as the tradesman went away, whistling.

Grady straightened, swung his camera. In fact the security was better here than it looked at first sight. The row of houses opposite extended to the left with Number 11 and two further doorways and four windows before it was blocked at the end of the street by Number 12 with a door and window that looked along the length of the street towards Whitehall. The bottom of the street was sealed off with gated iron railings. Steps led down by the side of the Foreign Office to Horse Guards, but the gate was obviously locked. Grady knew there'd be no way out there. Once you entered Downing Street you were trapped.

But they weren't going to enter. They weren't going after the Iron Lady. They would wait for her to come to them.

He and Maura stayed for perhaps half an hour. Some of the tourists left, others arrived. Meanwhile several official cars drew up outside Number 10 and their passengers went inside. A taxi came too, and delivered an elderly woman in an expensively-tailored suit. It looked as though there might be two policemen on duty in the entrance hall. Grady saw that even after they'd been alerted they'd have a good seventy-five-yard dash to get to the barrier.

He wandered down to the far end of the street. Behind the net curtains of Number 12 he could dimly see figures. Anyone in that room would have a view right down the street to Whitehall. That didn't matter either. Their operation would be over in seconds. They'd be away long before anyone in that room could do a thing.

He rejoined Maura. For the moment they had the pavement almost to themselves and they stood together, smiling and chatting quietly.

Maura indicated the barrier. "Just one bloody copper—that's all we have to deal with. And he looks half asleep."

Grady shrugged. "They all do. But it might be part of an act—keeping a low profile kind of thing."

"Don't you believe it." Briefly, her smile disappeared. "These bloody Brits—they never think it can happen to them."

"But it can—and it's going to." He relished the thought, then paused and glanced down at her. "That car we saw—the driver was a woman."

"So?"

"Maybe the driver on the day will be a woman too."

For a moment she didn't understand what he was getting at. Then she laughed.

"You mayn't have noticed it, Liam Grady, but so am I." She pointed up at the window opposite. "And so is she."

She was enjoying herself. It made him realize how childish this was, talking like this right in front of Number 10, just for the devil of it. He took her hand and hurried her away.

And he'd noticed she was a woman—he couldn't not have. His routine was shot to hell. She'd been in the bath that morning when he'd wanted to shave. And the previous night, at the restaurant, with her watching, he'd remembered his ulcer and gone for the poached fish instead of the curried lamb. Not that she'd said a word either way, but he'd be damned if he'd give her the chance.

39

As they went through the barrier she held him back while she asked the constable the way to Buckingham Palace. She didn't want to know. She was just like a kid playing with fire, and as soon as they moved away he told her so. She sulked all the way back to the car.

He let her, and drove up Whitehall, then round Trafalgar Square and down Whitehall again. He was noting the traffic, how it built up, which lanes were best, where the lights were. He hadn't yet checked on the underground garage where they'd be switching vehicles. On the day a lot would depend on where that was. But they'd have to get round one or other of the big squares, Trafalgar Square or Parliament Square, in a hurry. He must plan a route. O'Sullivan would be driving—as soon as he arrived Grady would send him down into town to drive round the area till he knew it like his own reflection. Then—

"Penny for them."

Maura had come out of her sulk and was smiling at him. She was good-looking all right. But she'd have to learn to accept criticism better than that.

"I was thinking about the Paddy factor."

"What's that for heaven's sake?"

"It's the Brits' word for the way we often balls things up. Lack of discipline, lack of proper planning, forgetting the significant detail." He met her gaze. "Here's one we aren't going to balls up."

Not that there hadn't been successes—Mountbatten, Warrenpoint. He'd reason to remember the latter—sixteen men of the 2nd Battalion the Parachute Regiment and two from the 1st Battalion Queen's Own Highlanders blown in all directions. He had watched it from the other side of the border. And there'd been countless operations in the North. Maybe the British had invented the idea of the Paddy factor just to cheer themselves up.

There was his own first job—that hadn't been a balls-up either. That time all the planning had been done for him. He'd simply obeyed orders, waited with his Armalite behind the upper window of a corner house till the patrol came into view. All the time in the world, fixing the soldier in the V of his back-sight, the soldier who'd been so busy down the Falls Road the week before, then squeezing the trigger. By the time the patrol had swung into action he was down the stairs and out of the house by the garden door and over into the neighbouring property. There a kid was waiting to take the gun while he made off through several gardens and out at the end of the street. In five minutes he was having a Guinness with a friend in the pub on the corner. The kid had got away too, the gun in his sister's pram. He knew it was his speed and efficiency that had set him apart from the other "lads" in the clubs of Derry and Belfast. Well, this time it was his own operation, and they were going to get it right. Planning. Discipline. It was going to be bloody perfect.

He circled Parliament Square for the second time and turned left into Birdcage Walk. It was eleven o'clock, time they were getting back to the flat. If they were going to use a Daimler then he'd better start looking. But the more he thought about it the less he liked it. A Daimler was too low slung. It restricted movement. And fixing the Iron Lady so she couldn't be seen in the back would be bloody impossible.

4

At eleven o'clock that Wednesday morning, not half a mile away, in his office in New Scotland Yard, Superintendent Arthur Whitaker of the Special Branch was also concerned with problems of restricted movement. He hadn't had a decent one in three days. Worry, over and above the usual toll of anxiety that his job exacted, had that effect on him. He wondered whether to send Sergeant Trew out for a dose of something, then decided against it. There were some intimacies he preferred not to share, even with his imperturbable assistant.

He returned to his desk and, for the hundredth time, re-read the report from one of MI5's undercover men with the London Provos. The order had come through from the Army Council in Ireland that they were to lie low and were not to engage in any overt actions until specifically told to do so. Now, Whitaker's subject was terrorism in general and the IRA in particular. It was his job to know all there was to know about Irish terrorism in Britain—whether planned by the Provisional IRA, the Irish National Liberation Army, who had murdered Airey Neave, or the UDA and the UVF, the Protestant extremists. But this latest report had got him worried. Orders of this kind weren't uncommon, but his long experience told him that somehow this was different. He couldn't get rid of the feeling that there was something behind it.

Admittedly, there were several possible explanations. A simple shortage of funds was the first. But frankly that was unlikely. Possible a few months ago, but the hunger strikes had given a fresh impetus to the funds flowing from America, and moreover his contacts in the Garda were of the opinion that the proceeds from a couple of big bank jobs done that month had found their way into Republican pockets. So he didn't really see this as a cost-cutting exercise.

He sighed, sat back, reached for his pipe, and began to fill it. Then again the Provo command might be switching personnel and wanting to break in the new men slowly. Fresh arrivals had a way of rushing into things, and that could be wasteful. But the immigration boys had turned up no significant movements in or out. And Whitaker himself, in one of his few recent successes, had personally stopped up the only established illegal route, the North Devon one, via Lynmouth.

There was always a chance, of course, that the Provos were planning something big, conserving their resources, and hoping to lull the authorities into a false sense of security. But what? The MI5 man had pushed hard and hadn't come up with a thing.

Next—and he'd kept this one pretty low on the list—it was just conceivable that the government's latest political initiative was having an effect. He lit a match, applied it carefully to the bowl of his pipe. Provisional Sinn Fein, the political wing, had started issuing statements in the North on social problems, and only last week *Republican News*, a fair barometer of the Provos' current thinking, had carried an article declaring that the withdrawal of British troops could be secured more quickly if, in addition to the IRA's "military thrust", resistance to British rule could be directed into a political movement. But he'd heard all that kind of thing before. Words . . . words . . . He shook out the match and tossed it into the heavy glass ashtray on his desk, a twentieth-wedding-anniversary present from his wife. No, he didn't believe in leopards changing their spots. They never had and they never would.

Finally, since the Army Council were bound to know that some cells were penetrated, there was the possibility that the whole thing was simply a ploy—a ploy aimed at hazing the security forces and the Anti-Terrorist Squad and, as he was the bloke who was supposed to know about it all, a ploy ultimately aimed at him.

Him against them. Whitaker didn't think he was being irrational, but in his heart that's how he saw it. He didn't have any delusions of grandeur. He would be the first to admit that, at the end of the day, he was no more than a buck-carrier for the Anti-Terrorist Squad (C.13) and for a large and immensely capable police organization. But in his heart—ah, that was another matter. His heart knew that, ultimately, it was him against them. His ingenuity, his experience, his determination and, if necessary, his ruthlessness against theirs.

Whitaker wasn't, in general, a bitter, obsessional man. Personal vendettas were no part of his thinking. To the world at large, and particularly to his wife and their two teenage children and their wide circle of friends, he was gentle, warm-hearted, and fun to be with. Although formidably good at his job, he still found it hard, in other matters, to take himself seriously. Nudging fifty, and slightly over-weight, he had tried jogging for the good of his health a few years back, when the craze had first hit London. He lived within easy reach of Wimbledon Common, and half an hour in the morning before he caught the underground in to work had seemed a small price to pay. But he'd found it boring, and faintly ridiculous, and he'd lacked the earnestness, the self-concern, to persevere. So he'd resigned himself to a few extra pounds of middle-aged spread and concentrated thankfully on his only other hobbies, his pipe and his painting. Of these two, surprisingly, his pipe was the less anti-social, for his painting consisted of portraits in a peculiar, lumpy style that was all his own, and the walls of his otherwise impersonal office at the Yard—his home he spared—were thickly hung with them. His colleagues called him Art, affectionately, and did their best to avert their eyes.

All in all, therefore, he was painstaking and compassionate in the things he thought mattered, and easy-going in everything else—a reasonable man in an increasingly unreasonable world. But there was a darker, less reasonable side to his nature, one that only Sergeant Trew, and his wife, and those few others who enjoyed his ultimate confidence, were aware of.

Him against them: he felt it acutely, a kind of personal crusade. When an IRA bomb factory was found, the victory was his. And when an innocent child had its legs blown off in a shopping precinct, the failure was his also. He should have prevented it. Although it wasn't his job to be there, he always felt he should have been. He should have dragged the child to safety with his own hands. And his rage against the perpetrators grew accordingly.

Him against them. And it worked the other way. In Belfast, in Dublin, after each pointless killing, he could hear in his head the toasts being drunk: "There's one for you, Whitaker. We beat you then, bloody copper." Them against him. So this latest order from the Army Council might even have been aimed at him personally, to keep him guessing, to wear him down.

He sucked at his pipe. It had gone out and bubbled sourly. He flung it down, scattering ash across the MI5 man's secret report, and got angrily to his feet. That was crazy thinking, and he knew it. Paranoia. In reality, the Provos were unlikely even to know his name, or his job, and even if they did, the Provisional Army Council had better things to do with their time than gloat over Superintendent Whitaker.

He went over to the window. From it he could see right across to the Victoria tower of the Houses of Parliament, and even to the car park of the House of Commons. Clouds were building up over Lambeth Palace. It would be raining by lunch time. Summer this year looked like going the way of all the others . . . He frowned. Parliament. The Irish Minister's new initiative. Could he have been wrong to cross it off his mental list?

He returned to his desk, buzzed Trew to bring in the Tyrie report. The sergeant appeared a moment later, sorting in a buff folder as he came. He produced the report, stamped "Secret" a great many times in an excess of someone's bureaucratic zeal, and gave it to Whitaker. The superintendent knew what was in it, but he read it again, just to win himself thinking time.

Andrew Tyrie was supreme commander of the Ulster Defence Association. He had just paid one of his periodic visits to Scotland, and the report summarized his activities and other findings by the MI5 agent. Naturally Tyrie had been briefing the Scottish Prods on the UDA's attitude to the new government initiative, which was inevitably one of almost hysterical opposition. But he had also—and this was more ominous—made a tour at the local unit level, and the MI5 man said these units had been gathering arms and ammunition from a number of sources.

Whitaker tapped the report.

44

"Now what the hell would he be seeing the local units for?"
Trew shrugged.

"They have these drives now and then, sir." He too knew the report almost by heart. He also knew the shape of his chief's thinking. "It could be routine. Pep talks all round—that kind of thing."

"It could also be, friend Goodie, that he's heard something. Something we haven't . . . Unless, of course, you count this." He picked up the MI5 document and blew the pipe ash off it. "Lie low, the Provos' Army Council says. And Tyrie's boys are laying in guns. What if the connection's politics? I don't like it."

"A shooting war, sir? I don't think so. Nobody wants that."

"Nobody ever wants that. But they do happen . . . I wonder now—who's more afraid of a political solution, the UDA or the Provos?"

Trew considered.

"The Provo politicos would like one," he said. "They've been busy enough recently, ranting on about unemployment in the North. They'd like to appear respectable, to offer a viable alternative. The question is, sir, how much does the military wing listen to them?"

"You know the answer to that one as well as I do."

Whitaker flung himself down in his chair. Trew was bright. He'd gone through the staff college at Bramshill in Hampshire like an express train, in spite of a public school manner that would have crippled a lesser man. Too good to be Trew had been his first instructor's judgment, and the epithet had stuck. Whitaker, a product of Bradford Grammar, knew that his sergeant was quickly destined for bigger things and meanwhile appreciated him for his outstanding ability, and had even grown fond of his upper-class vocabulary and strangulated vowels.

"It doesn't listen at all," the superintendent added. "Or at least it hasn't up to now."

"Then we're left with two possibilities, sir. And they're both pretty bloody." Trew cleared his throat apologetically. "Either the UDA aims to come out shooting again, and so force the Provos' hand, and put paid to any political advances for the next year or so. Or else the Provos have something big in mind, and the Proddies have got wind of it and want to be ready with the jolly old reprisals."

Whitaker grunted. That, more or less, was the conclusion he had slowly been coming to.

"We must put the pressure on, Goodie. Squeeze our poor bloody informers till the pips squeak. Someone's got to have something."

"I hope you're right, sir."

"I'd better be. What else is there ... ?"

"Yes, it's routine in the end, sir, isn't it? That pays off, I mean." Even Trew began to look a little reflective as he added: "I suppose, sir, it's the hardest lesson the brilliant and ambitious young police-man has to learn—that the best police work often turns out to be painstaking routine."

Whitaker half smiled: "Ah, the philosopher too, eh, Goodie?" The superintendent recognized that his sergeant was trying to head off his superior's gloom and the sudden bursts of anger it was liable to produce. But the fellow was right. There was no point in giving way to the fury that he could so easily feel. Better get on with the hard-slogging routine.

"All right then," he said with sudden firmness. "Get the machine turning—and see it's well oiled. I don't like having to wait for those other bastards to make the first move."

Three days later Sean O'Sullivan arrived at the flat in Colney Hatch Lane, and the team was complete. His first job was to pick up Farrell at Liverpool Street Station at five past eleven on Monday morning. His weekend Terrier classes disposed of, Farrell was coming to London for the day, in response to Grady's small ad in Colchester's *Evening Gazette*: *Having a wonderful time, wish you were here*, together with the Muswell Hill telephone number. When Farrell called they kept conversation to a minimum—no names, no ad-dresses, simply the time of his train's arrival—11.04. Farrell was the vulnerable one. It was important for everybody's sake that no direct trail should ever connect the army sergeant with his fellow conspira-tors.

Sean took the Mini. Unlike Maura, he had been in London before. Some five years earlier, after leaving school in Collinstown, he'd crossed to England and worked briefly in the Liverpool docks. Then woman trouble had caused him to hitch a lift south and he bummed around Earls Court for a while, stealing cars when he could, but mostly pushing dope in a half-hearted fashion for a smooth Aussie operator. His air of sandy-haired, freckle-faced innocence had been an asset in that trade, together with his capacity for casual brutality, but the hours were long and the rewards proved disappointing. So he'd drifted back to Ireland and taken a job as a bouncer in a Dublin club. It was there that the IRA had found him.

He'd been a mess. Going nowhere, drinking more than was good for him. But by giving him a cause, and discipline, the Army had made something of a man of him. The drinking stopped. They even found him decent, regular work, driving a van for a big market gardener near Athlone. That was the job he'd had to work out the week at. A man with Army backing had to be reliable. He never quit without proper notice.

Although the station was a long way from his old stamping grounds, Sean made it to Liverpool Street with ten minutes to spare. He parked the car, sat in it till the last minute as he'd been taught, then went quickly to the recently smartened but still grubby concourse. Farrell's train must have been a minute or two early, for he was waiting impatiently at the barrier, staring round, back straight, shoulders squared. Sean was surprised to see the sergeant in uniform, and felt the old familiar flare of instinctive hatred in his guts.

He strode forward, smiling warmly, both hands outstretched.

"There's a fine figure of a man you are, Sergeant Farrell. Indeed yes—a fine figure of a man."

Farrell winced, and eyed him sourly.

"You're late," he said.

Sean's temper flared, but he controlled it.

"Better late than never, Sergeant—as the actress said to the bishop."

The sergeant wasn't amused.

"Where's the car?" he demanded.

Sean started hunting theatrically in his pockets.

"Mother of God—where can it be? And I had it with me only a moment since . . ."

Sergeant Farrell swore briefly and pushed past him, his mouth in a thin hard line, towards the ticket offices and the road beyond. Sean followed him, whistling cheerfully. Sure, but there's more than one way of dealing with the likes of you, boyo, he thought.

When they reached the pavement he pointed to the car and Farrell got in, making no comment. He sat very straight in the tiny Mini, his knees nearly up to his chin. As Sean went round to the driver's door he glanced casually up and down the road. Two kids in jeans were hailing a taxi and an old lady was sitting on her suitcase. Apart from these, nothing. He sat in the Mini, waiting until the taxi had driven off, just in case. All the best policemen were kids in jeans these days.

Farrell turned to him. "What are we waiting for?"

"Standard security practice, Sergeant. There might be a tail. But then, a soldier like you wouldn't be knowing about things like that, now would he?"

Only when the taxi had been out of sight for a full minute did he move away from the kerb, and when he reached the street he turned in the opposite direction from that taken by the taxi. They progressed in silence for several minutes.

"You seem to know your way about London," the sergeant finally conceded.

Sean took this as a peace offering. He wasn't a man to bear grudges.

"I'm learning all the time. Tomorrow Grady's taking me down to Whitehall. He's got these photographs. You wouldn't believe."

"Photographs are a good idea." His companion sounded agreeably surprised. "Seems like he's got his head screwed on right, after all."

"I'd say you've got it, Sergeant." He nodded emphatically. "Liam Grady's got his head screwed on right, sure enough."

Sean had seen that in Dublin. But now twenty-four hours in London, at the flat, had confirmed it. Quick with the orders maybe, and a hard man . . . but weren't his sort always hard men? And if the three of them were to get on then there had to be some system about the place, who did what, even the cooking. This wasn't a rest cure they were on.

Sean appreciated system. Too much of his short life had been haphazard, going nowhere. The Provos had given him purpose and now Grady was focusing that purpose. In fact, more even than O'Sullivan realized, Liam Grady had his head screwed on right.

For the rest of the journey to Muswell Hill Sean chatted easily, describing the flat and its appointments, which had impressed him enormously, in glowing terms, and also describing—man to man—the sleeping arrangements as laid down by Grady, which had impressed him rather less.

"I ask you, Sergeant, one to a room and no exceptions. And him promising to do the rounds . . . I mean—Mother of God, if Maura's willing and I'm willing, then where's the harm?"

Farrell massaged his cramped shins. "And is Miss Lynch willing?" he asked drily.

Sean laughed. "Sure, and aren't all women willing?"

The sergeant didn't argue with that. But if he didn't appear to disagree, then he didn't agree either. Instead he changed the subject.

"What's your cover?" he asked. "If you get talking in the shops like—what's your story?"

"Liam's this freelance accountant, working from home." Sean fingered his open-necked shirt. "And he's got this smart blue suit to prove it . . . Maura's his girl, and I'm her brother. I'm supposed to be over here looking for a job, something in the construction line. Liam's got it all worked out—he says I look the part and nobody'll be surprised if I just sit back on my jacksy. There's always a Mick bumming a ride off someone somewhere." He laughed again. He didn't mind being cast as a layabout—anything Grady said was all right by him.

When they reached the house in Colney Hatch Lane he drove straight up the side entrance and into the garage. He'd had his instructions before leaving—there was no point, Grady said, in advertising their visitor. He took Farrell up, pointing out with proprietory pride the fitted carpet on the stairs, the stylish modern lighting. He'd been brought up in a three-roomed cottage backing on to a peat bog, he and his eight brothers and sisters, and the flat gave him a thrill every time he entered it.

Grady was waiting for them in the front room with Maura. He looked up at Farrell from where he was sitting, very neat and tense, in the corner of the brown leather sofa.

"The uniform was a mistake," he said coldly. "It draws attention."

For a moment antagonism sparked dangerously between the two men. Sean looked anxiously from one to the other.

"Sure, but it suits him, Liam," he suggested placatingly. "Wouldn't you say?"

Farrell eased off, moved slowly to the fireplace, shrugged.

"Grady's quite right. I should have thought . . . Still, the crafty way I was smuggled in here I doubt if there's any harm done."

Grady was unappeased. "And where're your gloves?"

"Gloves?"

"I said gloves, didn't I? You wear them whenever you come here. If this place is ever blown I don't want the police finding your prints all over it. Maura—get him a pair of those plastic examination ones from your medical kit. And Farrell—next time you come you bring your own."

Farrell stood to attention. "Will do."

"And the car—remember to wipe it off when you go. The handle, the seat, anything you touched."

Farrell saluted half-mockingly. "You think of everything, don't you?"

"I have to."

Maura returned with the gloves, and Farrell put them on. They were thin and pale pink, and reminded Sean of a packet of five.

The atmosphere became less tense. Grady sat back, stretched his legs. Maura stood by the door.

"I'll make some coffee," she said, as she left the room again.

"Glass of milk for me," Grady called after her. Then he turned again to Farrell. "And how's the hideout? You've looked it over?"

Farrell nodded. "It's fine." He sat down by the fireplace. "Everything's just as I thought. Abbey Field is a series of blocks of ground-floor and first-floor flats. The first-floor ones have an open balcony with railings running all along the front, with stairs at each end. There's a good view up there, and I think we should go for one of those."

Sean sat down, relieved that there wasn't going to be a quarrel. He hated quarrels. They made him do things that got him into trouble afterwards. He chose the low swivel chair and revolved it contentedly as he began rolling himself a cigarette.

Grady ignored him. "Dublin says their man's fixed it so there'll be water through to Block D. They suggest number six. Would that be upstairs?"

Farrell screwed up his eyes, trying to remember. "Yes . . . yes, six is ideal. First floor and near the centre. Our lot in Colchester must have done a good job."

"Can you get in and start stocking it at once?"

"Of course. Tonight, if you like."

"The area isn't guarded?"

"There's not a soldier near the place. You could even go there in daylight."

"What about kids? If they found the stuff we'd be in trouble."

"I'll fix the lock on the door. And, as I told you in Dublin, the windows are boarded up. The Army did a good job. Kids used to hang around, but now it's boarded up and there's nothing to break, they've got tired of it. Anyway they wouldn't bother with upstairs."

Grady considered. "Are you sure you won't be noticed if you—" he broke off. "I've told you before, O'Sullivan. Smoke if you bloody must, but not in here. The stink turns my stomach."

Startled, Sean hastily nipped the end of his roll-up between finger and thumb. Sure, Liam had told him, but he'd told him so much—a man couldn't always be remembering every single little thing. With a show of bravado he smoothed out the crumpled cigarette and stuck it jauntily behind his ear.

Farrell cleared his throat. "I won't be seen," he said. "Look—it's a garrison town. Who ever looks at a soldier in a garrison town? Besides, it's easy for me. My time's mostly my own. I'm a PSI—Permanent Staff Instructor—to the 95th Colchester Communications Squadron, Territorial Army. Yes, we have Terriers there too. My job's communications and admin. I run these courses, and as long as I'm there when I'm needed and the admin's done properly, the CO lets me get on with it. I can organize my own time off as long as it's not weekends—no trouble."

Grady drummed his fingers thoughtfully.

"We'll be needing army uniforms for myself and O'Sullivan."

"No problem. Just give me the measurements, and I can win them from the stores. Book them out to myself and then square the quartermaster's clerk."

Sean spun his chair delightedly. "Myself in a Brit's uniform now—won't that be something?"

Farrell frowned. "We should have something else to wear for the actual snatch, though," he said. "If they know they're looking out for army men, then—"

"I'm not a fool, Sergeant." Grady gestured irritably. "We'll wear our own clothes and change in the garage."

"Won't that take too long? I'd have thought—"

"Of course, it'll take time. That can't be helped."

Farrell rubbed his chin. "The vehicle switch is when we're most in danger. I'd have thought boiler suits . . . some sort of overall we can get out of quickly. Even change on the move if we practise it."

Grady gave him a cold hard stare. He didn't like being taught his business; he resented the sergeant's experience. But even Sean could see that what Farrell had said made sense. The moment was saved by Maura's return from the kitchen with a tray of mugs, a milk bottle, and a packet of sugar. She put it down on the coffee table, handed mugs of instant coffee to Farrell and Sean, and poured milk for Grady.

He watched her sourly. "Do we have to pig it? There're jugs, aren't there? And a bowl for sugar?"

Maura shrugged. "There's a fancy lace tray cloth, too, if someone cares to get it."

Sean leaned forward and helped himself liberally to sugar. Even in the short time he'd been there these two had squabbled now and then. It didn't worry him. They seemed to understand each other pretty well, and their rows never got out of hand. Liam and the sergeant were another matter, though. He'd sensed there was trouble brewing there, right from the start.

Grady turned back to Farrell. He'd got rid of his resentment elsewhere.

"Boiler suits are a good idea," he conceded. "Maura can go to Milletts up in the West End. Even if they remember her it won't signify." He paused. "But the car—we might look odd. I mean we'll have to get to Whitehall in good time and park for a while. That's why at first I'd thought of something official-looking—one of those Daimlers, maybe. But if we're in boiler suits and someone notices . . ."

Maura took her coffee over to the window seat. "What's wrong with a delivery van?"

"Doors at the back," Grady said. "Too awkward."

"We could always take a taxi," Sean suggested.

He'd meant it as a joke, but Grady looked at him with sudden seriousness.

"That's a good idea, O'Sullivan—a very good idea. Taxi drivers wear anything. And there'll be room for the three of us out of sight in the back. Not even the fuzz will look twice at a taxi waiting in Whitehall, yellow lines or no yellow lines. Don't they even turn into Downing Street itself? Yes, that's good."

Sean looked modestly down at his shoes and blushed with pride. Grady glanced at the others.

"Is that fixed, then? We steal a taxi, give it another number plate?"

"Wait a minute." Farrell had his eyes closed, remembering. "Taxis have another number. On the back . . . a hackney carriage number."

"We'll change that too."

"I don't expect you can buy them. You'll have to make it. And it had better be real and match the number plate, just in case some copper with nothing better to do checks up while we're waiting."

"You're right," Grady said. "Sean can see to that."

"I'll do the hackney number," Maura put in. "I got an A for art in my O-levels."

They all laughed. The barriers were disappearing. They were becoming—at least for the moment—a team.

"We need the taxi soon," Sergeant Farrell said. "We'll have to practise."

"Practise?" Grady got up and went to the desk set in the teak wall unit. "We need to be able to do it in our sleep."

He returned with the bundle of enlarged black-and-white snap-shots Sean had seen the night before and spread them out on the table. Farrell moved the coffee tray on to the slate hearth.

"We park the taxi here," Grady said, pointing to a position about forty yards up from Downing Street in a long shot of the end of Whitehall and Parliament Street. "That's just out of the line of sight of the copper standing by the Downing Street barrier. That's the Foreign Office alongside. We must be there by 2.20. She leaves any time between 2.25 and 2.50. I shall leave the taxi and walk to . . . here."

He changed to a close-up of the entrance to Downing Street. Maura was posing in the foreground, but the entrance was clearly visible, with the barrier and the policeman behind. "I can see into Downing Street to give the signal when she appears," he continued. "And I'll be in the best place to take out the copper when the time comes."

Sean was looking over his shoulder, but not at the policeman. He was staring at the picture of Maura. Christ, he'd like to part those thighs.

Grady went on: "When I see the Iron Lady's car move away from Number 10 I'll give the signal. It's the one bit we can't rehearse perfectly. OK, we can time how long it takes her car to get to the barrier, and we can time the taxi to the entrance. They've got to coincide perfectly. You can see from this picture . . . here. You've got to block her car off when it's just got through the barrier and just before the front wheels have begun to turn to the right. It's going to be tricky. These drivers are trained to reverse fast out of trouble. If we move too soon that's what he'll do. If we move a fraction too late, he might crash on past. Even if he tried to, and seriously damaged the taxi, we'd be in a mess. These drivers are good. O'Sullivan will just have to be better."

53

At the sound of his name Sean started, and turned his eyes guiltily to the photograph Grady was now referring to. If Maura was willing, and so was he, where was the harm?

"Once the car is blocked," Grady continued, "O'Sullivan will keep the engine running and stay at the wheel. By then, I'll have dealt with the copper, and you, Farrell, will be out of the taxi with Maura. You'll have the automatic because you've got the training. Maura will handle the sledgehammer. The glass is probably bullet-proof but it'll smash given a hard enough knock. We can't shoot from the front—we daren't risk getting the woman. It'll have to be from the side—that's the left-hand side looking into Downing Street. It's also the driver's side of the car, which means we can get him before he's had time to try the old Stirling Moss stuff. But we'll have to move on to the Special Branch man sitting alongside the driver in the same burst. These fellows can be quick, and he mustn't be given the chance to draw his gun."

Farrell sorted through the photographs.

"I see there's another policeman outside Number 10," he said. "He's bound to have a go, poor sod. We could gain time if we used a smoke canister."

"I was coming to that. Witnesses we don't mind. You two will both have stocking masks, and, I thought, long blond wigs. If they think you're both women, so much the better. I'll get into a mask myself, if there's time, but I doubt it. O'Sullivan's the only one at risk, and he'll just have to keep the window up and his head down. But we'll use smoke to create confusion. Maura will smash the side windows, and Farrell will fire in fast to deal with the driver and the detective. There'll be a lot of noise and a lot of panic. You must keep calm. Once the back side window is broken, you'll be able to get at the latch to open the door. I'll be there to help you get Herself into the taxi. Farrell follows, giving covering fire if necessary. Then it's up to O'Sullivan."

Farrell stared at the pictures.

"U-turn?" he queried. "Or straight on down to Trafalgar Square?"

"I'm not sure." Grady chewed his lip. "We're switching cars near Regent's Park, in Albany Street—that's where the underground garage is—but I've not yet worked out the best way to get there."

Farrell looked up. "Albany Street? That's where the barracks are."

54

"I know." Grady smiled and sat down again, complacently folding his arms. "The less you have to drive beforehand the better. It's also on the direct route for Colchester. Dublin's got this one right all the way. They're leaving no excuses."

A thoughtful silence pervaded the room. Farrell felt suddenly proud. He remembered his grandfather and 1916, and at last saw himself fulfilling what history required of him. He was strong, certain, determined. Maura was still on the window seat. She'd already heard Liam's plan and had looked at the photographs *ad nauseam*. She drank her coffee, stared into it, at the bottom inch or so revolving murkily.

"We sit here and talk," she said. "The sun shines, and people go about their business, and we make our plans . . . Sure, isn't it all just a game we're playing? D'you think it'll ever happen?"

Grady got up. He went to her and stood, one hand on her shoulder, looking quietly down into the street.

"Oh yes," he said. "Oh yes, Maura mine, it'll happen. It'll happen sure enough."

And Sean, watching the two of them, thought: So that's the way of it. Leader's bloody perks, is it? Right then, we'll see about that . . .

5

Maura had been putting it on a bit the first time she had met the English sergeant, telling him she didn't care what Mrs Thatcher was like. Of course she cared. She knew how she was going to treat her, no matter what, but the woman's character still mattered. Some of them accepted things more easily than others, but she hadn't said as much. She'd started out wanting to jolt him. He'd seemed so cold, so stuck up, taunting Sean the way he had. And also, maybe she had wanted him to notice her. But then something else had taken over . . . memories, haunting bitter memories, her hatred, her desire for vengeance; and the thought of it sent an unpleasant shiver down her spine. She hadn't realized the violence of her feelings.

Now it was the following Tuesday after the meeting in the flat. She was sitting in the Strangers' Gallery in the Chamber of the House of Commons. The scene below her was noisy, yet curiously timeless. She hardly noticed it. She was there to get a close look at the Iron Lady, and so she was waiting for 3.15 and Prime Minister's question-time.

It hadn't been difficult for her to get in. All one needed was a ticket from one's MP. Grady, who made it his business to know about these things, had warned her that the man representing the constituency in which she was now living was a Minister, and so might very well not be in the House. So she picked another MP, a Labour left-winger, bound to be a full-timer, filled in the green card given her by the attendant and sat patiently waiting in the central lobby, a kind of crossroads between the Lords and the Commons. In due course her name was called and she went over to the small standing desk in one corner, met the MP she'd asked for, and pretended to be from his constituency. They chatted briefly, mostly about the weather, and then he gave her the necessary ticket. Her shoulder bag was checked. She followed a group of other visitors along a corridor hung with portrait prints and up a flight of stairs to the back of the Strangers' Gallery. Another attendant, a gold badge hanging about his neck, handed her the Order Paper listing the day's business and an explanatory leaflet. He whispered that she was not allowed to take notes, and showed her to a seat about half-way down the steeply-raked gallery. And there she was, looking down at the symbolic heart of all that she hated most. Where it had all begun, where it had first been announced that British troops were going into the North—a decision that had ended, as inevitably as night follows day, in her brother's brutal murder.

The Prime Minister was not yet in the House. At the despatch box was the Secretary of State for Employment, the Right Honourable Norman Tebbit. His hang-dog expression gave him a permanently solemn look. He was a man who could quickly respond with a biting riposte, and today he felt he'd had more than enough of the sniping and simulated outrage of the Labour Opposition. For nearly forty-five minutes he had been answering a barrage of questions and criticism about the rising level of unemployment. As he sat down to hear yet another supplementary question he glanced up at the clock set in the oak panelling of the Press Gallery above the Speaker's chair. It was almost 3.15. The Prime Minister was unusually late. Normally she would have been sitting coolly on the bench beside him for most of his questions.

"Is the Secretary of State aware that the unprecedented rise in unemployment among school-leavers is going to condemn much of the youth of this country to the despair and degradation of the dole queue? Does he want to follow his predecessor as the man who led Britain into mass unemployment?"

During the Labour cheers that followed this piece of rhetoric, Mr Tebbit got patiently to his feet. He had answered the same question, differently phrased, at least a dozen times already.

"The increase in unemployment among young people," he began, "is a most worrying feature, and it is important that the motivation and commitment of young people be preserved. But I would remind Members opposite that—"

The rest of his reply was drowned by loud ironic jeers from the Opposition countered by loyal cheering from the benches behind him. He glanced round. Mrs Thatcher was moving calmly to her place on the front bench. The commotion continued as she sat down.

Mr Tebbit raised his voice. "And I would remind Members opposite that many jobs could be saved if we avoid wage increases we cannot afford and which price our goods out of markets. The only way to bring down unemployment is to counteract foreign competition with more productivity, better quality and lower prices. There are," he pressed on amid rising shouts of "Resign", "there are no magic formulas, no easy answers. And moreover . . ."

Up in the Strangers' Gallery Maura Lynch was leaning forward, staring down, her heart pounding. The rest of the House had blurred: its childish behaviour was forgotten, her entire attention focused on the figure in the immaculate honey-coloured jacket and skirt, the hair fixed in expensive blonde waves, seated below her with careful dignity on the buttoned green leather bench. So that was her. That was the Iron Lady.

On television, Maura thought, the woman had a chocolate-box prettiness. But down there it looked more like a cool dignity. That one will take some breaking, she mused. She's nobody's fool, and she's tough with it. And in a way Maura was glad. The time would come when it would be just the two of them. And the Iron Lady would make an interesting opponent.

Maura knew she herself would have to behave without mercy; not out of a need for vengeance, although that would be reason enough, but, she told herself, from simple expediency. The four of them, shut up together for weeks on end—something would snap if it wasn't made clear right from the beginning who was boss. Margaret Thatcher wouldn't break easily, but Maura knew how it could be done. She'd never personally worked with geriatric patients during her nursing days, nor on the psychiatric wards, but she'd seen how supremacy was established, and often with the very best of intentions—although there were inevitably, in any group of nurses, those whom the overcrowding and understaffing allowed to get away with almost anything. Yes, she'd seen how it was done . . .

Down on the floor of the House some degree of order had returned, and the Secretary of State for Employment was winding up his reply. He'd noticed the hands of the clock jerk round to 3.15 and so, with this last question before Mrs Thatcher took over, he was prepared to show his irritation and finish strongly.

"And I have to say," he declared, "when the nation is facing crucially serious problems, the country expects this House to behave constructively and responsibly, and not to have to suffer the useless bawling of the Opposition benches."

He sat down firmly. Protests and shouts resounded from the other side of the House, and broke into cries of "Apologize . . . Resign! . . ." Norman Tebbit ignored them. The Prime Minister remained seated while the Speaker shouted: "Order . . . order!" Then, above the din, he called out: "Questions to the Prime Minister!"

There was something like silence. A Labour backbencher jumped to his feet. "Number one, sir."

The question printed on the Order Paper was from a Labour MP for one of the north-east constituencies, and asked when the Prime Minister proposed to visit his constituency.

Mrs Thatcher rose calmly to the despatch box and stood, her feet precisely on the red line that ran the length of the green carpet that separated the two front benches, according to ancient tradition, by two sword-lengths.

"I have no immediate plans to do so," she answered courteously, and sat down.

The question, of course, was a much-used formula, a ruse to enable the MP to put a supplementary question about the matter that really concerned him, and so open up the subject to the House.

"Doesn't the Prime Minister think," he said, "that she should come and explain to my constituents why more and more of them are being thrown out of work by her government's inhumane policies?"

There were shouts and cheers from his colleagues. The Prime Minister, her hands lightly clasped at her waist, waited until these had died down. Then she waited a few seconds more until she had the House's undivided attention. And when she spoke it was quietly and with impressive sincerity.

"This is not a new problem," she said. "It has been developing over a number of years. This government has given first priority to fighting inflation. In doing this it is inevitable there should be a short-term increase in unemployment. The alternative is to print money— that's what the Right Honourable Gentleman opposite did—to print money," she persevered incisively above the Labour protests, "and that leads to a much bigger increase in unemployment in the long run . . . I would remind the Honourable Member that in the first year of his government unemployment rose by over a million, and—"

Uproar broke out again. She stood at the despatch box, patient and imperturbable. She spoke again, was interrupted again . . . And so the exchange continued. When the Prime Minister could make herself heard she delivered her points calmly and concisely and with conviction. Occasionally she was short with her questioners and, bending forward slightly from the hips, adopted the lecturing manner that had also earned her the name of "Headmistress". But she never allowed herself to be rushed, never permitting any serious disruption of her lucid marshalling of facts, and confronted by hostility and heckling, she remained cool and confident.

Maura watched her, filled with an uneasy mixture of dislike and admiration. Clearly, once this woman had made up her mind about something, nothing would shift her. Her handling of Northern Ireland was evidence of that. Admittedly, Maura reflected, the woman was only the last in a long line of British prime ministers who had perpetuated the injustices and misery of all Ireland by their imperialist obstinacy. But she would have met that responsibility, as she met the House now, with a certainty in her own rightness that was surely unique.

Who else but she would have let the hunger strikers die? Who else but she would have dared? And who else but the Iron Lady would have dared deny the most basic of common justice to Maura and her parents, justice for the murder of her only brother, and their only son? Ah, Michael, Michael . . .

Only seventeen he'd been, and not a thought of politics in his head—up in the North just to visit his uncle. Caught in someone else's war he'd been: shooting at a street corner, and his instinct sending him in all humanity to the aid of a man lying wounded in the gutter. And this British soldier coldly shooting him dead . . . There'd been a dozen witnesses at least. The fighting was over, no question of it, and the wounded man moaning his heart out in the gutter. And the British bastard had shot him dead, murdered him, murdered her Michael, her Michael who'd so hated killing, who'd never even owned a catapult, let alone a gun.

And the bloody Brits had admitted it. A tragic mistake, they said. In the heat of the battle, they said; and offered their deepest regrets. Their *regrets* . . . for a brother, for a son, lying dead. And they'd smuggled that murdering Tommy back into Britain quick as a flash, where he'd be strutting, free as a bird, to this very day. Denied common justice; offered regrets instead.

And all that, Maura told herself, the tears hot in her eyes, all that was the doing finally, when all was said and done, of that woman below her, with the fancy hair-do and the prissy English ways. You must love your enemies, the Bible said. But Maura had seen her parents, and seen the greyness fall over their lives. She had helped them all she could, given up her career, comforted them in their loneliness. But she wasn't Michael. She could never be their son. And he lay in the little Ballybrennan cemetery, a cold white stone marking his last resting place.

While below her, the Iron Lady was talking . . . talking . . .

Now she was answering the Leader of the Opposition. "The Right Honourable Gentleman thought differently when his government was in office. Then he supported his Right Honourable Friend, who said we could not spend ourselves out of a recession; who went to the Labour Party conference and said simply and unequivocally, 'Unemployment is caused by paying ourselves more than the value of the goods produced.' But now he asks for increased public spending. Of course he is concerned—as I am concerned—about the increase in unemployment. But what was true then is true now. If . . ."

Unemployment . . . public spending . . . could they talk of nothing else, while Ireland lay bleeding? Maura pulled herself together, dried her eyes, blowing her nose to cover the action. She glanced sideways: no one had noticed. And soon, very soon, the bloody Brits would be out for good and Ireland would be free, united and free . . . She turned back to watch Mrs Thatcher, the words spinning out of her like an endless silken thread. No longer did she listen to their meaning; their

60

fluency alone was remarkable. It continued, and so did the interruptions, for more than twenty minutes. Then Mrs Thatcher, a formidable opponent indeed, sat down. The Speaker called next business.

The Chamber rumbled into a hubbub of sound as some Members got up from their seats and made for the Members' Lobby. The Prime Minister left, followed by Mr Tebbit. She bustled, taking short steps and leaning slightly forward. It was an ungainly walk for such an obviously assured and attractive woman. Maura watched her thoughtfully. The headmistress going back to her study. But it was no school she was running. And she'd soon find out that some of its members were by no means children.

Maura herself only stayed a few more minutes. She could make little of the doings on the floor of the House. She referred to her Order Paper, but it wasn't much help. Besides, Liam and Sean would be waiting for her. Sean was getting his first look at Downing Street, and Liam had wanted to observe the Prime Minister's departure, to time it, and to take some more photographs. So Maura gathered up her shoulder bag and went down again to the central lobby.

Now the tiled floor beneath the massive brass chandelier was thronged with visitors and scurrying MPs and officials. Maura pushed her way impatiently through them to St George's Hall and out by way of St Stephen's entrance. She walked back to Bridge Street, crossed the road and went quickly up Parliament Street and Whitehall. The day was overcast and a cool wind blew her summery cotton skirt uncomfortably against the backs of her legs.

Liam and Sean were standing on the pavement opposite the entrance to Downing Street. She joined them.

"And isn't Herself the great talker," she said. "But she's got guts. She's a tough one. She'll stir up trouble between us if we give her half a chance."

But Liam seemed not to have heard her. He was staring across the road.

"It's perfect," he said. "The car's front wheels don't turn until it's well through the barrier. Getting to the doors will be easy. But the breeze blows away from Number 10, from the west. On the day that would mean any smoke canister would have to be thrown well up the street."

Sean looked at her sideways, shrugged and winked. She ignored him. Liam had his priorities right: first they must concentrate on getting the Iron Lady. They could worry later about what they were going to do with her afterwards.

Superintendent Whitaker was sitting hunched forward over his desk, a pen in his hand, his pipe neglected between his teeth, its bowl cold and spraying dead ash occasionally as he breathed. He'd begun some half an hour before to rough out a memo about security arrangements for the coming visit of a Saudi Arabian trade delegation. They would be staying at Claridges: their Embassy was undergoing extensive renovations—for which read installing new electronic anti-surveillance equipment. Just now the Saudis were unpopular with the rest of the OPEC countries for their pro-West stand on oil prices, and an incident on British territory was to be avoided at all costs. The memo, therefore, was important, and Whitaker was writing steadily. Recorders were fine for some, but the superintendent knew he worked better on paper. "How do I know what I think," he was fond of saying, "until I see what I've written?"

But now his back ached, the fingers holding the pen were cramped, and he was glad of the interruption when Sergeant Trew knocked and entered. He sat back, wincing as he eased his muscles.

"Well, Goodie? What brings you? A message from the Palace? Are they giving me my OBE at last?"

"Order of St Jude more like, sir. Wasn't he the patron saint of lost causes?"

"I wouldn't know, Goodie." Whitaker reached for the ashtray and began cleaning out his pipe. "All that bumf you've got—you wouldn't be trying to break something to me gently, would you?"

Trew fingered his sheaf of papers. "I'm afraid so, sir."

"IRA?"

Trew nodded. "I know you're jolly busy, sir, but I've just been going through the reports. The squeeze you ordered, sir, on all our Provo contacts. You remember, sir—following the Tyrie visit and the Council directive suspending mainland activities."

Whitaker groped in a pocket for his penknife.

"So it's come up with nothing, has it?"

"Almost nothing, sir. And what there is, isn't good."

He flicked through the papers, took one out, and put it on Whitaker's desk.

The superintendent opened his knife and began scraping lugubriously at his pipe bowl.

"A digest if you please, Goodie. Today isn't one of my reading days."

Trew sat down opposite his chief, carefully hitching up the legs of his Austin Reed slacks.

"Seems there's been a big Army Council meeting, sir. Chief of Staff himself—and all highly secret. Safe house, blindfolds, the lot—in that school just north of Dublin, actually."

"And?" Whitaker cocked an eyebrow.

"That's the funny thing, sir. And nothing. That's all we've got. We squeezed our poor bloody informer rotten, his last job for us, we'd shop him to his Provo bosses if he didn't come across, you know the form . . . and that's all we got. The fact of the meeting, nothing more. Who else was there, what was discussed—not a bloody sausage."

Whitaker grunted. "Odd."

"More than that, sir. Highly suspicious, I'd say. I mean, Paddy security being what it is, there's always something. A work of art, maybe, but there's always *something*."

The superintendent blew through his pipe stem. It rattled wetly. "If the clamp-down's so good, how come our man got to hear of the meeting at all?"

"It's really very simple, sir." Pipe ash had settled on the sleeve of Trew's jacket. He dusted it reproachfully. "You see, the man's sister is married to a Dublin postman. And *his* auntie's got a daughter who's between jobs at the moment. Now, Auntie's a cleaner at the school in question, and some evenings she lets her daughter stand in for her. And the daughter took a fancy to a tape recorder she saw in one of the class rooms, and a couple of Saturdays ago she decided to go back in the afternoon when the school was empty, and—"

"And it wasn't." Whitaker sighed. "Spare me the details, Goodie. I see it all." He reached for his tobacco pouch. "All I can say is, knowing the bastards, I'm surprised she lived to tell the tale."

"It cost her, sir." Trew cleared his throat. "By all accounts the guard who caught her wasn't gentle." He shrugged. "Still, I don't expect hers has been the only virginity lost behind those particular bicycle sheds. And a knee-capping would have been worse."

Whitaker didn't find that amusing. Not for the first time he felt sickened by the cheating and lying and petty exploitation on which so much of his work depended. And besides, he had a teenage daughter of his own.

63

He lit his pipe, taking his time about it. Finally: "I presume we have only the one informant for this meeting?"

Trew shifted uneasily. He'd been guilty of a lapse of taste and he knew it.

"But reliable, sir. If past experience is anything to go by."

"Only one informant," Whitaker mused, "and that one only by the merest chance. Unusually good security. And therefore an unusually important meeting. And what, I wonder, was discussed at this unusually important meeting? General policy? Or something more specific?" He tamped down shreds of glowing tobacco with a calloused thumb. "I'd plump for the specific. Wouldn't you?"

Trew didn't answer. He was sorting through his notes.

"One more thing, sir. Andy Tyrie's just given an interview—*Boston Globe* of all papers. Their columnist calls him 'an affable rogue'... Anyway, he's promising a moratorium on all UDA killings—even of the chaps on their special assassination list. Unless, so he says, there's blatant provocation. His exact words, sir: blatant provocation."

Whitaker frowned. "Obviously he knows something. He knows something's in the wind and that's his way of issuing a warning. He may know more than we do and he may not. He may just be putting two and two together. Either way, he won't tell *us*, that's for sure." He sat up straight, suddenly businesslike, his pipe forgotten. "Eyes and ears, Goodie—the policeman's best friends. We can't do much at this stage, but I can put out a plea for a special watch on all things Irish. We'll start with London. With the Provos sitting around idle there's always the chance that one of them will put his foot in it. And every London copper will be waiting for him to do so."

6

Sometimes the Prime Minister gave her aides and advisers the impression that she relaxed by taking on more work. Her compulsive energy had, from time to time, left more than one of them exhausted. She worked hard herself and expected nothing less from everyone else, but whereas she thrived upon it all and her blue eyes sparkled with the anticipation of more, there were those who understandably wearied at the pace. Among the staff at Number 10 there was an unmistakable relief—which they were careful to conceal in the presence of the Prime Minister herself—that the summer recess was upon them. It had been a tough, hard-slogging session. Not, it was realized with a certain foreboding, that Mrs Thatcher was proposing much of a holiday, but at least the pressure occasioned by an inexorable Parliamentary timetable would diminish, and the shower of terse Prime Ministerial memos should abate a little.

This morning the Prime Minister had been receiving a group of constituency workers in the White Drawing Room, dispensing morning coffee and emphasizing to these party faithfuls, in the privacy of Number 10, her strongly-held personal view that the country must be made to face major changes, both political and economic. Such transitional periods were inevitably painful, but she was convinced that the overall strategy was right. She might feel impatient sometimes, but she never felt doubt. If Japan could do it, Britain could do it. That was the message she offered her supporters and they received it warmly.

Now, for a few moments, she was alone among the delicate gilt chairs, the brocaded sofas and elegant Adam furniture, precious relics of a more gracious age. Among the pictures on the walls there was still the peaceful little Corot, in misty greens and greys, of cows standing in a marsh, which Ted Heath used to have hanging alongside his grand piano. She may have reflected on the sad contrast between its tranquillity and the storms that her predecessor had brought down upon himself. But it is more likely, since she now glanced down at the small round dial of her gold wristwatch, that her mind had already moved on ahead to her next appointment. The time was 11.30. James Prior, the Secretary of State for Northern Ireland, would be waiting to see her.

Briskly Mrs Thatcher left the White Drawing Room and returned to her inner office. She summoned Mr Prior.

In 1689 thirteen apprentice boys in the city of Londonderry had slammed the gates on the army of King James, thus beginning the famous three-month siege of the city. It was this act of rebellion, together with King William's later victory at the Boyne, that had led to the change of ownership of land in Ireland and had given the Protestants an ascendancy which they had ruthlessly used to ensure that all Roman Catholics were deprived of position and property, of education and power . . . And the Secretary of State for Northern Ireland had come to report to his Prime Minister that this year's commemoration of the event had passed off with agreeably little trouble. Some hooliganism, stone throwing, and the burning of a bus. The Army had kept in the background, and the event had been admirably managed by the Royal Ulster Constabulary. This low profile for the Army was part of a policy that his predecessor, Mr Atkins, with the help of William Whitelaw, had sold hard to the Prime Minister. Now he was able to point out that it seemed to be paying off.

Mrs Thatcher thanked him drily, and repeated her abiding determination to stamp out terrorism, from whichever side. They discussed ways and means, and then moved on to their party's commitment to some sort of devolved government for Northern Ireland. The role of Mr Ian Paisley was raised, as it had been raised before and would be again. Negotiating with him would be difficult, but then getting some kind of devolved government was bound to be difficult. Nevertheless, the Prime Minister was convinced that it could, and must, be done.

Sean O'Sullivan was out in the West End, looking for a taxi. He had completed his last watch on the Downing Street entrance in that current parliamentary session two days before. Herself had left at three o'clock. That was the latest ever; sometimes it had been as early as twenty-five past two. Well, he'd be ready whenever it was.

Today Sean had taken a 134 bus from Muswell Hill down into town. He had a look first at the underground garage in Albany Street. Liam had told him to check often on the vacant parking bays. The garage was under an expensive block of flats, Chester Court, but there was no attendant, and although the bays were numbered, Sean had noticed that there were some which were permanently empty. Two of them were conveniently at the end of a row.

When he'd finished looking round the garage and had confirmed once again the angle of the approach ramp, which he might one day be taking in something of a hurry, he strolled slowly along Albany Street, watching the taxis that passed him in a steady stream. There were more cabs in London, he thought, than black beetles in a strip-club basement.

He noticed there was a police station in Albany Street, as well as the army barracks. The idea of making the switch within a few hundred yards of a nick amused him. After a while a taxi stopped just ahead of him to pick up a fare. It was black with no particular identifying marks. He made a note of the number plate, and also of its hackney carriage number. Acquiring a cab itself proved less easy. It took him a long day's wandering until, well into the evening, he found one unattended, not far from where he'd begun looking. It was alone on the rank at the top of Great Portland Street, almost opposite the tube station. He still had the bundle of keys he'd used in his sideline back in his Earls Court days, and his hand hadn't lost its skill. He was into the cab and away in a matter of thirty seconds.

Back in Colney Hatch Lane the red Mini was already parked on the road. He drove the taxi into the garage and left it there, carefully closing and locking the doors. That night he removed the hackney carriage number plate and, after Maura had made a copy of the style of the numbers, scraped it clean. Then he painted it white again and left it to dry.

The following afternoon, while Maura was busy with a fine brush and a tin of black enamel, he went to a car accessory shop and ordered number plates to go with the hackney carriage number he had noted the night before. He left a false name and address and paid cash in advance. The plates would be ready, he was told by the bored assistant, in three days' time. On the way back to the flat he called in at a self-service ironmonger and bought a green-painted four-pound sledgehammer with a two-foot-six handle.

When he got home Maura was still at the kitchen table, hunched over her lettering. She looked up irritably.

"This is harder than it looks. Haven't I had to wipe it off and start again a dozen times at least?"

Her hair was untidy, there was a smudge of paint on her cheek, and he thought she looked enchanting.

"Cheer up, old darlin'," he said. "Haven't I brought you a fine present now?"

He showed her the sledgehammer. She took it from him and nearly dropped it.

"Christ, it's heavy. Who d'you think I am—Mr Universe himself?"

He laughed. "You and him together, and I reckon I could just about tell the difference. You'd be the one with the pretty face." He watched her stand up, heft the sledgehammer and swing it experimentally. The movement tightened the blouse across her breasts. "Where's Liam?" he asked.

"Out."

"I can see that. When's he coming back?"

"God knows. He's taken the Mini, gone looking for a place for us to practise. I've forgotten where—something like Upping Forest." She lifted the hammer shoulder high. "I'll soon get the way of it if I keep at it."

"No question, darlin'. And the name's Epping—Epping Forest. Sounds like swearing. I reckon it's maybe twenty miles. With the rush hour coming, he won't be back for hours."

Maura rested the hammer on the floor and sat down again. "That's a mercy. I'd like to get these blamed numbers done for him to see."

She reached for her paint brush. Sean put his hand gently on her arm.

"Where's the hurry? We won't get the plates for a couple of days—there's plenty of time."

She looked up at him. "Isn't it your day for the cooking?" she said pointedly.

"Sure, and there'll be time enough to boil up a few spuds after."

"After what?"

He sat down at the table, drew her arm closer, took her hand in both of his.

"Would you be saying, Maura me love, that I'm a bad-looking sort of feller?"

She met his gaze, answered him lightly. "Sure, but I've seen worse."

He tightened his grip. "I doubt you've seen better."

He pulled her towards him. Up to now she hadn't resisted. Now, suddenly, she stiffened.

"No, Sean. No—it wouldn't be right."

He'd heard that before a thousand times. "Nothing that's worth having's right," he murmured. "You listen to them priests, me darlin', and—"

"Not the priests, Sean. Us . . . you and me . . . here . . . the operation." She was pleading. "Didn't Liam say—?"

He exploded. "Liam! Who does he think he is—Saint Peter himself? And him not above a little tender loving care himself when he thinks nobody's looking?"

"Why, Sean O'Sullivan, I do believe you're jealous." Her words

68

were joking but her gaze was wary. "You're thinking Liam's got in first."

"And hasn't he? Christ—you were here together bloody long enough before I came. Hasn't he?"

"Him? He's like a monk, that one." She forced a laugh. "Besides, he'd have wasted his time trying. He's just not my sort, Sean. You know?"

Sean looked at her, at her flushed cheeks, her soft full lips, her breasts lifting provocatively as she breathed. He wasn't sure he believed her, but it didn't matter. He stumbled to his feet, dragging her up with him, and held her tightly against his body. Let them feel *that*, he thought. Let them know what's coming to them. It always does the trick . . .

She struggled, but only briefly: he was stronger than she. He felt her sag against him and his blood pounded with his need for her. He moved one hand to the back of her head, tilted her face up to his, and thrust his mouth down on to hers. And tasted salt tears . . .

She was trembling now, weeping uncontrollably. He hesitated, puzzled. She had seemed so eager.

She wrenched her head away. "No, Sean," she sobbed. "No . . ."

He stared down at her, angry. "Why not?" He had known teasers before, hadn't marked her as one. "If it's not Liam, and it's not the priests, then what the hell is it?"

She lowered her head. There was a long silence. Then, very softly, "I . . . can't."

"Of course you can. You were keen enough a moment since."

"That's not true." She eased herself out of his grasp, turned away. "There . . . there are things a woman doesn't like to have to explain, Sean."

He rubbed the back of his hand across his mouth, watching her as she walked slowly to the door. So *that* was it.

"Then why did you lead me on so, you bloody bitch?"

"I never led you on, Sean." She spoke quietly, over her shoulder, as she continued on out of the room. "Think back, Sean. I swear to God I never led you on."

When she was no longer there he slumped at the table, still staring at the now empty doorway. Oh, the bitch, the bloody little bitch . . . Sure, and she wouldn't catch him like that again in a hurry. Just let her wait till she really wanted it—two could play hard to get as well as one. And there were more good fish in the sea than ever came out of it.

He looked down, saw on the table the metal disc she'd been painting, and swept it with an angry gesture on to the floor. It landed paint-side up and slithered away into the corner by the refrigerator. A moment later, as his anger faded, he got awkwardly to his feet, stooped, and guiltily retrieved the disc. There were two numerals painted on it, and half of a third. The lettering was very good. He stared at it. Would she tell Liam what had happened, he wondered. Christ, he hoped not . . .

Maura closed her bedroom door behind her and stood for a while, leaning against it. Then she laughed softly and went to the pink-frilled dressing table for a paper handkerchief with which she dried her face. Real tears! If she was as good as that maybe one day she should go on the stage. But what a poor fool Sean was: *There are things a woman doesn't like to have to explain*—fancy him swallowing that, and she a nurse. A good few years had passed since any aspect of human biology could cause her embarrassment . . . Still, it was a good excuse, one that a man like Sean would never argue with.

She sat down at the dressing table and reached for her eye shadow. Seriously though—the three of them were in for trouble. Sean would be sure to try again. She hadn't given him the slightest encouragement, had dressed soberly, had always been looking the other way when he tried giving her the eye . . . if it hadn't worked before there was no reason why it should now. And she could hardly use that same excuse again. So what then? It was important that he shouldn't think she didn't fancy him: he was jealous enough of Liam as it was, and with no good reason, and the whole success of the operation depended on the three of them trusting each other. Imagine them holed-up in Colchester for weeks on end, with something like this simmering in the background! And besides, she almost *did* fancy him . . .

But Liam had strong views on the subject, and Liam was boss. She accepted that. So how she was to handle Sean she didn't know. How complicated life was. She finished making up her eyes and sat back to see the effect. The scene with Sean, she realized, stretching sensuously, had made her feel in the mood. Well, was that wrong? Maybe she should have been above such things, but wasn't she only flesh and blood? Michael would never have blamed her. Michael, who was innocence itself, would never have blamed her for that. Ah, Michael, Michael . . .

70

She stayed in her room an hour. When she came out she was bright and brisk. She went back to her lettering. Neither of them referred to what had happened. Sean was morosely frying onions, and a haze of burning hung over the kitchen. She was glad of it. A pile of dog-ends lay in a tin lid on the draining board, and if Liam smelt cigarettes about the place when he returned he'd go through the roof.

He got back shortly after seven, and was in good spirits.

"I've found the ideal place," he said. "Couldn't be better."

In a lonely farmhouse at the foot of a hill in County Wicklow a group of serious, determined-looking men were watching a replay of the previous night's BBC nine o'clock television news. Whiskey was on the table, but they drank sparingly. Several minutes of the broadcast were taken up with an end-of-session interview with Mrs Thatcher. Many of the things she said, and also the confident, superior British way in which she said them, were almost certainly laughable to the men gathered in the low-beamed parlour. None of them laughed, however. In a country of jokers the Army Council guarded its serious-mindedness.

Early on, though, while the talk was still of unemployment, inflation, the money supply, one of them did nudge his neighbour and point to the screen.

"Will you look at them flowers. From a grateful admirer, is it?"

Another grunted. "She asks for them—did you not know that? She reckons they warm up the empty, barn-like studio interiors. I read that in the paper."

"Bugger the studio. Couldn't she do with some warming up now?"

A ripple of amusement. A hand was raised. Silence.

". . . I wonder," the interviewer was saying, "if we could now turn to Northern Ireland, Prime Minister? With the two communities still holding to entrenched positions, is there the slightest chance of your government's proposals making any progress?"

Mrs Thatcher had listened politely, her head tilted intently to the right. She was wearing a dark, almost royal blue dress, a double row of pearls at her neck. Now she leaned earnestly forward.

"Oh, I hope so. When we came to power we said, in the Queen's speech, that we would strive to restore peace and security, and that we would seek an acceptable way of restoring to the people of Northern Ireland more control over their own affairs . . ."

71

The interviewer rustled his notes. "But—"

"If I may just finish." Mrs Thatcher smiled at him ruthlessly. "And those two aims we are going to fulfil. And you know, there is a great deal more security than there used to be. We have been able to give much more authority to the police, to the Royal Ulster Constabulary, and to hold the Army in reserve, and the people of the province, the great majority of them, they don't want terrorism on their streets: they want to be able to live happy, normal lives like everyone else . . ."

There was a stir of anger in the room. "Normal lives, is it? With an army of occupation lording it like—" And again the hand was raised, while from the loudspeaker Mrs Thatcher's words continued in a quiet, relentlessly mellifluous stream.

". . . and you know, there is so much more co-operation than many people realize, and so many more occasions when Protestant and Catholic work together. We don't hear of these things, but there is something to build upon, and if only we can continue to improve the security, then I think there is a chance. There must be a chance. Because, you know, no one wants to live in an atmosphere of uncertainty and fear. And there's no doubt that the IRA, the Provisional IRA, have lost some support and authority. And I have welcomed the way the Irish Prime Minister has made it clear that the terrorist is as much an enemy to the Republic as he is to the people of Northern Ireland—"

A finger went compulsively out to the "pause" key, and Mrs Thatcher's image froze on the screen.

"He never said that, did he?"

"Sure he did, though. He's a politician, isn't he? And what did Ireland ever get from her bloody politicians but double-talk and schemin'?"

"Ah. But you're right there, Patrick. You're right there."

The finger was removed, and Mrs Thatcher continued as if the interruption had never occurred. As indeed it hadn't in her well-regulated television world.

"Yes, I really do believe that with goodwill—and I am an optimist, you know—we can at least make some progress, and bring peace. And then, with peace, prosperity to that most troubled province . . ."

For a moment the interviewer seemed uncertain whether Mrs Thatcher had finished. Then, "Thank you, Prime Minister," he said hastily. On a close-up of her smiling face the screen went blank.

72

One of the men in the farmhouse parlour got up and turned on the bare overhead bulb.

"Jaysus! Doesn't it make you want to spit? More security than there used to be, indeed."

"But it was a Council decision to hold off." The voice was calmly insistent. "It *was* a Council decision, wasn't it?"

"Sure, and did I say it wasn't? But to hear that woman's self-righteous—"

"Ah, it's the pride that comes before a fall, so it is."

"She'll be laughing on the other side of her face come the winter."

"She'll see then the authority we've got, all right."

"So it's still agreed?" As always, the quiet, almost hypnotic voice, bringing them back to the matter in hand. They had been called together so that they could understand the short-term effects of their planning. "So it's still agreed? We go ahead?"

There were a few seconds of nervous silence, then a muttered chorus of agreement.

"I'm sorry for our team, though," one of them offered. "That woman—sure, she'd try the patience of a saint."

Their leader smiled. "Don't doubt they'll find a way of coping. They're not exactly saints themselves. And to lose his patience is no great burden to the man who has no need of it."

7

Grady stood naked, save for his briefs, in front of the wall of mirrors in his bedroom, rubbing Ambre Solaire Duo Tan lotion into his face and neck. Then he treated the backs of his hands, and his arms up as far as his elbows. Finally he darkened his feet, also to an overall golden brown. He stared at himself in disgust. When first suggested, this had seemed a good idea. Now its theatricality made him feel a fool, and he was tempted to turn the whole project over to O'Sullivan. The oaf would love it.

He tilted his head and studied his reflection. No. If either of them were to pass for an Arab it must be he. His face was lean, his eyebrows sloped, and there was even the suggestion of a hook to his nose. Sean's amiable moon face would never pass muster.

Quickly he turned to the bed, took up the webbing harness Maura had made for him, and fixed it over his shoulders and round his waist. That was for the automatic rifles, and anything else that wouldn't fit inside the slim briefcase, which was all he would carry. Then he slipped on sandals and the white Arab burnous he had found in a trendy shop on the Portobello Road. He debated whether he should remove his wristwatch, and decided not to. Arabs wore watches like everyone else these days.

With one final look in the mirror—and the overall effect was reasonably convincing—he picked up his briefcase and quickly left the room. The sound of Sergeant Pepper's Lonely Hearts Club Band blasting out of the sitting room told him where O'Sullivan was. That, and the faint smell of the man's foul roll-ups. Maura he found in the kitchen. She'd pushed the table back and was holding the sledge-hammer out at arm's length, her face crimson with the effort.

"Tell O'Sullivan it's time we left," he said curtly.

She turned to him, and lowered the hammer with a sigh of relief.

"I was counting," she gasped. "I can get up to forty, but I'll make a hundred yet." She examined him critically. "You'll do," she said, restraining a smile.

Grady twisted his shoulders self-consciously inside the long flowing robe. "That was the idea, wasn't it?"

She sighed. "Did anyone ever tell you, Liam Grady, you're the hardest man to get along with? No—don't answer that." She retreated from his glare, laughing gently. "I'll go and fetch Sean."

Grady waited in the kitchen, looking out at the blue sky above the rooftops opposite. At least he had a good day for it. He'd have felt even sillier in this bloody outfit if it had been raining. Behind him the sound of the record stopped. There was a long pause, then O'Sullivan appeared, Maura watchful behind him. She must have warned him to keep his jokes to himself, because all he said was, "The Mini's out front, boss. I'll back it round to the door." But laughter was ready to burst out of him at any minute, and he turned quickly away.

"Not the Mini," Grady called after him. "I'm walking no further in this get-up than I have to. We'll take the taxi—then you can pick me up outside the place afterwards." He turned to Maura. "You might as well stay here. Keep on with the exercises."

He hesitated. Having her about the place wasn't as difficult as he'd feared.

"You did a good job on those numbers," he said. "I reckon you'd do a good job on anything you set your mind to." Praise didn't come to him easily. He frowned. "I wish I could say the same about O'Sullivan."

She stepped aside to let him pass. "Sean's all right," she said. "It's only an act. He's serious enough where the operation's concerned. And he thinks the world of you."

Grady went down the stairs without answering, and waited behind the closed door, briefcase in hand, until he heard the clatter of the taxi's diesel outside. Then he opened the door and went quickly down the steps and into the waiting cab. The alleyway was very private, but there was no point in taking chances. An Arab seen leaving the flat might cause talk.

He leaned forward, tapped on the glass. O'Sullivan slid it back. "You know the address?"

"Sure I do, boss. 22 Queen's Gate."

"Drop me off a couple of hundred yards before you get there. Then drive slowly round the block and wait. I shouldn't be more than twenty minutes."

He sat back, well out of sight, as the taxi drove down the alley and into Colney Hatch Lane. He relaxed, put the briefcase on the seat beside him, and crossed his legs. The robe felt strange: cool, almost as if he were naked. He glanced at the back of O'Sullivan's head. So the oaf thought the world of him, did he? A pity he didn't try a bit harder then, always arsing about . . . Still, he'd done a good job getting this taxi and fixing it up, and he was driving it now briskly and with assurance through the dense London traffic. And he'd be a hard one in a fight, not much doubt about that.

Grady left the taxi at the corner of Queen's Gate and Bremner Road. He checked the street numbers and walked on down past Prince Consort Road. The sandals and the flapping burnous forced an unfamiliar pace upon him—leisurely and, he hoped, typically Arab. He felt horribly obvious, like a man in a bad fancy dress, but nobody gave him a second look.

Number 22 was like all the others in the stately terrace of cream stuccoed houses, each with its pillared entrance porch and balustraded balcony. The number was painted boldly on the two front pillars. Outside it the black, white and red flag of Iraq hung from a short flag-staff, limp in the still afternoon air. Behind all the windows were trellised steel shutters, and mounted each side of the porch were small television cameras. A third camera was fixed high on the wall two porches further down, giving a general view of the street. A large blue Mercedes was parked outside, and between it and the porch stood a young police constable.

Grady had expected him: he would be a member of the Diplomatic Protection Group of A Division. The Irishman squared his shoulders and slap-sandalled boldly past him and up the four steps to the front door of the Iraqi Embassy. He rang the bell and waited, feeling the policeman's eyes on his back. The door stayed closed for an anxiously long time. Finally it was opened by a burly Arab in a Western suit.

"Yes?"

Grady leaned forward. "I have an appointment."

"You have papers?"

Shit. He'd forgotten to have them ready. "I'll be getting them out." He lifted his briefcase.

"No."

The Arab held out his hand, took the briefcase, opened it. He looked inside and then returned it to Grady, who took out the papers he'd been given in Dublin. The Arab examined them carefully, stepped back and motioned him in. Grady entered, and the door closed behind him with a dull metallic sound. Sweat was running coldly down beneath his arms. The Arab searched him for hidden weapons, then led him to a waiting room, watched by another TV camera.

"You will wait here. Not long, I think."

Grady sat, leafing blindly through that week's European edition of *Arab World*. After ten minutes or so he was taken into a high well-proportioned room, thickly carpeted and furnished with magnificent Moorish antiques. A slim, elegant man, also in Western dress, sat behind a massive desk. He had sallow, well-boned features, dark eyebrows and moustache, sleeked-back hair, and a dazzling smile. He rose courteously, and they shook hands.

"Welcome, Mr Grady. Your papers are in order, and your . . . 'goods' are being made ready at this moment."

Grady sat down. "They have been paid for?"

"But of course. Your . . . friends are men of honour, are they not?"

Grady relaxed. There'd always been the possibility, knowing

bloody Arabs, that they'd try to screw him for more cash. There was money, in an envelope in his briefcase, against that contingency.

The diplomat's smile widened. "We too are men of honour," he said, as if he had read Grady's thoughts. "A deal is a deal." Then he pointed to the burnous. "I see you like dressing up, Mr Grady."

"No." Grady controlled his irritation. "I just thought it better."

"Ah." The Arab pondered. "Then perhaps you are like the conjuror—positively nothing up your sleeve?" He laughed extravagantly, saw Grady's unsmiling face, and laughed some more. "Clearly, Mr Grady, you are *not* a man who relishes fancy dress. But believe me, I do understand my national dress is useful for hiding things other than white rabbits . . ."

Still laughing, he pressed the bell on his desk and a moment later two swarthy men, both in chauffeur's uniforms, came in, one carrying several small but heavy boxes, and the other a cloth bundle that contained two sub-machine guns.

"They are from our strongroom," the Iraqi explained. "And from the Israelis before that. Such things do come our way from time to time. UZIs, of course. We ourselves use Russian PPS-43s, but it is wiser that we do not give you those. The UZI, too, is an excellent weapon."

The guns were placed on the desk and Grady got up to examine them. Both had folding metal butts and were in excellent condition. He lifted his burnous, aware suddenly of the whiteness of his body, and fitted them into the harness Maura had devised. They were cold against his skin, but reassuring.

The boxes contained a hand-gun, smoke grenades and magazines of ammunition. The gun and five of the UZI magazines, each with twenty-five 9-millimetre rounds, went into his briefcase. Another five magazines, together with two smoke grenades, joined the UZIs in his harness. By the time he had lowered his robe, checked that it hung loosely, with no sharp edges, and picked up his briefcase, he was a walking arsenal.

The Iraqi diplomat was delighted. "You must be careful you do not trip, Mr Grady. With such a clattering of metal people would think you are the famous Irish tinker. Is that not so?"

Clearly the man liked to show off how well read and cosmopolitan he was. But Grady, having got what he had come for, was prepared to be forgiving. "The Irish are famous for other men than tinkers," he suggested mildly. "Our history is full of heroes. And Bernard Shaw was an Irishman. So was James Joyce."

"Ah, but wasn't Joyce—" now the Arab was laughing so much he could hardly speak "—wasn't Joyce the greatest tinker of them all?"

He collapsed against his desk. Grady smiled discreetly. The joke, if joke it was, escaped him. He'd always thought James Joyce was a writer. He picked up his heavily-laden briefcase.

"I'll be on my way, then."

The Iraqi diplomat collected himself and shook hands warmly.

"Good luck, Mr Grady. It has been a pleasure meeting you. Something tells me we share many of the same enemies."

"Sure we do." If it was an attempt to pump him, it was a clumsy one. "Well . . . goodbye, then. And, thank you."

The Arab showed him to the front door. "No, no—it is I who should thank you. A man must help his friends. It is by doing so that he gains virtue . . . And remember, Mr Grady, walk very carefully. There are steps outside. Please do not trip in front of the noble British policeman."

He opened the door and stood there, chuckling softly, as Grady went down the steps, past the policeman, and as quickly as he could manage in the direction of Cromwell Road. After thirty yards or so Grady looked over his shoulder, saw a cab pull out from the kerb a long way behind him. He paused. As the taxi approached he recognized the number plate, and hailed it. It stopped beside him and he leaned forward briefly, as if giving an address. Then he got in and the cab drove off, turning almost immediately into Imperial Institute Road.

O'Sullivan already had the interior sliding window open. "That bloody copper had his eye on you," he said.

Grady arranged the weapons under his robe so that he could sit more comfortably. "Only doing his job. He'd have stopped me if he'd thought there was anything funny."

"And what then? Christ, boss, I was shitting blue lights, so I was."

"I was safe enough," Grady said easily. "They don't like to harass embassy visitors. Certainly not in front of senior embassy officials."

His belly, too, was giving him hell, but he didn't care to admit it. His ulcer always played up when he was under stress.

"What do you think we've got?" he said. "It's bloody ironical. They've given us UZIs—the things Garda Special Branch men carry round in those blue attaché cases."

Sean looked back over his shoulder, chortling with delight. "I've always wanted to play with one of those," he said.

Grady frowned. "You'd better pray you don't have to. If you need to come out shooting on the day, then there'll be something badly wrong. Farrell's the man with the artillery. You stick to your driving."

He reached automatically for one of the bismuth tablets he always carried, but he'd left them at home in the rush. And besides, the burnous had no pockets.

Later that afternoon PC Richard Crome, Diplomatic Protection Group A Division, sat behind a typewriter in Cannon Row Police Station and slowly tapped out: ". . . At 14.45 a young man about five feet six inches tall, slim and tanned, of Middle East appearance, wearing white flowing Arab dress, and carrying a black leather briefcase, arrived at the Iraqi Embassy on foot. At the door, he spoke quietly to an embassy official, but not in an Arab accent. What little I heard sounded more like an Irish accent. He stayed about 20 minutes, and then left, walking in the direction of Cromwell Road. After a few moments, he hailed a taxi and was driven off down Imperial Institute Road. The cab's registration number was WYE 608S . . ."

8

Farrell had arranged to spend the following day—Thursday—in London. It was convenient for him, and Grady had decided it was a good day for their first practice. There was less chance of Epping Forest being crowded with picnickers. He had chosen a very secluded spot, but there was no sense in taking unnecessary risks.

It was nearly three weeks since the sergeant's last visit, and he had filled the time well. He'd broken into the flat at Abbey Field and had fitted the door with a good new lock, undetectable from the outside. He had checked the sheets of thick plywood on all the windows, and carefully stuffed newspapers into what few cracks there were. It was now safe to shine a light inside. He'd also been stocking the place with tinned goods, cornflakes, instant coffee, just a few at a time, all that he could carry without making himself noticeable. There was grass sprouting through the cracked tarmacadam surrounding the blocks of flats, and the grass of the central drying area had been left uncut and stood now as over-ripe hay. So he was careful always to approach by a different route, so that he didn't wear a revealingly beaten path.

The flat itself had one double bedroom and two small singles. Paper hung in long shreds from its walls, plaster had fallen from the sitting-room ceiling, and there was a stink of damp and neglect that wasn't helped by the warm weather and the closely covered windows. But the toilet flushed, and water came out of the taps. So Farrell bought disinfectant and did his best to clean the place up; and he reflected wryly that if the others were there well into November they would be grateful for the stuffiness to help them keep warm. Colchester could be a windy, bitterly cold town.

He was glad of the work to keep himself busy, his mind occupied. He even wished it had been a little more difficult, but his PSI's job made it easy for him to organize his own time. But to keep his evenings free he had cancelled his twice-weekly snooker date with a REME sergeant—ricked his back, he'd said, and wasn't up to all that stooping. And his woman out in the town was having to get used to going to the pub on her own, too. He wasn't worried. If she found herself another bloke there . . . well, he himself wasn't going to be around all that much longer.

But in spite of his new activity, he still had a strong sense of being left out of the main centre of action. Maybe that was a good thing, he told himself. He'd made a real effort to get on with Grady the last time, but the man was as touchy as a colour-sergeant with piles. In fact, the less they saw of each other the better. And he didn't really need all Grady's bloody practising—he was a trained soldier, not an IRA amateur. But his isolation up in Colchester still irked him, and he put on his civvies that Thursday morning with an almost schoolboy feeling of eager anticipation. At last he was going to accomplish something. And he'd show those buggers a thing or two in the process.

He took the army uniforms Grady had asked for, and Sean met him in the Mini at Highgate underground station, and drove him right up the alleyway to the flat's entrance. The Irishman talked all the way about the guns they'd got from the Iraqi Embassy. Farrell thought he sounded like a kid with a new train-set, but he kept the thought to himself. He was glad he'd brought the thin plastic gloves as well as the leather pair he was wearing for the car journey. If he was going to handle guns he would need something sensitive.

The weaponry was upstairs, laid out on the leather sofa in the sitting room, curiously incongruous in such plush surroundings. Farrell approved of the stubby-barrelled UZIs. He was familiar with them: the West German army used them. They were very compact guns, with folding butts and ten-and-a-quarter-inch barrels. The magazine, pushed into the pistol grip, lay at right angles to the body.

"We've got ten magazines," Grady said. "That's two hundred and fifty rounds. The guns fire six hundred a minute."

Farrell knew that. "One magazine's enough," he said. "The two men will be close together." He tried to imagine it, the detective and the driver sitting in the car, himself firing the bullets which killed them. Somehow the image refused to sharpen.

"You'll carry three," Grady said. "There may be others you have to deal with."

"Twenty-five rounds spread pretty wide. Still, if you say so."

"I do say so."

Farrell shrugged. He changed his gloves, pushed back the coffee table, took the first UZI, got down on the floor in the classic firing position. He stripped the weapon, checked it meticulously, then reassembled it. He slipped in a magazine of the 9-millimetre cartridges, making sure the change lever was pushed to "S", then detached it again. He performed all these actions crisply, methodically, with the minimum of movement.

Maura came into the room. She watched him.

"Sure, and it's nice to see a man who knows what he's about." Grady rounded on her.

"If he lies down like that in the middle of Whitehall he'll have the coppers pissing themselves laughing."

Farrell reached for the second gun.

"Not for long they wouldn't," he said quietly, and repeated his drill. In his mind, suddenly, the picture was no longer blurred. He was squeezing the trigger, there was a rippled crack and two bodies crumpled into the fire-power.

When he'd finished with the gun he unwrapped the parcel containing the army uniforms. Grady was unimpressed.

"We'll see if they fit when we get back from Epping," he said.

Sean had already loaded the taxi. He had managed to track down a Rover similar to the one used by the Iron Lady and he had measured it carefully—the size of its side windows and their height from the ground. Now, in the back of the taxi, there were two window-sized pieces of plywood cut from the remains of an old packing case he'd found under the stairs, an expanding measure, some nails, and Maura's sledgehammer. There was also a piece of wood trimmed to the rough shape of a UZI. Grady said that, practice or no practice, there was no point in risking being caught with one of the actual guns. For once Farrell agreed with him.

They drove out to the North Circular, and round it to the turn-off for Epping. During the journey, Farrell reported on his activities up in Colchester. Grady was satisfied, and the atmosphere in the back of the taxi eased. When they reached the forest, Grady led them through side roads and finally down a long leafy track. The trees closed about them. The taxi stopped at the edge of a small depression that looked as though it had once been a quarry but was now thickly overgrown.

Under Grady's instructions Sean nailed the pieces of plywood between two trees at the correct height, then angled the taxi close against them. Farrell saw the amount of space left between them and the side of the taxi. It was small, only just enough to get the taxi door decently open.

"If that's really how it's going to be," he said, "then you'll have to drag the Iron Lady round the back and in at the other side. There's never room for us all here."

Grady smiled. "We were going to anyway. With me coming from the back it'll be far quicker. And it'll leave you a free field of fire, Sergeant."

Sean was sent back along the track to keep watch, and they practised piling out into the restricted space while Grady timed them. First Maura led, and struck at the front piece of ply with her sledgehammer while Farrell was getting past behind her. Then they found it was quicker if Farrell led. But it was still very slow. Farrell suggested that Maura break only the rear side window: then the men in the front seats would have to turn to shoot and he could get them with no chance of hitting the Prime Minister. Grady thought about it, then agreed.

They practised again and again. At first they bumped into each other and it was impossible not to laugh, but they were soon too tired for that. Farrell's hands sweated unpleasantly inside his gloves, but he saw the point of them and didn't complain. Maura too, swinging her sledgehammer, was obviously glad of the breaks necessary now and then while Grady re-attached the plywood panels to the tree. But Farrell had to hand it to her. It cost her a visible effort even to lift the hammer, but she wouldn't give in. By the time they finished for the day she was landing two in three blows squarely on target and had splintered it until it was useless. When they were done Grady flung both pieces far out of sight into the undergrowth.

Sean came back and they rested, sitting on the ground, their backs against a low mossy bank. Grady took the opportunity to deliver a lecture, recapping for Farrell's benefit the progress made so far: the pattern that had emerged in the timing of the Prime Minister's departures for the House, the underground garage, and the place he had chosen in Whitehall where the taxi must wait.

"Farrell," he said, "next time you have to bring a Land Rover to London check on the car park. Just drive in and out again. Make sure you know the approaches. On the day you must have parked by 1.45 at the latest. We'll pick you up in the taxi at the top of Portland Place at two o'clock. Check how long it takes you to get there."

He paused. "We'll be wanting plastic explosive and detonators. Can you arrange that?"

Farrell hesitated. He didn't like it. Up to that moment there'd been no mention of explosives in the plan, and he'd have preferred to know what he was letting himself in for. A glance at Maura's face told him that she too was puzzled. Still, for better or worse Grady was the leader.

He nodded. "Can do." He'd have to steal the stuff. But he could arrange things so it wouldn't be missed till the next inventory. By that time he'd either be safely out of the country or . . . or what? Or dead, he supposed. Certainly he'd never let them take him alive and then lock him away for the rest of his days.

"Right." Grady glanced briskly at his watch. "We'll get back to the flat now. Then you can give O'Sullivan a lesson in handling the UZI. If things go right, he shouldn't have to use it, but it's best to be prepared."

Sean backed the taxi out and turned it. Then he drove slowly back along the track while the others walked behind, scuffing the ground and spreading dead leaves over the tyre marks. They would be coming there again, Grady said, and often, but there was no point in advertising their visits. Once more Farrell was reassured. The Irishman might not be the easiest man to work with, but he knew his business.

Superintendent Whitaker was spending that Thursday away from the office. His previous weekend had been shot to hell: there'd been a bomb hoax down in London Docks and he'd spent most of Saturday and Sunday learning about fruitless searches of bonded warehouses by the Anti-Terrorist Squad and deciding what further action was necessary. So he was taking this Thursday in lieu.

This had worked out rather well. His children's school was holding its Open Day and Field Day, and for once he was able to get to it. But before he had left for home the previous evening, he had been intrigued by the report of PC Crome. At last there was a link—he was convinced of it. So he'd left the headmaster's telephone number with Sergeant Trew with firm instructions to ring him the moment more information came in. As he watched the afternoon's races his attention kept wandering across the wide lawns to the school building and the window of the headmaster's study.

The call, typically, came through just when his son had come second in the long jump, and he was unable to stay to offer his congratulations. By the time he reached the telephone he was out of breath and sweating. Maybe giving up his jogging hadn't been such a good idea.

He leaned weakly on the desk and picked up the receiver. "Trew?"

"Sorry to bother you, sir, but they've found the taxi driver."

"Well? Our Arab with the Irish accent—where did he take him?"

"He didn't take him anywhere, sir. The driver was nowhere near Queen's Gate all day. He had a succession of short fares south of the river, then a long trip out to Isleworth, and then up to Hampstead."

Whitaker groaned. "Is he telling the truth?"

"Yes, I think so, sir. The station sergeant knows him well. Good, honest bloke. Anyway, he's given us the Isleworth and Hampstead addresses if we want to check."

"Don't bother."

Whitaker knew when a trail was dead. He sat down heavily at the headmaster's desk. And it had seemed just like the breakthrough he needed—an alert copper, a phoney Arab with a briefcase, and a taxi that had obviously been waiting for him. There was no doubt in Whitaker's mind why the man had gone to the Embassy. A bunch of Iraqi diplomats had been kicked out in the summer of 1978. Information had come both from the Israelis and the PLO confirming police enquiries about Iraqi links with Palestinian extremists. He was tolerably sure the diplomatic bag was being used to smuggle arms, and he didn't doubt that the Provisional IRA would be a customer. If only they could have discovered where the taxi had taken the bastard . . .

He sighed. "So the taxi was as fake as the Arab?"

"Spot on, sir. But someone's got an eye for detail. The registration number was right, *and* it matched the taxi licence."

"Then circularize them. With two taxis on the road with the same numbers, some bright copper might spot the wrong 'un."

"It's a lot to hope for, guv." Trew sounded doubtful. "There's an awful lot of cabs to choose from. And if we pick up the right one again, he's not going to like it."

"Then he can lump it."

Through the open window of the headmaster's study came the sound of cheering. Whitaker looked up. He tried to remember what the next event had been: the 420, he thought, and his daughter with a good chance of winning.

"You still there, sir?"

He closed his eyes. "Of course I'm still bloody here. Have the CID started checking the licence plate suppliers?"

"Yes, sir, that's in hand."

"I want to know immediately anything comes up."

"Of course, guv."

"Oh, and Trew—set the wheels in motion. Tomorrow I want every known IRA contact in London pulled in. We'll find those bloody guns if we have to turn London inside out."

"Our lads are already nosing around, sir."

"Good, Trew, good."

"Anything for the Foreign Secretary, sir? A complaint to the Iraqis?"

Whitaker thought about it.

"No—not yet. Later perhaps. But at present, we've nowhere near enough to go on. If that constable had only had the sense to stop our Irish Arab—"

"Difficult, sir. Not enough to go on."

The echo of his own words infuriated him. He controlled himself. In criticizing the constable he'd simply been looking for someone to blame.

"I suppose you're right, Goodie. Keep in touch. I'll be in sharpish tomorrow."

He rang off. *Looking for someone to blame* . . . when the fault was his own. Knowing what he did, fearing what he did, he should have expected something like this. Now there was an Irishman somewhere in London probably with enough fire-power to mow down the entire Royal Family if he had a mind to. But what could he have done?

Wearily he got to his feet and went out again to the flags and rosettes and the excited children. But for him the sunny summer afternoon had lost its joy.

It was Tuesday of the following week, and Grady was driving on his own to Colchester. He had chosen that day, even though it was the holiday season, because it was the closest he could get to a rehearsal of the actual snatch. He took the Mini and started from Chester Court at half-past three, timing himself. He hadn't told Farrell he was coming. Surprise spot checks were good for morale. It would be broad daylight when he reached Abbey Field and presumably the sergeant wouldn't be around. He wanted to inspect arrangements undisturbed.

It was one of those grey July days with a suggestion of thunder in the humid air. Grady had the driver's window open and was irritated by the tiny black thunderbugs that blew in and lodged in his hair. He was irritated also because the previous day, on one of his frequent visits to Whitehall, he'd caught the Prime Minister arriving at Number 10 in a new Daimler Sovereign. If she was going to change her car they'd have to practise with a whole new set of dimensions. The Daimler was longer and lower — less easy to drag her from. That was just the sort of detail that haunted him. Plan as he might, there was always the possibility of some last-minute hitch.

The journey to Colchester, going against London's incoming traffic, was easy, and he reached the area of the barracks in an hour and three-quarters. He had made a careful study of the town map Dublin had given him, which he now had open on his knee, and he first drove slowly round the whole vast, scattered conglomeration of army buildings. It accommodated about nine thousand people these days, and he could well believe that somewhere in all its five thousand acres there must be some disused building where they and the Iron Lady could safely disappear.

Colchester was the oldest recorded town in Britain, sacked while under Roman occupation by Queen Boudicca and her Iceni warriors. And now he and his tiny group, in their own way, were going to bring it to its knees, humiliate it in the cause of banishing a foreign oppressor.

When finally he came to the derelict married quarters in Abbey Field he saw that Farrell had described them well. Abbey Field itself was situated at a main road junction, standing in a triangle made with another major route, the Mersea Road. Just before the junction there was a turning in between broken concrete bollards, running across to the Mersea Road. Alongside the access road, now virtually unused, were the married quarters partly hidden behind a high brick wall with two brick pillars at the open entrance. Grady drove on, past the road, turned right, parked half a mile further on, and walked back.

Where the brick wall ended there was a stretch of high white-painted railings. The access road might possibly be used by pedestrians as a short cut to the Mersea Road, but the shabby entrance led nowhere. Just inside it was a grassed area with clothes-line posts still standing in stiff military rows. On the buildings themselves faded letters were visible: to his right Block B, to his left Block E, with Blocks D, C and A beyond them and screened by them from the entrance.

Grady walked casually in, glancing up and down the road. No one was in sight. He went through to Block D. Just beyond the building, bordered again by high railings, was a footpath and beyond that some playing fields. Doubtless people would occasionally use the path as a short cut, and the playing fields would obviously be used in the winter, but they didn't seem any threat to the deserted nature of Abbey Field. He climbed an outside staircase to flat number six, off a railinged balcony that ran the length of the whole terrace. The peeling yellow door was securely locked, but yielded easily to the key Farrell had provided.

The door led into a narrow dark passageway, living room straight ahead, with kitchen and bathroom beside him on the right. The rooms were inky black, the only light filtering in through the tiny broken window panes in the front door, which Grady had carefully

87

closed behind him. He waited until his eyes were accustomed to the gloom, then checked the three bedrooms. There were single mattresses leaning against the walls of the two small ones. Everywhere seemed very clean, and the musty smell of the place was overlaid with disinfectant. One of the kitchen cupboards was nearly full of provisions, and a new plastic washing-up bowl stood by the chipped sink, together with a bottle of detergent. Grady clicked his tongue thoughtfully: Farrell had a long way to go yet, but he was doing well.

It was too dark to examine the provisions. Grady made a mental note to be sure there was plenty of tinned and dried milk. He disliked both, but his ulcer wasn't so fussy.

He chose the room they'd give to the Iron Lady and examined its window. The casement was securely blocked by the thick plywood that had been nailed firmly into position. The Army had done a good job. It would take a man with a crowbar to shift that wood. Behind it, however, were still the jagged shards of broken window panes. The sergeant would have to remove every single piece of broken glass. An enterprising prisoner could do a lot of damage with one of those.

Grady went through to the bathroom, flushed the toilet. As he'd expected, its noise seemed thunderous. They'd have to be careful. Even though nobody was supposed to come near the place they'd have to take care about noises generally. They'd have a transistor radio, but there'd be rules about that too, otherwise O'Sullivan would have it blasting out rock at all hours.

He considered observation points. On the balcony side, the window in the front door would do, screened by a piece of heavy blanket. That gave a clear view over the footpath and the whole playing-field area. The back, which fronted the drying area, the access road and the main road, was more difficult. They'd have to make a hole in the boarding at one of the windows. In Maura's room perhaps. She could be relied upon to make sure it was blocked before she used a light. It was, after all, from that side that any intruder was likely to come.

He returned to the sitting room and stood in it, trying to imagine what it would be like when they were living there. He'd be sharing the bigger bedroom with O'Sullivan and the prospect didn't please him. He'd always guarded his privacy, but here they'd be in each other's pockets day in day out. And then there were O'Sullivan's foul cigarettes. He'd have to cut those out for a start. A daily routine was what was needed: tasks for everyone and fixed periods of quiet. He must work out a timetable.

Grady made sure no one was in the vicinity when he left as quietly as he had come. Large splashes of thundery rain were just beginning to splatter on the cracked tarmacadam of the yard. He paused in the entrance between the two brick pillars. *Always leave a way out*, the Chief had said, and here there was none. They could prise a gap in the railings of the balcony, but that would be dangerously exposed. No, when they finally left it would be by the same route as they'd gone in—through this entrance. So they had to remain undiscovered to the end. As he gave the whole scene a final glance, he felt confident that they could.

By the time he reached the Mini rain was falling heavily. He drove into Colchester and bought himself a sandwich in the High Street. He wanted to get the feel of the place, even though he was unlikely to see it again. As he ran back to the car, he stopped in at Martin's the newsagents for the local paper. The *Evening Gazette* was running on its front page: RAPIST CLAIMS THIRD VICTIM. He glanced at it in the Mini before driving off. "Colchester's rapist struck for a third time last night. His victim was an eighteen-year-old girl who was walking home alone from the Tudor Disco. Police are looking for a man in his middle-twenties with dark hair and a thin growth of beard . . ."

Grady flung the paper into the back seat. That sort of thing disgusted him.

He was back in Muswell Hill by half-past eight. Maura had dinner on the table waiting for him. He told them about D Block and the conditions they would all be living under, and they seemed interested. But the atmosphere in the flat was strangely tense. After dinner, when Sean had gone into the kitchen to do the washing-up, Maura closed the sitting-room door and purposefully sat down opposite Grady.

He was reading the Colchester *Evening Gazette*. Now he put it down and looked across at her. "Something's happened," he said.

She smoothed her skirt. "Nothing really . . . but it might have." She met his gaze squarely. "These separate rooms, Liam. I don't think they're such a good idea."

He recoiled. "For Christ's sake—you're not suggesting you and I should—"

"Of course not." She managed a weak smile. "But Sean and me, we—"

"God Almighty, have you gone mad? 'Sean and me . . .'," he mimicked her cruelly. "'Sean and me'—I'll bet you all the bloody punts in the Republic it's not your hand he's after."

Now she was on her feet again, as angry as he.

"And what the hell's that got to do with it, Liam Grady? We're not talking about marriage. We're talking about fucking." She saw him wince, as she went on furiously: "We're of age, aren't we? Just because you don't want to, who do you think you are, talking like a bloody father confessor?"

Grady took a deep breath, controlling his anger. He spoke with a steely coldness.

"I made it clear, right at the beginning. No sex. I made it clear."

"And I agreed with you." She softened. "But we're only flesh and blood. And where's the harm in it?"

"The harm in it, Maura, is that sex and work don't mix. It disturbs the concentration. It saps the vital forces."

She stared at him. "That's nonsense—the most incredible bloody nonsense I've ever heard."

"It's *not* nonsense. Fornication. Godless self-gratification . . ." Pictures flashed in his mind of a man in his middle-twenties with dark hair and a thin growth of beard—plunging, plunging. "This is not a stinking whore house, d'you understand? For as long as you're under my command—you and that half-wit O'Sullivan—you will behave yourselves decently. I will not have . . ." He turned away, bit his knuckle, leaving deep white marks. "Do you hear me? Do you hear me?"

"I hear you." Her voice was very distant.

He swung round. "And you'll do as I say! You're not indispensable, you know. It's not too late—I could have you replaced tomorrow. There's a hundred women, good Irish girls, who would jump at the chance."

She waited, eyeing him with something close to pity.

"At least I came and asked you," she said at last. "I thought you might . . . listen to reason."

"Reason, is it? That's what you call it—you and that stud in there—" he gestured wildly—"it's reason, is it, that the two of you should . . . should . . . ?"

She was staring at his hands now. He looked down. They were shaking violently. He lowered them on to the chair, spoke with controlled quietness and calm. "Yes . . . yes, it's good that you came and asked. It shows openness. It shows a proper spirit. But I'm afraid the answer's the same. It has to be. No . . . It's this waiting, Maura, that's what it is. It's getting on your nerves. Things will be better soon. You'll see."

She stood up and went to the door. "Then you do trust me?"

He lifted his hand, was pleased to see it still again.

"Of course I trust you. You're not in this for yourself. You're in it for Ireland."

She nodded. "That's all right then." But the oddly pitying look that had been in her eyes as she watched him remained. She went out then, softly closing the door behind her.

He listened resentfully for sounds from the kitchen: conversation, anger, amusement. But none came. So she'd gone straight to her room. He picked up the newspaper: RAPIST CLAIMS THIRD VICTIM . . . He massaged his forehead, slowly round and round, back and forth. He'd been right, hadn't he? Fucking, she'd called it. Fornication. No purpose . . . just self-gratification . . . Godless . . . They'd have enough on their souls without that.

He sat alone for a long time, staring blankly at the headline, his mind in turmoil. He wanted her for himself, and that was the most shameful thing of all.

9

September came, and at last the day had been chosen. Grady had decided it should be the last Tuesday in October. By then the political party conferences were over and Parliament would have returned to its routine. If he left it later than that he knew it would be difficult to maintain the discipline of his team. And still seven difficult weeks of waiting remained. He filled them as best he could. Weight-training sessions for Maura, trips in the Mini with O'Sullivan, trying different versions of the escape route, setting arbitrary time limits just to pass the hours. The man had few resources within himself, and he would be cooped up soon enough.

.   .   .

For Superintendent Whitaker also the time passed slowly. Every day held the possibility of disaster. The threat of the IRA was like a nagging pain, a rotten tooth to be probed at constantly.

During August officers from Special Branch, the Anti-Terrorist Squad and the Special Patrol Group carried out raids in many parts of London. There had been other police raids in Birmingham and Liverpool. In London alone twenty people were pulled in for questioning. But the IRA cell system, which broke up members into self-contained groups of three or four and had been initiated — according to a document captured by the Garda back in 1977 — when Seamus Twomey was Chief of Staff, proved its value: what they didn't know they couldn't tell. And not even the Special Branch's one-time methods, declared unjustifiable by the International Court, could have done anything about that.

What was even more disturbing was that none of the raids produced arms likely to have come from the Iraqi Embassy. One haul was made of highly sophisticated equipment for the assembly of remote-controlled explosive devices, which was shown off to the Press as a major find, but that was Belgian in origin and almost certainly obtained via South Africa. So whatever weaponry the Irish Arab had taken away with him was still around, and to no benevolent purpose.

In addition, the IRA's continued inactivity did nothing to ease Whitaker's anxiety. Since INLA's killing of Airey Neave and the assassination of Mountbatten, there had been no comparable action, even though the British Press at the time had quoted "a Provisional IRA terrorist" as saying: "We will continue to hit prestige targets, without apology, and we will hit the next one just as hard." And, since in Whitaker's experience the Provos were not given to vain boasting, such an operation was by now long overdue.

The duplicate taxi, too, had eluded him. But that meant nothing at all, except that a copper on the beat had better things to do with his time than stare at taxi number plates. In the matter of the plate itself he'd had more luck. It had been traced to an auto-accessory shop in Bounds Green Road, but there the trail had gone dead. The purchaser had paid cash, had left what turned out to be an imaginary address, a name which was probably false too, and the man behind the counter was not even able to remember whether he'd had an Irish accent or not. "I mean to say," he grumbled, "they all have accents of one kind or another in these parts. Proper little United Nations. Makes you sick."

So there the trail ended. Short of a massive house-to-house search, on a matter of undeniably low priority, especially since the purchaser would have come from the other side of London if he'd any sense, Whitaker was no further advanced than when he'd started.

Until, in the third week of September, an event occurred that changed his fortunes.

What worried Grady most was the precise timing necessary to get the taxi and Mrs Thatcher's car to the Downing Street barrier at exactly the same moment. That, and the success of Maura's weight training. The car's window had to be shattered at the first swing, and if it was bullet-proof then more than a tap with the sledgehammer would be needed. Also, Maura's aim was still shaky, and there was nowhere in the flat for them to set up a proper target.

The timing he worked at with Sean in quiet nearby back streets. He would set the taxi at varying distances from a corner and then pace off down the side turning the seventy yards from the door of Number 10 to the barrier. Then, with that position marked firmly in his mind, he would wait at the corner. He imagined the Prime Minister coming out, getting into the car. Still watching her, in his mind's eye, he would give the signal. The imaginary car would approach him and pass through the barrier. Only then would he look up to see where the taxi had got to. Sometimes it wouldn't have reached him, and sometimes it would have overshot. The difficulty was that Sean would not be able to see the official car until the last minute, so he must judge his speed entirely from what they had worked out in advance.

Finally, in the middle of the third week in September, he thought they had it right. Now they needed a dress rehearsal.

Maura had been expecting to stay at home. In the weeks since their stormy discussion Liam had been even less approachable than before—a brooding figure who spent most of his time, when he wasn't out with Sean, morosely watching television. And he found in it, especially the news broadcasts, little to cheer him: IRA men, together with valuable equipment, picked up all over London, not to mention other cities; the Iron Lady receiving a standing ovation at a Conservative Party meeting. His ulcer, she knew, was bothering him.

He would glower at the screen, rub his gut and mutter with a cold venom, "*Bastards*", and then retire to his room, slamming the door behind him.

But today he was in good spirits. And outside, for once after endless days of grey skies and drizzle, the sun was shining.

"You'd best come with us, Maura—see what it's going to be like. And afterwards, if all goes well, we'll drive out to Epping. It's a pity Farrell isn't with us, but there's no harm in you putting in some practice on your own." He turned away, paused. "And bring some sandwiches. I've been working you all too hard—maybe we'll make a day of it."

She stared at his departing back. Wonders would never cease. He'd be dancing a jig next.

In Whitehall he stopped the taxi at the planned position, got out and leaned in on Sean as if he were a passenger paying his fare. "You know what to do. The main thing is not to hurry it. Nice and easy, and you can't go wrong."

He walked away. Maura, keeping well back out of sight, watched him through the windscreen, over Sean's shoulder. He went just past the corner of Downing Street by the Privy Council Office. He had a folded newspaper in his hand and he held it thoughtfully up to his chin. The policeman at the barrier ignored him. Maura found her hands were sweating. She looked away: this was ridiculous. If she got as tensed up as this now, what would she be like on the day?

Over on the opposite side of Whitehall she noticed another policeman walking slowly along the pavement. Well, if there was one there on the day, she told herself, they'd just have to deal with him as they'd deal with the other.

The policeman stopped. He seemed interested in the taxi. She shrank back, her feet scuffing the battered plywood panel on the floor, ready for her afternoon's practice. After the first occasion they had taken the wood back with them each time. There was no point in having to buy more if the stock under the stairs ran out. She peered cautiously through the side window, and saw the policeman begin to take out his notebook. She was about to warn Sean when suddenly the engine revved and they were off. She glanced back to Liam—his newspaper was lowered.

Through the tinted rear window she saw the policeman flipping the pages of his notebook. Then, a few feet away on her left, the barrier to Downing Street flashed by. They drove on and stopped outside the Whitehall Theatre. Behind them the policeman was invisible, lost in the traffic. Three minutes later, Liam caught up with them, hailed the taxi, and climbed in. He ignored Maura, leaned forward cheerfully and tapped on the glass. "To Epping, driver, and don't spare the horses." And then, once they were moving, "Fine. Perfect. Do it like that and we'll have the Iron Lady where we want her."

The drive out of London had almost the feeling of a school outing. Maura didn't spoil it by mentioning the policeman and his notebook. Everything was going to be all right. They had nearly a month still to wait—but Farrell needed that time to finish stocking the flat in Abbey Field. He'd be down just before the final weekend, to make his report and have a last run-through. Everything was going to be all right.

They reached the track, drove along it to the overgrown quarry. Sean tacked the plywood to the trees at Rover height. If the Daimler was used, Liam said, its window would be lower, and therefore easier for Maura to swing at. Sean moved the taxi into position close by the trees and then went back along the track, as always, to keep watch.

But there was a different feeling to the day. Maura tried to take her practice seriously. She piled out of the taxi, swung her sledge-hammer, and missed completely. Suddenly it all seemed so ridiculous. She leaned against the taxi mudguard, laughing helplessly.

But Liam's face was like thunder. "You see how it is. Ease up for a moment and you've lost it. Do it again. We're not stopping till you get it right three in a row."

She did it again. The next time was perfect. And the next. She climbed back into the taxi, rested, her forehead on the long sledgehammer handle. Through the side window she saw Liam watching her. It's all right for him, she thought bitterly. All he's got to do on the day is take out the bloody copper. She braced herself, flung open the door yet again, and—

"I do hope you don't mind my asking, but I'd love to know what you're doing."

She froze. Slowly she turned. Beyond Liam, a few yards down the track along which they had come, a man was standing. And beyond him, to one side, doing up his trousers as he emerged from behind a tree, was Sean. She felt like laughing, like crying—was it really on such a silly, simple thing as a man taking a pee that their whole operation was going to be wrecked?

Liam was the first to recover. "Doing?" he said gruffly, playing for time. "What do you mean, doing? What business is it of yours what we're doing?"

"Oh, none at all. None at all, really . . ." The man was elderly, in loden breeches and walking boots, with a small haversack on his back, and expensive binoculars hanging round his neck. "It's just that . . . well, is it something to do with television, perhaps?"

"Television?"

The man came forward a couple of paces. "You TV people get up to the oddest things, I know. And I couldn't help watching. I mean . . . well, the young lady appeared to be rehearsing something. Hmmm? Is that not so?"

Maura jerked into movement. Television. If they could just get this silly old man to believe they were something to do with television, then—

"You mustn't tell a soul," she said. "It's all supposed to be terribly secret. Our producer would be furious if he knew we'd been spotted."

It sounded horribly thin to her, but the old man shuffled his feet delightedly.

"My dear young lady, you can rely on me entirely. But my gracious, how absolutely fascinating. I . . . er, I don't suppose you could tell me what programme it is you're—?"

"I really shouldn't." She shook her head vehemently. It was a gesture meant for Sean, who was creeping up behind their visitor, moving silently on the soft brown leafmould, murder in his eyes. "No," she said, speaking more loudly. "No. No, you mustn't—"

Now the old man had caught the direction of her gaze, and started to turn. But he was too late. Sean's arm came round his neck from behind, crushing his windpipe. His eyeballs bulged, wept instant tears. His arms flailed hopelessly. Then, as Sean adjusted his grip, the old man let out a thin, bleating scream. There was a sharp click, clearly audible across the leafy clearing. The old man's legs gave way, kicked briefly, and were still. A trail of spittle dangled from his chin.

Maura sank down on the ground. Her legs, too, would no longer support her. She watched, like a rabbit mesmerized by a ferret, as Sean casually lowered the body and stood over it, grinning.

"They shouldn't scream," Liam said coldly. "If you do it properly they shouldn't scream."

Sean tilted his head, still grinning. "Ah, but where's the fun in it, boss, if they don't scream?"

Maura shuddered silently. Liam crossed the distance between him and Sean in three quick strides. He struck Sean's wide grinning face savagely with his open hand, first one side and then the other. Sean's head rocked on his shoulders.

"That's enough," Liam snapped. "We're professionals—don't you understand? A scream attracts attention. You can keep your 'fun' for when you're on your own. And much good may it do you."

The two men confronted each other, their faces scarcely a foot apart. Maura felt the bile rising in her throat and swallowed it down. *Hail Mary, full of Grace, the Lord is with thee. Blessed art thou among women, and blessed be the fruit of thy womb* . . . And *that*, she thought wretchedly, staring at Sean, that is the man I almost went to bed with.

Eventually Sean backed off. He lowered his head. "That silly old goat," he muttered. "We couldn't let him—"

"Of course we couldn't. I agree with you. You did the right thing." Liam stepped forward over the crumpled body, suddenly very small and insignificant. "So we'll have no more talk of 'fun'. I shall put in a report to Dublin, praising your presence of mind."

He put an arm round Sean's shoulder and for a moment the two men stood close together, not speaking. Maura got slowly to her feet. She felt bruised all over, but very calm. Liam was right, the man had had to die. That was all that mattered.

"What now?" she said, her voice unnaturally loud in the forest stillness.

"We don't come here again." Liam disengaged his arm. "That's for certain."

"And the body?"

"We bury it."

"We don't have anything to dig with." And men were supposed to be the practical ones. "Only my sledgehammer, and you don't dig with a sledgehammer."

"Then we hide it in the bushes. They're thick enough."

"We could always fetch a spade."

"No." Liam looked round. He was taking command again. "There's no need. It's not worth the risk. Who comes down here anyway?"

She gestured abruptly. "*He* did."

"And how long have we been coming here? Eight weeks? Eight weeks and one old man . . . And besides, even if there's a search and he's found we'll make sure there's nothing to connect us with it."

And suddenly they were busy, and life moved on again. Sean picked up the body, slung it over one shoulder, and forced his way deep into the undergrowth at the bottom of the quarry. When he returned he removed the plywood from the tree and put it into the back of the taxi. Meanwhile Maura searched the ground for anything they might have dropped, one of Sean's dog-ends, for example, and Liam reversed the taxi out and turned it. They worked hard at the tyre marks, scrubbing them with broken branches. They continued this task back to the road, then retraced their tracks, kicking leaves about and scuffing their footprints till there was only a confusion that would settle into the ageless patterns of the forest floor. Liam kept them at it for a full hour. Maura didn't complain. At least they were occupied, and accomplishing something.

When they left they took the broken branches with them. These Liam threw into the woods a couple of miles away. While he was out of the cab Sean tapped furtively on the glass and grinned again, showing her a well-worn leather wallet. The old man's. He opened it to display a thick wad of bank notes, then lifted one finger to his lips and put the wallet quickly back in his pocket. Maura stared at him, appalled. But when Liam returned to the taxi she said not a word. Why should she, of all people, deny Sean his one small rebellion?

As they were driving back into London she noticed the packet of sandwiches she had made up, tucked into the corner of the seat beside her. She didn't mention that either. She was afraid that if she reminded Liam, he would make them stop somewhere and have their picnic. And she didn't think that, just then, she could face a picnic.

That night, a few hours after sunset, when the moon was high, the body of Henry St John-Smythe was found by a scavenging fox. As the following week went by various smaller carnivorous animals visited it. Apart from them, and the flies that laid their eggs in its increasing putrefaction, it was undisturbed. By then a police search was under way, but it lacked conviction. St John-Smythe was a widower and his daughter, with whom he lived, was vague. She thought he'd gone birdwatching, and it might have been to Epping. But he might very well have taken the bus to Burnham Beeches instead. He was an independent old codger, and she still half believed he'd turn up again, safe and sound.

Grady had been right: the track to the old quarry was seldom travelled, and the undergrowth anyway provided virtually impenetrable cover. He had not counted, however, on a cheerful black Labrador pup, brought to a glade some half-mile away by its owner and his girl, and allowed to wander while the two of them occupied themselves agreeably on a tartan car rug under the trees. The shoe that the pup joyfully brought back to them was less joyfully received. It had a most curiously unpleasant smell and, when examined, was found to be not entirely empty.

The discovery in Epping Forest of the dead body of Henry St John-Smythe, sixty-nine-year-old retired ophthalmic surgeon, made headline news. The police admitted signs of foul play, and gave out that the motive for his murder was presumably robbery, since his wallet was not found. But the CID superintendent in charge of the case in fact presumed nothing of the sort. In his experience robbery with grievous bodily harm seldom involved the breaking of the victim's neck from behind in a manner so expert as to suggest more than a basic knowledge of the skills of unarmed combat. No, this was a professional job. And it was for that reason that the advice of Superintendent Whitaker of the Special Branch was asked for, in a matter that otherwise would have remained entirely the concern of the Essex CID.

It was a long time since Whitaker had been out to the scene of a crime. But this was something special, and he took Sergeant Trew with him early on the morning following its discovery. The normal screens were up to keep the Press and the public at bay, but set at an unusually unhelpful distance. Whitaker and Sergeant Trew showed their cards and were allowed through. A path was marked with ribbons to one side of the main track, on which a number of policemen were already busy, meticulously sifting its surface. For once it was a fine morning and sunlight slanted down through the leaves, dappling the soft brown leafmould of the forest floor.

Trew and Whitaker trudged for upwards of half a mile before they reached the edge of a small overgrown quarry and were met by Superintendent Blackhurst of the Essex CID. Courtesies were exchanged. Blackhurst was a shrewd, quietly-spoken man whose style Whitaker warmed to immediately.

He declined Blackhurst's offer to show him the exact place where the body had been found. He'd already seen the photographs and he had the police pathologist's preliminary report in his pocket. His eye wandered round the clearing.

"Those will be the trees," he murmured.

Blackhurst nodded. "A bit of a puzzle. I'd welcome your opinion."

The beaten area in front of the two trees had already been examined. The three men crossed to them, and Whitaker squatted down.

"I agree with you completely," he said after a moment's pause. "They have to be nail holes. A large number of them."

Blackhurst stooped beside him. "And you'll see how the bark has been crushed. Some flat surface has been attached. The lab's got some bark for analysis. There'll be fibres . . ." He tailed off.

Whitaker straightened. "It's probably got nothing to do with the crime, of course."

"Of course. But it's a rum do. Wouldn't you say?"

Whitaker would say. Something repeatedly nailed to two trees in the middle of Epping Forest, and recently, and in the close vicinity of a violent crime, was a very rum do indeed.

"Was the body brought here?"

Blackhurst shook his head. "Pathology doesn't think so. It's not in the report, but the general feeling is that the body was disturbed only minimally after death."

"Which took place about a week ago . . ."

"The bruising of the branches on the way in matches that estimate. And some of the nail holes can't be much older. You can see for yourself how white the wood is."

"Only some of them?"

"Oh yes. That one . . . and that one . . . and those down there. The others are older. We found three nails, incidentally. Quite rusty. They seem to have been driven home by something with green paint on it."

Whitaker turned to the track. "Tyre marks?"

"A large number, but carefully obscured. And right out to the road too. Somebody did a good job. Their distance apart would fit several vehicles, but the turning circle is very small. Which might suggest a London taxi."

A bell rang in Whitaker's head, but he ignored it. Coincidences like that didn't happen. He sighed. "Footprints gone too?"

"Pretty well. A few deep impressions of a small heel, almost certainly a woman's. Oh, and two excellent prints, male, size ten, close to and facing that tree back there. Usual purpose. Rubber-soled gym shoes, worn smooth. Might be connected. Even if they were, and we found the original, I doubt if we could swear to a match. Nothing that would stand up in court."

Whitaker turned back to the tree. "A target of some sort?"

"We've found no slugs."

"Anyway, why all the precautions? It's no great crime, potting at a target deep in the woods."

Sergeant Trew cleared his throat. "The body, sir. I know the old man wasn't shot, but there has to be a connection."

"There doesn't *have* to be anything, Sergeant." Whitaker rounded on him, untypically. There was something sinister here, and he didn't like it. "First rule of police procedure—nothing is connected until it can be proved to be so. What the hell did they teach you at Staff College?"

Trew was spared answering by a constable who emerged from the bushes and approached them, panting. He spoke to Blackhurst.

"Sorry to interrupt, sir, but the sergeant said you ought to see these, sir. I found them over there—" he gestured behind him "—more than half hidden by new growth. They look to have been thrown, sir. One of them had its corner sticking in the ground."

"These" were two roughly oblong pieces of discoloured plywood that the constable was holding discreetly by their extreme corners. On both of them one short side was ragged, broken away where nails had clearly been pulled through the wood. Visible beneath the staining on one of them were the stencilled letters "Blessing" and under it, thickly handwritten in black, probably with a heavy felt-tipped pen, were the numerals seven and two, enclosed in a circle. The seven was crossed, in the Continental fashion. The second piece of plywood had the letters "stock", also handwritten in heavy black, beginning at its very edge as if they were the continuation of some longer word.

Sean was out with Maura in the West End. Only eight days remained now, and they were doing some last-minute shopping. They travelled by bus. First they went to a Milletts in Oxford Street where Maura bought four dark blue boiler suits of different sizes. The shop was crowded with tourists buying T-shirts and pack-away plastic macintoshes. Maura chose the boiler suits she wanted off the shelf and took them to the cash desk. The assistant scarcely looked at her.

The boiler suits made a heavy, awkward parcel, which Sean carried. It was for this reason that Maura had insisted he go along with her—insisted, that is, to Liam. Sean himself was delighted with the chance to be alone with her. He'd noticed that in recent weeks Liam had gone out of his way to keep them apart. His hero-worship had turned to resentment. The bastard's jealous, he thought. He wants her to himself. Though he had to admit, in his calmer moments, that there was precious little sign of that.

He'd heard them quarrelling in the sitting room the night Liam had got back from Colchester but he hadn't guessed the reason and Maura had resisted all his attempts to pump her. That had been the day he'd nearly got her in the sack. He would have if he'd only had a rubber—but he'd counted on her being on the pill as all good Catholic girls were these days. He'd been willing to chance it, but not her. And he supposed he couldn't blame her. Who'd be a woman, for Christ's sake?

After Milletts they went across to the wig department in Selfridges. Maura bought herself a long blond wig and another for Farrell. There was difficulty in finding one big enough—she made Sean try it on to be sure. It perched on the top of his head like a pimple on a round of beef, but she said she could fix it. She told the assistant they were going to this fancy dress party as the Heavenly Twins. He felt a bloody idiot, though, standing in the shop with the wig on while everyone stared. And the assistant would remember *them* all right, if it ever came to that.

Next Maura went upstairs to Ladies' Lingerie. First she bought two pairs of flesh-coloured 15-denier nylon stockings in the largest size the shop carried. Then she looked at a stack of nightdresses, but none of them was what she wanted. They tried three more stores down Oxford Street. Finally Maura bought a length of rough white flannelette at John Lewis and said she'd make it up herself.

In John Lewis she also bought a cake of coarse carbolic soap and a scrubbing brush. She refused to say what she wanted these last three items for and Sean was puzzled: he couldn't imagine her wearing the flannelette, and surely Farrell was supplying cleaning things for the flat?

They paused on the crowded pavement outside the shop. "What now?" he asked her.

She hitched up the strap of her shoulder bag. "Home."

"Ah, but where's the hurry? A pretty girl like you, a handsome man like me—let's find a fancy place and I'll buy you a cup of tea and a Danish."

"No." She hesitated. "It's time we were getting back."

He took her arm. "You think I can't afford it? Sure, but I'm rich now. Himself was loaded—didn't you see?"

She stiffened. He thought she was going to pull away but she simply stood there. "I . . . it's that story in the paper. I can't help it, Sean—it's as if everyone knows and they're staring at me. Hating me. Let's go home."

He didn't believe a word of it. She'd been happy enough up to that moment. "Look, Maura love—what is it? The last few days it's scarcely civil you've been." He smiled, tried to jolly her up. "BO? Is that it? What my best friends won't tell me?"

She laughed then, but even he could see the effort it cost her. "It's the waiting, I expect. I'm a bundle of nerves. I . . . I'll be better once we get started."

And with that he had to be content. They took the bus back to Colney Hatch Lane and she spent the evening doing needlework. She cut the length of flannelette in two, then folded each piece in half on the living-room floor and stitched up the sides, leaving a gap by the fold on each side. Then she cut a hole in the middle of the fold and roughly hemmed it. She did the same with the second piece. Liam, sparing her a moment's attention now and then from the TV, made no comment. But to Sean's way of thinking they were the saddest pair of nighties he'd ever seen.

For Whitaker the Epping Forest investigation progressed with agonizing slowness. But for the manner of the old man's death he'd have backed out gratefully and left it to Blackhurst. He'd enough on his plate without that. But the crime had spy or terrorist stamped all over it, and nowadays they were becoming increasingly one and the same thing.

By the end of the week his interest had narrowed down to the two pieces of plywood. In this he was contradicting his irritated words to Sergeant Trew, but the sergeant tactfully never reminded him. After all, the panels were all he had.

They were turning out to be a mine of information, but whether useful or not remained to be seen. They had lain in the forest for at least a month: that could be deduced from their soggy condition and the growth of black mould on them. They had also been struck often and forcibly by a heavy blunt instrument bearing the same green paint as had been found on the nail heads. Fibres adhering to their rough edges indicated that they had at some time lain on a nylon-based carpet, the type of carpet identical to that used in most London taxis. And, inevitably, in several other commercial vehicles.

As to the markings on them, the "Blessing" had been found to be the stencilled trade mark of the Heinrich Blessing Gesellschaft, a firm of international removal agents centred in Frankfurt—which Continental origin was borne out by the cross on the handwritten figure seven. From this it had been easy to deduce that the piece of plywood on which it appeared had once been part of a packing case supplied by the Heinrich Blessing Gesellschaft—a blessing in disguise, as Sergeant Trew had felt obliged to remark—and that the packing case, since it was numbered seventy-two, had been part of a fairly large consignment.

The word, or part-word, "stock" was rather less revealing. Laboratory analysis of the plywood had suggested that this second piece was sufficiently like the first to be in all probability from the same source, and the ink used for the numerals and the letters was found to be identical. Therefore it was safe to assume that the two panels came from the same consignment. And on a numbered packing case the most likely additional information would be the consignee's name. Therefore the lack of a capital letter at the beginning of the "stock" confirmed what had been already supposed, that the beginning of the word had been cut off when the panel was trimmed to its present size.

Via Interpol Superintendent Whitaker had contacted the Heinrich Blessing Gesellschaft. He was looking for a customer of theirs whose name ended in "stock". The consignment would probably have come to Britain, but even that was not certain. And as to the date, whatever guess he might make would be frankly worthless. He could only suggest that they started in their records for a month or so ago, and worked back.

The Heinrich Blessing Gesellschaft, mindful of their international obligations, agreed to do their best. They were a large organization, however, with sub-offices in eight European countries, so the search was likely to take some time. They had a computer, naturally, but it filed its information alphabetically. There was no chance, they supposed, of obtaining also the first letter of the customer's name?

Whitaker sighed, and said of course there bloody wasn't, or he'd have given it them in the first place. And then apologized for his bad manners to the helpful Interpol officer on the line from Paris. But the Heinrich Blessing Gesellschaft was asking for time, and time was the last thing he felt he had.

He put down the phone and looked across at Trew. "Our smash-and-grabbers don't know how lucky they've been. A couple of inches to the right with the saw and we'd have had them. Or at least we'd have been on our way . . ." He reached for his matches. "But what exactly are they planning to smash and grab?"

It was a recurrent discussion. "Something pretty jolly important, sir. They've been practising a month at least—and six or seven times, according to the nail holes. And they were prepared to kill when they were interrupted."

"A puzzle, Goodie. A target centre twenty-seven inches up from the ground. What does that suggest to you?"

"The same as last time, sir. A copper's bollocks."

Whitaker winced, and closed his eyes. "An Irish Arab bearing arms from Iraq . . . an IRA go-slow . . . a duplicate taxi . . . that man Tyrie and his warning . . . a green-painted sledgehammer . . ." He stiffened, opened his eyes, glared accusingly at Trew.

Something was expected of him. The sergeant shrugged. "At least half the sledgehammers sold in Britain are painted green, sir."

"I know that." Whitaker struck a match, held it over his pipe bowl, spoke round it. "I was waiting for you to tell me that it needn't have been the same taxi. That I've got the IRA on the brain."

"But I don't think you have, sir. It's all too pat."

Whitaker waited till his pipe was well alight. "All the same, have a man ring round the commercial security organizations. Ask if this twenty-seven inches makes any sense to them. After all, we may have a straight gang of bank robbers on our hands, with an ex-SAS unarmed combat man riding shotgun."

Trew got reluctantly to his feet. This was busy work, and they both knew it: something to give the illusion of useful activity. At the door he paused, turned back. "That twenty-seven inches," he said. "Wouldn't that be about the height of a car window?"

On Friday Farrell took the train down from Colchester, and then the underground to Highgate, where Sean met him with the Mini. The snatch was only four days off now, and if young Sean seemed less than his usual extrovert self and chain-smoked from a store of roll-ups all the way, Farrell put it down to last-minute nerves.

He himself had never felt better, never more exhilarated and determined at the same time. The long period of planning had been tedious after the heady atmosphere of the Army Council briefing, and he feared the hiatus held the danger of the Paddy factor—some bloody stupid thing one of them at the London end might do that would blow the whole scheme sky-high. But now, suddenly, it was really going to happen. At last he was going to fulfil his destiny, honour the memory and faith of his grandfather, and become part of the glorious history of Ireland.

They talked very little in the car. Farrell had read of the murder—for a day or two the papers had been full of little else—and he'd put two and two together. Indeed, at first he'd expected it to be the mistake he'd imagined might happen. But as a week passed, and then ten days, and no arrests were announced, he came to believe that they'd got away with it. He'd have liked to ask Sean for details, but the man was so surly that he decided to wait until they reached the flat. Or, better still, avoid the subject altogether. He had preached need-to-know long enough; now he should practise it. So he folded his gloved hands in his lap and wisely kept silent.

Grady had the UZIs out on the living-room floor.

"Thank God you've come. Knock some sense into O'Sullivan, will you? I've been at it all morning and he's still all thumbs."

Which explained Sean's ugly mood. Farrell hid a smile. So they needed the professional after all.

"Let's do it at the kitchen table," he suggested. "He'll be sitting up in the taxi, won't he?" He winked at Sean. "I'd have thought if he lay down in Whitehall the fuzz would piss themselves laughing."

Scoring off Grady got him and Sean off to a good start. Half an hour's patient revision and Sean was handling the gun like an expert.

Maura served lunch then. She seemed cheerful enough, but the meal was uneasy and Farrell observed that she directed most of her remarks at him rather than the others. Trouble in the nest, he thought, and wasn't surprised. Ten weeks or so of Grady would be enough to drive anyone round the bend.

After lunch Maura produced the boiler suits and they practised getting in and out of them quickly. She'd taken them to the launderette to soften them and fade their bright blue newness. Grady would have to stand out on the pavement in his and she reckoned if it looked well used he'd be less noticeable. He tucked the 9-millimetre Browning automatic from the Iraqi Embassy in his right-hand pocket. As he'd already established, it fitted well and unobtrusively. The smoke grenade in his left-hand pocket was bulkier, but less immediately identifiable. Then Maura and Farrell put on the stocking masks and over them the wigs. The lining of Farrell's had to be cut down the back before it would fit. They made a grisly pair, with long blond hair and flattened, distorted features.

Farrell thought how bizarre the scene must look—the four of them in that classy sitting room. But bizarre or not, this was important, deadly serious.

Maura suggested that Sean should pull on a stocking mask at the last minute. Grady said no—he needed all his concentration for getting to the Downing Street barrier at exactly the right moment. Sean didn't argue. His good spirits had returned: anything that spoiled his manly beauty was a sin, he said.

They went over the schedule. Farrell parked in the vacant bay at Chester Court by 1.30, then was ready to be picked up at the top of Portland Place at 1.45. He'd be in uniform, and they'd have his boiler suit and the rest of the equipment in the taxi. The journey to Whitehall should take no more than twenty minutes, although Grady was allowing thirty. But if the taxi was in position by 2.20 that would be all right. She'd only rarely left before then, but had invariably gone by 2.50. After they'd negotiated Parliament Square, Grady would leave the taxi at the bottom of Whitehall and walk up past King Charles Street and the Cenotaph. He'd be in position, outside the Privy Council Office by the corner of Downing Street, only a few seconds after Sean had parked the taxi. Then they had to wait. When he saw the Prime Minister's car begin to move he would give the signal.

"That's it then." Grady sat back, looked round the group. "But what have I missed?"

There was a long silence.

"What if Herself crashes into us?" Maura asked.

"We pray that the taxi's still drivable. If not, we take the official car. Either way, it'll be a bloody mess and we'll have to play it by ear."

In Farrell's opinion "a bloody mess" was an understatement. They'd be as good as dead. But he kept that thought to himself.

"What if we're blocked on the getaway?" he put in.

"We can make a U-turn if we have to. We only need to get clear by a few hundred yards and we'll disappear. Among all the taxis going up and down Whitehall what's one more? The dangerous part is five minutes later, when the police have had time to radio our licence number."

Farrell nodded. The plan was for them to switch plates in St James's. The delay was supposed to be worth it. Personally he couldn't see that, but he muttered drily: "Nothing's perfect. Anyway, with luck, they might not even see it."

They relaxed. Farrell handed over the list of provisions and equipment now in the Abbey Field flat. Grady checked it as Maura looked over his shoulder.

"Can I give you a pair of scissors and some other things to take up?" she said. "I shan't be carrying my bag or I could take them with me. And I'll need them as soon as we get there."

The scissors were a new requirement, but Farrell didn't question them. He could take anything she gave him to the flat on Monday night, when he made his final inspection.

"I'll be over every few days once you're installed," he said. "I thought maybe I'd whistle *The Wearing of the Green* so you'd know who it was."

Grady conceded one of his rare smiles. "Very suitable," he said softly.

Towards the end of the afternoon Maura and Farrell were left briefly alone. He leaned across and touched her arm.

"Well?" he asked. "Are you sorry you joined?"

She looked across at him. Suddenly her lip trembled and her self-control fell away.

"It's a bloody nightmare," she whispered. "Liam's nothing but a machine, and Sean's a vicious psychopath."

"*Sean?*"

She nodded vehemently, still close to tears.

Farrell thought about it. Sean had always seemed a thug, but hardly . . .

"It's a bit late to back out," he said doubtfully.

"I couldn't do that." She got up, moved away, nervously massaging one arm. "And I'm not sorry I joined. The ends justify the means—isn't that it?" She swung round. "But I'm glad you'll be coming now and then. I've a feeling I'll be in need of a little sanity."

Across the hall the lavatory cistern flushed. Their moment alone together was almost over. "I'll come whenever I can," Farrell said urgently. "And don't worry—things'll get better once you're up there."

"Better?" She laughed with a show of her old gaiety. "I'm telling you, Patrick, things'll get worse before they get better, and that's the truth of it."

Behind them the door opened and Grady came into the room. "I've been thinking," he said. "Maybe Farrell should keep away. Every visit increases the risk. Maybe we should arrange a signal and him only come when we really need him."

Tuesday morning found Whitaker and Sergeant Trew still beating their heads against a brick wall. No word had come from Europe, and Trew's belated realization of what, Whitaker told himself, should have been immediately obvious—that they were threatened with an assassination in a car, or perhaps a kidnap—only served to increase their anxiety.

Whitaker's first thought had been for the Queen, or one of the Royal Family. Ever since the Mountbatten killing that had been his most abiding fear, and one about which he could do very little. The royal engagements had been carefully checked, the routes gone over thoroughly, and security surreptitiously and discreetly increased, but there was a limit to what Her Majesty, conscientious in her concept of duty, was prepared to accept.

From the Royals Whitaker moved down through other possible targets: the Prime Minister, the Home Secretary, the Secretary of State for Northern Ireland. Protection had been stepped up for all of them, but to provide anything that was foolproof was impossible. And, in the present situation, what could he tell them? Nothing but an improbable mish-mash of fact and fiction, of events linked only by the merest guesswork. He and Sergeant Trew might believe it, but he couldn't honestly expect anyone else to. Even the Commander of Special Branch had looked at him askance and resignedly supposed that he knew what he was doing.

He fingered a report sheet that had finally reached him after lying for more than two weeks on some station sergeant's desk. On the twenty-third of September, at 11.17, a constable on pavement duty had thought—had only thought, mind—that he'd seen one of the taxis there was a call out for, waiting in Whitehall, outside the

Foreign Office. He hadn't had a chance to question the driver. He'd needed to confirm the registration number, and by the time he'd got his notebook out, the taxi had driven away. He hadn't radioed in—the identification was too uncertain. And a similar uncertainty had marked the progress of the report: a series of fits and starts until at last Whitaker had now received it.

The Foreign Office? Any number of suitable targets for the Provos came and went from there. But the entrance that was used was not in Whitehall, but through the archway in Downing Street. Oh, my God, it might even be some bloody Middle East terrorist group if the FO were involved. He shuddered at the thought that it might not be the IRA after all. Or they might have two—

On his desk the telephone rang. He picked it up absent-mindedly. "Whitaker."

A second later he had reached for a pad and was writing urgently, the receiver held between chin and shoulder, all earlier speculations banished from his mind.

His conversation lasted six minutes. Then he rang off, thanking his caller profusely, and buzzed for Sergeant Trew.

"We're in business, Goodie. I've just had Paris on the line. The Blessing Gesellschaft have traced their mystery customer."

"Jolly good, sir." Unbreakable nonchalance was one of Trew's least endearing attributes.

Whitaker pressed on. "Apparently they took so long because the order was originally booked in a company name, some engineering firm, on behalf of their employee. They were sending him to England so they made all the arrangements. Chap called Capstock."

"Doesn't sound very Irish, sir."

"What's that? No. As a matter of fact he gives his birthplace as Cornwall. But that's neither here nor there. Capstock himself is out of the country again. They've sent him to one of the oil states—Saudi Arabia, or some such."

"That wouldn't be Iraq, would it, sir?"

Whitaker peered at his notes. "No, Saudi Arabia . . . Look here, Goodie, if you're trying to be funny you can just pack it in. The point is, Blessing Gesellschaft have given us the address they sent his goods to. It's in London, up in N.10. Colney Hatch Lane, to be precise."

"N.10, sir?" Trew's off-handedness cracked. "That's round Muswell Hill, isn't it? Near where those number plates—"

"Exactly so. A connection at last. A tenuous one, admittedly, but a connection all the same." Whitaker got briskly to his feet. "We're going to take a hand ourselves, Goodie. Long time since we've seen a bit of action. Oh, you'll have to tell the CID and C.13. But we're going to take a look ourselves—go in with them. *And* we'll be needing the Smith and Wessons."

The time on that last Tuesday of October was exactly 12.41.

10

At 11.15 that Tuesday morning Charlie Patterson was idly dusting the fluted radiator of his immaculate Daimler Sovereign in the managing director's car park of a factory in Brentford, on the western outskirts of London. He was also keeping a watchful eye out for a sign from the modern, glass-walled foyer of the factory's main administrative building. He had delivered the Prime Minister there exactly an hour ago, and she ran her visits to a very tight schedule. The factory manufactured advanced electronic equipment and had recently won a multi-million pound contract in the Middle East against stiff international competition. This had been judged well worth an hour of Mrs Thatcher's time: one hour, no more and no less.

Charlie Patterson had been a driver with the Department of the Environment for ten years, and had been driving the Prime Minister for the last eleven months. The title "chauffeur" he had never aspired to: Charlie had strong socialist convictions, and the word carried an aura of inherited wealth and privilege that he detested. That he should be serving a Conservative Prime Minister, however, held no difficulties for him. He was above all a democrat, and if a Conservative Prime Minister was what the country was misguided enough to want, then so be it. He did his job, and that was that. Personally, he had nothing against Mrs Thatcher. In the months he had been driving for her he had always found her thoughtful and considerate. He had to confess he rather admired her.

He glanced at his watch. 11.20. He had to get her back to Downing Street for lunch with a delegation from the CBI, the

Confederation of British Industry. But that shouldn't present much difficulty. Then his time was his own until he was on stand-by at 2.20 to take her to the House. His wife had put him up some sandwiches and a slice of apple pie, so he'd skip the canteen, and if the weather stayed fine he'd eat them in St James's Park.

Movement caught his eye. The factory PR man was signalling urgently from behind the big glass double doors. Charlie nipped round the car, got in, stuffed his duster into the walnut-veneered glove compartment, and pulled smoothly away. By the time the Prime Minister's detective emerged, closely followed by Mrs Thatcher herself, the Daimler was waiting, neatly positioned at the end of the short length of official red carpet.

Superintendent Whitaker caught the Commander of Special Branch at ten to one, just as he was thinking of having some lunch. The duty officer would have issued him with the necessary firearms, but Whitaker wanted to talk the whole thing over with his superior who, up to now, had evinced a certain scepticism. The slight delay was worth it. The case had gone on for nearly three months already from the date of the Iraqi Embassy incident. Another hour or so wouldn't make much difference.

At 12.45 Sean O'Sullivan, in British army uniform with the boiler suit over it, had finished loading the taxi. Grady, similarly dressed, went down to the garage with his check list. When he returned to the house he looked up at the sky. The forecast had been for bright periods. So far he hadn't seen any, but at least there was no sign of rain. And with the wind light, and in the north east, the smoke from his grenade would drift back along Downing Street, masking them from anyone watching at Number 10 and Number 12. Everything was going to be all right. He leaned for a moment in the doorway of the flat, bent over slightly, massaging his belly. Then he straightened and went quickly up the stairs. Maura, wearing her boiler suit over slacks and a dark woollen sweater, was in the kitchen, making coffee. He stopped her.

"If you're thirsty, take a mouthful of water. Nobody should go on a job like this with a full bladder."

O'Sullivan was waiting for him in the sitting room, smoking feverishly. Grady crossed to the window, flung it open, fanned the air.

"I told you to cut that out. Chew gum if you have to do something."

He sat down. "The taxi's fine. Everything's going to be all right." He drummed his fingers. "You checked the fuel?" O'Sullivan nodded. "Bloody fine we'd look," Grady went on, "if we ran out of gas half-way round Berkeley Square."

O'Sullivan nodded again. He was scrubbing his soggy cigarette stub back and forth in the ashtray. Suddenly he looked up.

"D'you think Farrell will make it?"

"Of course he'll make it. You can always rely on the British Army." O'Sullivan didn't smile.

Maura came in from the kitchen. "The coffee—d'you think Farrell will have some in the Land Rover?"

All these questions: Grady saw how they both depended upon him.

"I told him to. And I was just saying to O'Sullivan here—you can always rely on the British Army."

Maura too had lost her sense of humour. "I hope you're right," she said anxiously. "We're going to need it."

"And whiskey?" O'Sullivan brightened at the thought. "A nice drop of Irish—that's what I'll be needing."

Grady shook his head. "No. Nobody drinks till the operation's over. And that means when we're finally shot of the Iron Lady."

O'Sullivan subsided. Maura drifted over to the window, and stood there, staring out. Distantly a police car siren blared, then faded. Grady looked from one to the other. It was far too early, but if he kept them hanging about much longer they'd be climbing up the walls.

They were leaving the flat just as it was. When and if the police ever found it there would be nothing to help them. Plenty of fingerprints, of course, but none that was on file. And the only thing that might have linked them with Colchester, the *Evening Gazette*, had been burnt in the back yard weeks ago, and the ashes spread around.

He slapped his knees briskly and stood up.

"Well," he said, "what are we waiting for?"

He led the way downstairs. O'Sullivan drove the taxi out, waited while he closed the garage doors behind them. When he had settled himself in the back seat Grady checked his pockets for the Browning and the smoke grenade. Then he turned to Maura.

"You never did get to plant your shamrock, did you?" he murmured.

.   .   .

Farrell arrived at the Albany Street barracks shortly before one o'clock. He delivered a radio transceiver surplus to requirements, and spent some time chatting with the quartermaster sergeant. The rest of the day was his own, he said. He was going to look up a bird. She lived in Hampstead and worked nights at the Royal Free Hospital. By now she'd be rested and warm and willing. The quartermaster sergeant wished him luck.

At 1.30, Farrell drove the Land Rover down into the Chester Court underground car park, found the empty bays at one end, and reversed carefully in beside a pillar. The place was deserted.

He checked that the blankets were out of sight in the back, and the two vacuum flasks of coffee Grady had asked for were tucked safely under the front seat. Then he left the Land Rover, taking the ignition key with him, but not locking the side doors. When it came to the change-over, every second would count. Of the whole operation, that was the moment that worried him most.

He walked out through the back of Chester Terrace into Regent's Park, and set off briskly in the direction of Park Crescent at the top of Portland Place.

At two o'clock, an hour and five minutes after the Irish had left, a small convoy of unmarked police cars drove up Colney Hatch Lane. They stopped just short of the house, the upstairs of which had once been occupied by John Capstock. Whitaker waited until the men had deployed themselves discreetly front and back, then climbed the four steps to the front door and rang the bell. Something about its sound told him there was nobody at home.

At ten to three Charlie Patterson was sitting in the Prime Minister's Daimler already drawn up to the kerb outside Number 10. While he waited he had the car radio playing, softly tuned to Radio Three. He was partial to a bit of classical music. Nothing heavy, mind. Not Wagner, for instance. He couldn't abide Wagner.

By shortly after three o'clock the gothic oak Chamber of the House of Commons was packed: the green leather benches, the Strangers' Gallery, and the Press Gallery at the opposite end, above the Speaker's chair. The time was approaching for Prime Minister's questions.

The Speaker noted the hands of the clock at the far end of the

Chamber, and the jumping digits of the television screens at the side. As yet Mrs Thatcher had not arrived. By now she was often sitting on the front bench alongside Mr Whitelaw, with the Leader of the House further to the left, in the corner seat by the gangway. The Speaker assessed for himself how many more questions and supplementaries he might squeeze in before 3.15.

The House usually got fidgety and noisier as Prime Minister's question-time approached, but today the Speaker's long experience told him he had a particularly difficult, agitated House on his hands. It had not helped that it was the Industry Minister who was taking the current set of questions. The Opposition invariably reacted testily to what they regarded as the ruthless monetarist policies of the government and, as the pained expression on the bespectacled and aged boyish face of Patrick Jenkin showed, the Minister was having a rough time of it.

The Speaker had already decided which MP would next "catch the Speaker's eye". He called the man's name, and the Member jumped to his feet.

"Is the Right Honourable Gentleman aware," he shouted, "that he has a manic obsession with ripping off publicly owned, profitable enterprises? We've seen the Post Office suffer. Now it's this. Is he aware that it's the taxpayer's money he's giving away?"

The Minister returned to the despatch box.

"I'm afraid the Honourable Member has got it wrong," he said crisply. "As he invariably does. The investment in this nationalized industry comes almost entirely from the cash flow provided by the customer, not the taxpayer. The cash flow will continue; the source of investment will remain the same."

Opposition shouts broke out again. The Speaker observed that it was now 3.14 and there was still no sign of Mrs Thatcher. He called another MP, this time from the government side of the House, for a further supplementary question, and saw the Leader of the Opposition give a questioning glance to the Leader of the House, who pursed his lips and raised his eyebrows. The Opposition Leader then glanced at Mr Whitelaw, who imperturbably shrugged his shoulders and made a small gesture with his hands. They both conveyed the silent message: "I don't know."

By five minutes to three, Liam Grady, standing near the northern corner of Downing Street, felt literally sick with the agony of waiting. His ulcer was giving him hell. She had never, in all their months of observation, been as late as this. What if she was ill? What if, on this day of all days, she didn't come?

He steeled himself not to look yet again at his watch. From a few yards away he could hear the gurgle and hiss of static from the radio of the policeman on duty at the open barrier. He glanced back along Downing Street. The official Daimler was still parked outside the door. At least that was a good sign. For the hundredth time he checked that the Browning in his pocket was free, ready at a moment's notice.

He moved casually to the edge of the pavement, as though he were looking for a taxi. O'Sullivan was still in position, engine running. He'd been waiting there for more than twenty-five minutes. Christ. It would be just their luck if some interfering copper were to come along and take an interest. He moved back, his whole body tense as a spring near breaking point. A couple of tourists passed him and wandered through the barrier. The policeman on duty directed them along the pavement opposite Number 10. He glanced at Grady, and then turned away. The tourists walked down the pavement on the Foreign Office side of the street. Grady got out one of his bismuth tablets and chewed it slowly. Another five minutes. They couldn't wait longer. It would get too bloody obvious. Something had gone wrong—something different he didn't understand. Christ, would she never come?

The police constable's pocket radio crackled into the sound of a voice.

Of all those immediately involved, perhaps only Charlie Patterson was neither worried nor surprised by the Prime Minister cutting it fine. He had seen the CBI blokes leave, late and glum, and now she wasn't going to have the usual time to go over the day's questions and the answers that had been provided for her. But Charlie reckoned she probably didn't need to anyway. And if she was keeping him waiting . . . well, that was her privilege.

At three o'clock precisely, the door of Number 10 opened. Charlie touched his engine into life. Mrs Thatcher's Special Branch man skipped lightly across the two shallow steps and opened the rear door of the car. The Prime Minister followed him closely, and climbed in. She had red folders in her hand and, in his mirror, Charlie saw her flick over the pages almost before she was properly seated.

The detective closed the door, checked the automatic lock, then moved forward, opened the Daimler's front door and lowered himself into the passenger seat beside Charlie. He cast a professional eye round Downing Street. Then: "We're running late. On your way, Speedy Gonzales."

Charlie was ready, the automatic transmission already in "drive". He accelerated smoothly away from the kerb. Ahead of him the duty policeman stood close by the open barrier. He slowed, nosing the Daimler through the gap as he looked right for traffic coming up from Parliament Square. A taxi was approaching. There was a gap behind it, and he decided to wait, angled across the Downing Street entrance until it was past, before he turned out across the wide roadway.

Suddenly the taxi lurched in towards the pavement. Its nearside door appeared to be hanging slightly open. Charlie stared at it, open-mouthed, as it screeched to a halt across his bows, only inches from the Daimler's front bumper. Two men in dark blue piled out. Close behind him he heard the sharp crack of a pistol. No, they weren't men, they had . . .

Charlie's training took over. The car was being attacked. He couldn't go forward, so he jammed the transmission into "reverse". Time stretched. The figures in blue were inches away. They had long blond hair and flat, obscenely featureless faces. One had a gun, the other something he couldn't see. The car's transmission took up and he stamped on the accelerator. Something smashed into the window pillar by his head. His window glass sagged, then shattered. In his mirror he could see thick white smoke billowing.

He spun the wheel. The Daimler was on the move now, slewing back sideways, grinding into the barrier on his left. The detective beside him was cursing, as he struggled to free his gun.

Charlie saw the muzzle of the automatic for no more than a second. It swung wildly as the car lurched backwards and jammed against one of the tilted supports of the barrier. Charlie screamed, and tried to duck. The bullets caught him above his right ear, blowing off the top of his head. His foot slipped from the accelerator. He died instantly.

Jack Radley was something not very successful in advertising, and he hated it. But it paid for his share of a flat in the fashionable part of Islington, and his sporty two-year-old TR7, which—in such difficult times—was not something to be sneezed at. At three minutes past three that Tuesday afternoon he was driving up Whitehall, returning from a long and indigestible lunch with a troublesome client, and hating his job, and himself for doing it, with peculiar intensity.

Unusually for Whitehall, the road ahead of him was clear for three or four hundred yards. He noticed a taxi, parked at an odd angle. A taxi, and smoke . . . a body lying on the pavement, a knot of people apparently struggling round the door of a car . . . Instinctively Radley lifted his foot from the accelerator.

Three people staggered round the back of the taxi. Two men in blue, and a woman. No, two women. There were tourists gawping on the pavement. One of them had a camera. Christ, these people will photograph anything.

He was closing now. Suddenly there was the unmistakable clatter of a machine gun. The tourists scattered. Several of them fell, including the one with the camera. The three people round the outside of the taxi had climbed in and the taxi was moving off. Now he could see a tall woman running after it, grabbing at its swinging nearside door, dropping something as she hauled herself up.

Radley had no doubt what he had seen. A kidnap, in broad daylight, there in front of him. As he drove by there was blood on the road . . . screaming . . . people running . . . drifting smoke . . . a Daimler jammed against some sort of barrier, its rear door open, both its windows smashed. He wasn't, in most circumstances, a brave man. But today he had something to prove—that he was worth more than expense account lunches and earnest discussions about TV jingles.

The taxi was clearly in sight, coming up with a red London bus. He put his foot down and the car's rear wheels spun noisily as it accelerated away in pursuit. The taxi was past the bus now, which was pulling away from the kerb. He swung out, was confronted by a bollarded island, passed it on the wrong side. But an articulated truck was bearing down on him, coming in the opposite direction, and he was lucky to get back on to his side of the road in time, and the bus was still there, almost in the middle of the road, and people were shouting at him, and he couldn't get past.

He blasted his horn. Incredibly, even this short distance from the noise and confusion and sudden death, it seemed that nobody was aware of what had happened.

Finally the bus moved over, its driver shaking his fist at him, and he hurtled by. And there the taxi was. Or was it the same? He cursed himself for not getting its number. But it was travelling fast, overtaking when it could. It had to be the same. He went after it, his palm flat down on his horn.

At the top of Whitehall there were three cars between them. The traffic was thick now, hemming them in. Entering Trafalgar Square the lights were green. They joined the slow crawl along the bottom end of the square, past Admiralty Arch and the entrance to the Mall. The TR7's horn was attracting attention. Radley leaned out, shouted explanations, meaningless appeals that were lost in the roar of engines. He looked for a policeman. Christ, they were always there when you didn't want them ... The taxi was keeping to the left, entering Pall Mall, passing the end of the Haymarket. Radley's heart leapt. Ahead, along past Waterloo Place, the road was wide, and one-way, the cars few. He'd be able to get through, block off the taxi, herd it up on to the pavement. He edged the sports car forward, containing his impatience.

Suddenly and inexplicably the traffic froze. Nothing moved. A haze of exhaust fumes gathered between the tall buildings. Radley craned out. The taxi was six or seven cars away from him now, utterly unremarkable, hemmed in on all sides, quietly waiting. And beyond it, on the zebra crossing at the junction with Waterloo Place, he saw a seemingly endless procession of school children.

He drummed his fingers on the window ledge. The delay gave him time to think. He'd assumed that the taxi would go straight on down Pall Mall towards St James's, but what if it turned right instead, into Lower Regent Street? By the time he reached the corner it might have turned off again, doubled back into the maze of streets around Jermyn Street, and he'd have lost it. Distantly he heard a police car siren, then another. He glanced over his shoulder. Even if they knew what they were looking for they'd have an impossible time of it, getting through this mess. He hesitated. Abruptly he came to a decision.

Inside the taxi there was an agonized stillness. The sliding window was open, and Grady was crouched down on the floor, out of sight. The Prime Minister, tightly wedged between Farrell and Maura, was deeply unconscious, breathing stertorously. Farrell had wrenched off his wig and stocking mask. Maura, quite unnecessarily, was cleaning her finger-prints off the hypodermic syringe. Her hands shook so that she could scarcely hold it.

"You dropped the gun," Grady muttered. "I might have bloody known you'd drop the gun."

"You weren't so fucking clever yourself," Farrell told him. "I thought you were going to wear a mask like the rest of us."

Grady swore. "And the taxi was nearly too late. Christ—what a balls-up."

Only Sean seemed unperturbed. "The Daimler got there sooner than you said. But we managed pretty well, considering."

"Pretty well?" Grady screwed his head round. "How many swings did Maura have to take? We could've had half the police force in London round our heads." He tried to look in the nearside mirror. "And where's that bloody Triumph?"

Sean laughed easily. "Miles back. I'll turn up right and right again. He'll never find us."

"And the number plates?"

"Don't worry, boss. There'll be plenty of time."

"You're crazy. We had the place picked out. You'll never—"

Farrell cleared his throat. "We'll do the best we can. Nothing ever goes exactly the way you think it will. We mustn't lose our heads, that's all."

Sean looked back, grinning wolfishly. "That driver lost his though. And the bloody dick. Mother of God, did you see the way—?" Suddenly he stiffened. "That's torn it, boss."

"What?" Grady's voice was almost a scream.

"That bastard in the Triumph. He's getting out. He's going to come after us. What'll I do?"

"Nothing."

"Shall I let him have it? When he gets here, shall I let him have it?"

"What, in this bleedin' traffic? You do nothing, nothing. No shooting, d'you understand? We'll try to take him with us. Maybe nobody'll notice. It's—"

"Ah, the saints preserve us, will you look at that now?"

Grady got to his knees and stared round wildly. A young man in a fawn blazer was approaching fast. Incredibly the cab began to move. The young man quickened his pace. Running flat out, his hand was on the door handle. The door began to open and Grady caught at it from the inside.

"Sorry, mate," Sean shouted. "We're not for hire."

The taxi increased its speed and the young man's grip was torn away. They passed a zebra crossing. On either side of them children waited. The teachers in charge had made a gap in the crocodile to allow the traffic through. Behind the taxi, in the midst of the moving traffic, the young man stood staring after them, his shoulders heaving. Several drivers hooted at him. While further back others blasted his empty sports car.

"Some gents will do anything to get a taxi," Sean chuckled. "Now he's lost us for good. You should see the snarl-up."

The cab lurched as it swung right. Grady hung on to the door and finally got it shut.

"If he's out of it, what the hell are we going up here for? Straight on was the plan."

Sean was cheerfully giving two fingers to the irate driver of a Renault he'd cut up.

"Better safe than sorry, boss. I can easily get over to St James's further up. Oh, and how's Herself now?"

Farrell smiled grimly. "Herself is fine. You stick to your driving."

Up at the top of St James's Street, just a few yards down from Piccadilly, there was a tiny turning off to the left called Bennet Street. It was little used, and served Arlington Street, which joined Piccadilly opposite Dover Street, and was also something of a backwater—except between five and six, when the car park at its bottom end discharged all the businessmen wealthy enough to afford it.

Sean drove sedately up St James's, turned left into Bennet Street, and double parked. He got out of the taxi and trotted round to the back. The street was quiet. Two people on the opposite pavement never even glanced in his direction.

It took Sean less than thirty seconds to cut the thin black twine holding the false number plates over the cab's original ones. He did the same at the front. The hackney carriage number screwed to the boot he left as it was. Covering it in the first place would have been too difficult. Who looked at such things anyway?

Inside the taxi Grady was struggling out of his boiler suit. They'd practised changing, but not in the back of a cab with three other people, one of them unconscious. Sean returned to the driving seat, tucked the two false number plates down beside his leg, and drove off. The whole switch had taken less than ninety seconds.

As they waited at the top of Arlington Street a police car went noisily by, travelling as fast as the traffic would allow, in the direction of Piccadilly Circus. Sean saluted ironically.

· · ·

The Speaker had allowed supplementary questions to the Industry Minister to run over to 3.19, and the House was in uproar.

"Where is she? Where is she?" came shouts from the Labour back benches.

The Speaker called for order and explained patiently that, in the unexpected absence of the Prime Minister, he had considered it reasonable to allow a few more questions.

The Opposition were unappeased, and the hubbub broke out again as Ministers on the government front bench exchanged anxious glances. The Speaker was again calling for order when the Leader of the Opposition decided to take the matter into his own hands. Turning towards the government front bench, he said, "Perhaps the Leader of the House could give Members an explanation?"

The Leader of the House rose to the despatch box and put on a wooden face.

"It will be within the knowledge of all Members," he said, "that the Prime Minister is meticulous in her respect for the traditions of this House, and I am therefore confident there must be some overriding reason why she is not here in time for her questions. I'm sorry to tell the House that I do not know what that reason is . . ."

"Disgraceful!" someone shouted from the other side, and more Opposition Members took up the cry. "Disgraceful . . . treating the House with contempt . . . where is she? Why isn't she here?"

Now the Leader of the Opposition had risen again and was demanding to know from the Home Secretary and Deputy Prime Minister what was the explanation for the Prime Minister's absence.

"Willie" Whitelaw, as he was affectionately known at Westminster, was well used to all kinds of scenes in the Commons, but now he was unmistakably annoyed. His cheeks reddened as they invariably did on such occasions, but he did his best not to show his irritation and to present a calm and reasonable demeanour.

"It should be clear to the House that I can do little more than apologize for the Prime Minister's absence. Neither I nor any of my colleagues," he said with a frankness that was designed to disarm criticism and perhaps even evoke sympathy, "know why the Prime Minister is not here. She should be. She normally is. I know she would wish to be. Clearly something totally unforeseen has happened. This is very disturbing, and enquiries are being made at this moment. . . ." He pressed on through the rumbling cries of annoyance from the Opposition. "I do not have the Prime Minister's replies with me, but if it is any help to the House, I am quite prepared to carry on and take Prime Minister's questions—should that be the wish of the House, Mr Speaker?"

The Leader of the Opposition was on his feet again, making the most of the government's embarrassment.

"This is a quite unprecedented situation," he said. "The Right Honourable Gentleman owes the House an explanation. Perhaps he will undertake to provide one as soon as possible."

Mr Whitelaw indicated that he would, and Labour backbenchers set up another chorus of indignation. The Speaker called for order. It was partially restored.

"Can we get on?" he demanded. "I am going to call Prime Minister's questions. Mr Cryer?"

The Labour backbencher with the first question called out: "Number one, sir."

Mr Whitelaw was half-way through his impromptu reply when a note was passed to him along the front bench from Minister to Minister. He unfolded it and placed it on the despatch box as he was speaking. When he had finished, and before he sat down, he looked at the message he'd been passed. As he read it, his face took on a look of utter horror. He remained standing, staring at the paper in front of him.

The noise of the House subsided. Raucous and unruly it often was, but it could still be a surprisingly sensitive body of people. As Members watched the stern figure of the Home Secretary, they began to sense something momentous. Mr Whitelaw looked up at the suddenly hushed MPs, and turned slightly towards the Speaker.

"Before I answer the next question, Mr Speaker," he said grimly, "I think I should tell the House of information that has just been passed to me. There has been a shooting in Downing Street. People have been killed. The Prime Minister is missing. It is not known if she was injured, or killed. It is presumed, however, that she has been kidnapped." He spread his hands helplessly. "There is no more information I can give the House at present. Perhaps, Mr Speaker, I might catch your eye to make a statement as soon as more information is available."

From the public in the Strangers' Gallery there had been audible gasps. Reporters rushed from the Press Gallery. The Leader of the Opposition moved to the despatch box.

"The Right Honourable Gentleman and all his colleagues will have the most sincere sympathy of the whole House. Does he know at this stage how the shooting occurred, or who was responsible?"

"No, Mr Speaker, I have no more information at all. I shall tell the House as soon as I have."

Again the Opposition Leader rose: "In these unique circumstances, Mr Speaker, the Opposition would raise no objection if you considered it appropriate to suspend the sitting for a time."

The Speaker, in his wig and gown, got to his feet beneath the imposing canopy of his chair.

"I am much obliged to the Right Honourable Gentleman. I was going to suggest that, in the first instance, we suspend for half an hour."

It was 3.45 before Sean drove the taxi smoothly down the ramp of the underground garage at Chester Court and into the unoccupied bay by the pillar next to the parked Land Rover. Maura, now in slacks and sweater, and carrying her medical kit, returned to the entrance to keep watch. While Sean got out of his boiler suit, Grady undid the straps at the back of the Land Rover, held up the canvas flap, and Farrell quickly transferred their captive on to the blankets spread out inside. She should stay unconscious for at least six hours, but Maura would travel with her in the back with a second loaded hypodermic syringe, just in case.

Farrell then retrieved the three other boiler suits, the wigs and the stocking masks, tossed them into the back of the Land Rover and himself climbed up behind its wheel. There, finally, he removed his plastic gloves. Grady joined him from the other side, taking the centre seat. Farrell turned, inspected his uniform closely. "You'll do," he said at last.

Sean bundled in his boiler suit, then darted back. He'd forgotten the UZI down on the floor in the front of the taxi. He returned with it, grinning cheerfully. Farrell started the engine, swung the wheel over and scraped the pillar lightly in passing.

"You should watch where you're bloody going, mate," Sean told him with a chuckle.

At the foot of the ramp they picked up Maura, and Sean ran round to fasten the buckles on the rear flap after her. Grady called impatiently for him to get rid of his boiler suit and gun, which were still on the front seat. He fetched them and stuffed them in under the canvas. Farrell waited for him, and then drove out into Albany Street. Half-way along he glanced sideways.

"For God's sake, Sean, you've got your cap on backwards."

Sean roared with laughter. "Sure, and I always knew I'd never make a decent, Queen-fearing British soldier."

The switch was over. Farrell heaved a sigh of relief. Now they had nothing to worry about—two soldiers and a sergeant in an army Land Rover—until they came to the first road block. And behind them they had left an unremarkable black London taxi, with a registration number that only someone looking for a vehicle stolen back in July would recognize.

I I

In the House of Commons the Chamber was empty. Immediately the Speaker had announced the sitting suspended, MPs hurried through the Members' Lobby to the Library corridor and the tape machines ticking out the news from the Press Association. Others went to the television viewing rooms on the upper corridor. Normal programming had been suspended to be replaced by a steady stream of information, much of it confused, from the newsrooms of the BBC and ITN. Outside broadcast units were already on their way to Whitehall equipped with ENG—electronic news-gathering—which could shoot pictures straight on to video tape, and then either beam them back to the studio or immediately on to the air.

Other Members of Parliament had left the building, drawn instinctively towards Downing Street. They found all of Whitehall, and the area of Horse Guards behind the Foreign Office, cordoned off, and had to content themselves with joining the rest of the public, craning over the barrier. Whitehall was unnaturally quiet. Then the rattle of the winch of the tow truck, and the sudden inhuman blare of an ambulance siren.

Mr Whitelaw had gone straight to the Prime Minister's room in the Commons, followed by those Cabinet Ministers who were in the House. Lord Carrington, the Foreign Secretary, was already there.

Within minutes the Metropolitan Police Commissioner was on the telephone. His report was brisk, and to the point.

The police at Number 10 had been in constant radio contact with Cannon Row police station. As a result, within four minutes of the first shots, squad cars were in Whitehall. But the terrorists—he used the word deliberately—had already got away, driving a black London taxi that had been used in the attack. Its number was known and its nearside front wing might be marked. There was some confusion as to whether the Prime Minister's car had struck it or not. An all-cars alert was out, road blocks were being set up to ring London, and all seaports and airports were being closely watched. The taxi might be of little importance. The terrorists would almost certainly have switched to another vehicle. But, whatever they were driving, they wouldn't get far.

It was too early to say how many witnesses there were. Probably not many. A group of tourists on the pavement had been machine-gunned and two were dead, four others injured. He didn't yet know how badly. The policeman on duty at the barrier, the Prime Minister's driver, and her detective had all been killed. There was no blood in the back of the car, however, so the Prime Minister was probably unhurt. A smoke bomb had exploded at the entrance to Downing Street, and the most reliable witness was the Special Branch man who had run through it from Number 10. He too had been shot and had fallen, wounded badly in the upper thigh. He remained lucid, however, and immediately had given a detailed report. There were three assailants and a driver, who never left his seat. All wore some kind of blue overall. Two of them had stocking masks and were either women or men in wigs. The principal weapon used was an Israeli-made UZI, which had been left at the scene of the crime. The man without a face mask might have had a hand-gun as well. He was of average height with sloping eyebrows, otherwise unremarkable, but a police artist was working with the Special Branch man on a picture at this minute.

From the policeman's position on the ground the face of the taxi driver had been invisible. Descriptions were still being taken from tourists, but already they varied enormously; so did their estimates of the number of terrorists involved. A sledgehammer, used to break the windows of the Prime Minister's car, had been left in the roadway. A preliminary examination showed excellent fingerprints, and—

The Commissioner broke off. News had just come in of a member of the public who had witnessed the assault from his car and had gone in pursuit of the taxi. He had lost it at the bottom of Lower Regent Street, but he was now in Cannon Row police station, and his evidence was expected to be extremely valuable.

Mr Whitelaw cleared his throat. "They might not try to leave London," he said. "What if they go to ground instead?"

"Contingency plans for a hostage situation are always ready, sir." The Home Secretary sighed. "The Provos or INLA?" he asked.

"We don't know yet, sir. It might not be either. It's not their style, Home Secretary." As a former Northern Ireland Minister, Mr Whitelaw knew that. "They almost certainly weren't Arabs anyway," the Commissioner continued. "Could be some psychotic European lot—West German perhaps. Their army have UZIs."

"We've got to find them quickly, Commissioner," Mr Whitelaw said with sudden firmness.

"Of course, sir."

"You've got all the power you need under the Prevention of Terrorism Act. Anything else you need, Sir David, let me know."

"When we do find them—I take it the SAS will be available if I need them?"

The telephone receiver rested in a loudspeaker cradle, and Mr Whitelaw barely glanced across to the Secretary of State for Defence, who was already nodding affirmatively, before he said: "Of course, of course."

As he rang off, he glanced at his watch. Time was flying. There was the Queen to be informed. And the Prime Minister's husband. And then a full Cabinet meeting at Number 10. Meanwhile the House was waiting for his statement. He told his colleagues he'd be calling a Cabinet meeting for six o'clock, and then hurried off to the Commons. At the door, he turned.

"Somebody get the Northern Ireland Minister back from Belfast. We shall need Jim here."

Superintendent Whitaker was upstairs in the flat in Colney Hatch Lane, watching morosely as four of his men quietly and systematically pulled the place to pieces, when a driver trotted up to tell him he was wanted on the radio down in his car. Whitaker was glad of the diversion. What they'd already found in the flat—traces of a familiar green paint, an off-cut of similarly familiar plywood in the cupboard under the stairs, suspicious signs of thin lubricating oil, possibly from an automatic weapon, on the sitting-room carpet . . . all this told him they'd come to the right place. But there was something else, a feeling in the air, some sixth sense, no more, that also told him they were too late: the birds had flown.

He stumped downstairs, pulled the handset out on its long expanding cord, leaned on the car roof and stared up at the narrow strip of sky above him.

"Whitaker here."

When he heard his superior's voice he stiffened. And when he heard what the Commander had to say he almost wept, silently pounding the car roof with his fist in his rage and frustration.

"Dear God, I knew we were too late. I knew it. Oh, we've found where they came from. Not a doubt of it. But they'll not be back . . . Hole out here? No chance, sir. The Prime Minister's kidnapped, you said. If they'd been planning to bring her here there'd have been some preparation . . . No. No, sir. Not a thing."

He closed his eyes. *The Prime Minister kidnapped*—he'd nearly gagged on the words. He'd been so close, so bloody close. And still the bastards had beaten him to it. What now? Where would they be taking her? If he only knew that he could order his own medal.

He pressed the receiver to his ear. "Suggestions, sir? Well, we can pull in all the old gang. In fact we must, but it won't do any good. This lot's taking its orders straight from Dublin, and no messing . . . Am I sure it's the IRA?" Slowly he rubbed the back of his hand across his mouth. "Yes, I *am* sure it's the IRA. Nothing has happened to make me change my mind since we talked this morning. All the signs at this end are positive . . . Yes, I'll be coming in at once."

He stepped back to replace the handset, then returned it quickly to his ear. "Commander? I tell you one thing: one of the bastards has a bad case of rot-gut. The flat here is cluttered with Rennies, Bisodol, that sort of thing. I just hope his stomach's giving him hell right now."

The first police check Farrell came to was alongside Finsbury Park, shortly before the road divided to the left on to the main A10. Two police cars were parked in the middle of the road. The traffic leaving London crawled into a solid block, edged forward, stopped again.

Farrell had been feeling good. It had all worked. It didn't matter that he'd lost his gun. He'd done his job, squeezed the trigger, and the men had fallen. A woman too—one of those bloody stupid tourists. But that was the way it went. It was a war, had been since the Rising and before that, and people died in a war.

He glanced over his shoulder. He was glad the Iron Lady was out of sight in the back. His ride beside her in the taxi had been disquieting. He felt no hatred for her in her drugged helplessness, but no pity either, only an irrational discomfort that anyone so self-contained and seemingly invulnerable should have been brought so low. Touching her had bothered him, as if it made him more intimately involved in her humiliation.

He turned back to face the front, his gaze resting briefly on Grady. Sean they'd sent back to be with Maura a few streets ago. She might need help if her captive regained consciousness. Also, the fewer people directly involved in any police check the better. Grady appeared utterly calm, his eyes staring straight ahead, his jaw firm. Farrell had to hand it to him: apart from that moment's panic in the taxi, he'd behaved like the machine Maura had accused him of being. The delay at the beginning had been bad enough for the three of them waiting in the cab; what it must have been like for Grady, standing beside the copper he was eventually going to kill, Farrell couldn't imagine.

He edged the Land Rover forward. He had his papers ready—his army paybook, the movement order for the vehicle, signed by his CO. He even had forged paybooks for Grady and Sean. And even if the police insisted on looking in the back, which was very unlikely, there was an excellent chance that they'd see only what they were intended to see—a soldier and his girl, and a pile of radio equipment.

The Land Rover came to the front of the queue. Behind it the traffic was backed up for a mile or more. Farrell held out his paybook, open, as he coasted to a halt.

"Colchester," he said. "I—"

The policeman's radio was rasping at him. He glanced down the line of waiting vehicles, waved Farrell on impatiently.

"Move it, Sergeant. For fuck's sake move it."

Whatever he was looking for, it wasn't two soldiers returning to barracks.

There wasn't another road block on their route out of London until towards the end of Forest Road, on the edge of Epping Forest, just before the Waterworks roundabout and the main junction of roads leading north and east. Because of the congested traffic, it had taken them another three-quarters of an hour to get there, and already the sky was darkening into dusk.

As one Cabinet Minister after another approached the black door of Number 10, it was automatically opened by the policeman in the entrance hall. Each made his way to the Cabinet Room, where Sir Robert Armstrong, the Secretary to the Cabinet, his slightly jutting jaw looking more determined than ever, and Mr Whitelaw were already waiting. And each took his place at the long table behind a red leather blotter bearing the words: "Cabinet Room, 1st Lord". But the Prime Minister's chair, the only one with arms, beneath the portrait of Sir Robert Walpole, remained empty. Mr Whitelaw, out of good taste perhaps, although he would be deputizing for Mrs Thatcher in her absence, sat in his normal seat.

The powerful figure of Sir David McNee, the Commissioner of the Metropolitan Police, was also there, but he left as soon as he had given his report and answered what questions he could.

Then the Ministers reviewed the situation. The presumption was that Mrs Thatcher was to be held hostage, but clearly nothing could be done until the kidnappers' demands were known. And by then she would almost certainly have been found. The group's origin remained uncertain. There was nothing at this stage to link it positively with the IRA, but no connection had been discovered with any other known terrorist organization. Mr Whitelaw's private view was that either the Provos or INLA were involved.

Meanwhile a vast police operation was in progress, and special units of the Army and the Royal Air Force were on stand-by. As soon as dawn broke the police Bell 222 helicopters, with direct television links to Scotland Yard, would be in the air, together with army helicopters. The sledgehammer found at the scene of the crime had indeed yielded excellent fingerprints, and a search through the Yard's computerized records was under way. The UZI that had been found had been less helpful. The manufacturer's number was known, and the authorities were investigating, but meanwhile the number was passed to the Foreign Secretary.

The Cabinet broke up after agreeing that the Home Secretary should immediately accede to requests for television interviews from the BBC and ITN so that he could explain the whole situation to the country and seek to allay any public fears. Thus by nine o'clock, a solemn Mr Whitelaw—displaying at once confidence and determination tempered by deep concern—was addressing the nation on the nine o'clock television news. He ended by warning the terrorists that, whatever the purpose of this outrage might be, they would gain nothing save their own downfall.

His remarks were watched appreciatively in a small suburban villa on the outskirts of Dublin—where direct reception of BBC programmes was excellent—because it was precisely what the Chief of Staff had been waiting for. A prime rule of Operation 10 had been that, from the beginning to the end, there should be no communications from the field whatsoever and, although news reports of one kind or another had been pouring out on the air waves for the last five and a half hours, Mr Whitelaw's official statement was the first firm indication that the lads had achieved unqualified success.

The Provisional IRA had their demands already drafted. The document was locked in the concealed safe in the basement of the Chief of Staff's present hideout, and he left it there. The British Government should be made to sweat out their uncertainty for a full twenty-four hours. That had been the Army Council's decision. So the Chief of Staff did nothing at all, except, in the loneliness of his room, to drink a silent toast in good Irish whiskey to the brilliance of his planning, and to the four brave patriots who were carrying it out.

Superintendent Whitaker and Sergeant Trew returned to Muswell Hill during the evening. The Home Secretary had told the Commissioner that he wanted their very best terrorist expert on the case. The Commander of Special Branch responded laconically with, "That's you, Art." It suited Whitaker anyway. He'd like to get these bastards.

So it was that he and Trew watched the Home Secretary on the large colour television set in the kitchen of the flat in Colney Hatch Lane. The set had been moved there to give the Yard's forensic team full rein in the sitting room. The carpet, the chairs and the sofa were receiving special attention. Dust and fibres were being gathered meticulously and placed in sterile plastic bags.

There was now no doubt in anybody's mind that the flat had been the headquarters of the terrorists who had kidnapped the Prime Minister. An oily towel in which, to judge from the markings, two sub-machine guns had clearly been wrapped, had been found in a drawer. A bag from the Oxford Street branch of Milletts' store, together with a bill for four boiler suits, was discovered in the dustbin downstairs. Together with these were other significant bills, including one from Selfridges for two wigs. Obviously the terrorists had been so confident they had done nothing whatsoever to cover their tracks. And there were even the remains of the Blessing Gesellschaft packing case to provide a firm link with the Epping Forest murder.

In the face of such confidence Whitaker found the Home Secretary's assurances less than convincing. There were signs of a professionalism at work here that made him uneasy. The terrorists had disappeared, which suggested that they intended to avoid a siege by remaining elusive. And to know where they had come *from* was one thing, while to find out where they had gone *to* was quite another. And for the evening to have gone by with no word of their capture only reinforced his misgivings. If they were going to be found, it should have happened quickly.

One factor alone gave him genuine hope. A late edition of the evening paper had come out with headlines screaming: BLOND TERRORISTS SNATCH PM. This matched with his evidence of the two wigs, yet the flat showed clear signs of occupation by only one woman. Furthermore, only three people had lived there: the beds told him that, together with the evidence of neighbours. Therefore the fourth member of the team—and the injured Special Branch man had been positive of that number—must have come from outside. Whether that member was a woman, or a man in a wig, was unimportant. He or she provided the most probable link with the team's eventual destination. In an operation as well planned as this, the hideout would have been carefully prepared, and someone would have been responsible.

It was, Whitaker knew, tenuous reasoning. If the final hideout were to be in Central London, then any member of the team could have got it ready. But in that case, why the outsider? And anyway, Whitaker's bones, which he had long ago learned to trust, told him that the Prime Minister had somehow already been taken through the road blocks ringing London and was far, far away.

Therefore the team's fourth member was his best hope. If he or she had ever visited the flat, and that seemed very probable, then he or she would have left some trace. Fingerprints there were in plenty—so obligingly many that Whitaker had little faith in their helpfulness. No, he was trusting that something else would turn up. He had no idea what. Just . . . something.

He leaned forward wearily and turned off the television set. Trew got up, went to a cupboard. "Care for a cup of terrorists' coffee, sir?"

Whitaker shrugged gloomily. "Why not? Seeing as they were kind enough to leave it."

"I doubt if they meant to be kind, sir." Trew filled the kettle. The kitchen had already been checked. "They could hardly have known we'd be here so soon."

"I wouldn't be so sure, Goodie. They know a lot, these bastards."

Whitaker settled himself, listened to the faint murmur of activity from the next room. It was going to be a long night for the experts, and he and Trew could quite well be spending it at home in their beds. Common sense, in fact, suggested that they should be: if any major discovery were made then they'd need all their wits about them in the morning. But this was Whitaker's case from way back, and he intended to stay with it. And where Whitaker stayed, Sergeant Trew stayed also.

By nine o'clock the Operation 10 team had been safe in the Abbey Field flat for over an hour. Their army camouflage had got them through successive road blocks with little difficulty. The closest call had come a couple of miles along the A12. Farrell was asked to get out of the Land Rover and his documents were closely examined. Meanwhile, a second policeman wandered round to the back of the vehicle. Out of the corner of his eye Farrell saw the copper's hand go up to the retaining buckles on the rear flap. But at that moment, the driver behind gave a series of quick blasts on his horn, leaned out and shouted that he was a doctor, and in a hurry, and it was bloody obvious he didn't have the Prime Minister in the boot of his bleeding MG, and would they please get that bloody Land Rover out of the bloody way. The policeman turned away then, and Farrell breathed again. On such tiny incidents did the success of great enterprises hang.

The moon was in its last quarter, the night dark. On Colchester's Circular Road East Farrell had chosen his moment, turning off onto the Abbey Field access road when no car headlights were approaching from either direction, dousing his own lights immediately and coasting to a halt in the deep shadow of the wall just inside the entrance. From there, led by Grady, Sean had carried their still unconscious captive. To drive any closer would have been to risk leaving tyre marks which they might not have seen until morning, when it could easily have been too late. Farrell and Maura followed, clearing the Land Rover of all their impedimenta. Farrell left them then and went to the barracks. He would look the vehicle over carefully by daylight. Then he would take it into Transport for a service. That would ensure that it got a good wash and clean up.

Now Grady sat in the back room, his eyes closed, trying to relax. He'd been listening to the radio. The police had found the Muswell Hill flat. This surprised him, but he wasn't worried. He'd always known they would dig it out sooner or later. He sat in silence. From the room along the passage he could hear confused voices. The Iron Lady was coming round. Grady stayed where he was, delaying the moment when he would have to face her.

The room was comfortable. Farrell had his own car, a Hillman estate, and he'd used it under cover of darkness to bring in an enormous amount of stuff: three folding canvas chairs and a table, a gas room-heater, a two-burner stove together with its own gas bottle, as well as the four mattresses. The floor was carpeted with army surplus blankets. Planks rested on bricks by the wall, bearing an assortment of paperbacks, playing cards, a cheap chess set, magazines, including *Penthouse* and *Men Only*, obviously for Sean, and the transistor radio. Above the gutted fireplace, Farrell had even hung a picture, a print of St Stephen's Green in Dublin, at daffodil time. A camping gas lamp hissed on the table. Its bluish glare was harsh, but Grady supposed he'd get used to it. And the windows were completely light-tight. He'd been outside to check.

He sat there, his eyes still closed, reviewing the day. They'd done it. Perhaps not in copybook style, but they'd done it. And most of the faults were his own. He should have anticipated that if the Prime Minister were late then she'd be in a hurry, and given the signal sooner. He should have reckoned on her driver trying to reverse out of trouble. And he should have expected some have-a-go lunatic to follow them. He should have—

He sat up straight, opened his eyes. Along the passage O'Sullivan's voice was raised now. He was shouting obscenities. Grady got wearily to his feet. He'd coached the oaf, coached him a thousand times. They would only hurt themselves, losing their tempers. The Iron Lady would simply laugh at them. He'd made it clear again and again—dealing with her should be left to Maura. Yet already, after less than an hour . . . Slowly and calmly he went out of the "sitting room" and along the corridor.

Though he had thought he was prepared, the appearance of their captive shocked him. Before she'd regained consciousness Maura

134

had been busy. She'd stripped the Prime Minister of her outer garments and dressed her in one of the flannelette shifts, scrubbed her face vigorously with carbolic soap and cold water, and had cut her hair to a jagged two or three inches all over. The woman Grady had steeled himself to face had seemingly gone, and in her place was the inmate of some turn-of-the-century charity ward, colourless and almost without identity, her fine-boned features deathly pale under the relentless glare of the gas lamp.

She was sitting on her mattress on the floor, her back against the wall, her bare feet sticking straight up below the unhemmed edge of the nightdress, her head bowed, her hands folded in her lap. At Grady's entrance O'Sullivan's stream of abuse cut off in mid-flow.

"Thank Christ you've come, boss. This bloody bitch here—"

"That's enough, O'Sullivan." Grady spoke quietly. "I'll take over now. You can—"

"But boss, she—"

Grady's self-control snapped. "That's enough, I said. Just get out and stay out."

O'Sullivan hesitated, then went. Grady glanced questioningly at Maura. She shrugged. He returned his gaze to their prisoner and coughed lightly. She lifted her head and their eyes met. Hers were icy blue and rock steady. She spoke first.

"What are you? Who are you?"

Her words and their scornful tone instantly dispelled whatever impression of meekness he had gained from her previous attitude. Mrs Thatcher had not been cowed. She had simply been waiting, and was utterly self-possessed.

"You wear British Army uniforms," she went on, her voice soft but firm and calm. "They're obviously disguises. You've got Irish accents. May I assume you're members of the Provisional IRA, or INLA?"

Grady was nettled. "You may assume what you like," he flashed back.

Mrs Thatcher looked back at him penetratingly and patiently as though to emphasize that, whatever her present physical condition, she was going to lose none of her authority.

"Well, what do you hope to gain by holding me like this?" She gestured at the furnitureless room. "You'd be foolish to expect too much, you know. It won't be forthcoming. Governments don't behave in that way. You should have learned—"

"I do not intend to discuss with you what the British Government will or will not do."

Grady had himself under control again. He'd decided long ago how he would address her, and he intended to stick to it. Never bandy words. Respectful but firm.

"My duty is to hold you here for as long as is necessary, while others make the decisions, including your government. You can make that duty easy for us all, or—"

"Moreover, young man," she interrupted quietly and insistently, "you have murdered people, and civilized governments don't tolerate that either. No government of mine will. And it will not surrender to blackmail, so it's not much good you trying that. You have placed yourselves beyond the law, and you will be hunted down and caught. I think you should understand that from the very beginning."

Grady was about to disregard the interruption and continue his prepared speech when Maura intervened.

"We're a bit on edge tonight," she said brightly, as though she were addressing a hospital patient. "Perhaps we'll feel a bit more co-operative in the morning."

She eased Grady towards the door, then turned back to the prisoner.

"I'm going to take the lamp away now, dear," she said. "We don't want to be tempted to do ourselves an injury, now do we?" Her tone was kind. "There are plenty of blankets, a torch on the floor there, and toilet paper should we need to use the bucket. See you in the morning, dear. Sleep tight."

She picked up the lamp. Grady's last sight into the room was of the Prime Minister still sitting on her mattress, looking up at them with an expression of tranquil determination. Maura closed the door and locked it.

"She hasn't seen herself yet. In the morning I'll take in a mirror. That should help, but you mustn't expect miracles."

Grady chewed on his lips uncertainly. "How is she?"

"Hard as nails. She recovered from the injection like a twenty-year-old. She's not going to die on us, if that's what's worrying you."

"Shouldn't we feed her? Won't she be hungry?"

"Do her good. Wasn't Bobby Sands hungry, God rest his poor soul?"

She went quickly through to the back room, where O'Sullivan was morosely listening to Radio One. She put the lamp down beside the other one on the table.

"Look, Liam," she said, "you've got to trust me. She's my responsibility now. We discussed it, didn't we? I'm going to have to see a lot of her, one way and another. She's a woman who needs to be boss. So am I. If I don't get her licked into some sort of shape she'll drive me crazy. OK?"

Grady frowned. "There's to be no violence."

"I won't lay a finger on her." Maura smiled sourly. "Kill 'em with kindness, that's my way."

O'Sullivan switched from his stream of pop music to Radio Four for another news bulletin, but Grady left the room, closing the door carefully behind himself. He didn't need to hear the news. It was enough that the men in Dublin should hear it and know of his success. He went down the passage in the dark, and out on to the balcony. Clouds were covering the last sickle of the moon. It was very dark. He leant on the railing. Four weeks, they had. Four weeks exactly. And then, unless a miracle occurred, it wasn't going to be kindness that killed the Iron Lady. He didn't believe in miracles. Neither did the men in Dublin.

The atmosphere at the meeting between the Foreign Secretary and the Israeli Ambassador the next morning was cool, if not prickly. Lord Carrington had recently been critical of the Israeli Government's intransigence in its negotiations with its neighbours, and had in consequence suffered accusations that the Foreign Office remained, as it traditionally had, unequivocally pro-Arab. In the circumstances, the Israeli Ambassador offered expressions of concern politely and correctly, and they were received in a similar manner.

The Foreign Secretary tactfully emphasized that both governments had a prime interest in defeating terrorism, and he was sure he could rely on the Ambassador to give any help in his power to Her Majesty's Government in apprehending the terrorists who had abducted the Prime Minister. Having received wary agreement on this basic principle he then handed the Ambassador a note of the serial number of the UZI sub-machine gun found at the scene of the crime.

"It would be helpful," he said, "if you were able to assure us that this weapon did not come from Israeli sources."

The Ambassador bridled instantly. "I trust you are not suggesting that my government could in any way be involved in—"

"Of course not." The denial was sincere. "But we are anxious to trace the source of the weapon, as a step towards discovering how and by whom it was acquired."

The Ambassador, not wholly appeased, departed after a further exchange of frigid pleasantries, promising to supply the Foreign Secretary with what information he could.

Lord Carrington decided to postpone a meeting with the Irish Ambassador. Police liaison with the Garda was at present excellent and had produced the assurance that the weapon had never been one of theirs; so until the kidnappers could be positively identified as the IRA there was nothing further to be gained from that quarter. Lord Carrington was profoundly worried. Fully eighteen hours had gone by since the crime, and there was still no word from the terrorists. Had something gone wrong? Was the Prime Minister in fact already dead?

As the terrorists' silence lengthened the same thought occurred to Superintendent Whitaker. He dismissed it. The further the investigations progressed the more impressed he was with the professionalism of the people he was seeking. Every lead seemed to end in a blank wall. Only three sets of fingerprints could be identified, and none was on record. Of the fourth member of the group there was still no trace at all. The landlord of the flat had been interviewed. His tenant had called himself Murphy and had taken the flat early in June for a six-month period. The landlord had called for the rent personally, and had always received it in cash. He had seen no one else on his visits, but he understood that a young woman and her brother were also in occupation. He could give a reasonable description of the man Murphy—not much more than average height, lean and wiry, with the nervous habit of pressing his fist into his stomach—and had been able to help the police artist to produce a working portrait. PC Crome identified it as probably the same man as the Irish Arab who visited the Iraqi Embassy. The injured Special Branch man was less positive. This told Whitaker nothing he didn't know already. The face was unremarkable, the sort of man one passed in the street a dozen times a day.

There was a red Mini parked outside the flat. It bore countless sets of the same three fingerprints. It had been bought in June by a man also calling himself Murphy, and had been paid for in cash. The change of ownership had never been made official, and no insurance had been taken out, so there was no record of an address or a bank account. The only fact to be deduced from all this was that the name Murphy was obviously false. Immigration had come up with several Murphys who had entered Britain in late May and early June, but unsurprisingly none of these fitted the description.

And of the rest of the team and, more importantly, their present whereabouts—nothing. Not the smallest hint. No, these people were professionals. The killing of their victim so soon would be a mistake that professionals simply would not make.

That afternoon the Foreign Secretary received a message from the Israeli Ambassador that the weapon in question had been one belonging to their army, but had been lost in an action with Arab terrorists about a year before. With the police report of the Iraqi Embassy affair on his desk, Lord Carrington felt justified in summoning the Iraqi Ambassador immediately.

The meeting got off to an effusive start. His Excellency was extravagant in his expression of sympathy for the government and, in fact, for the whole British people in having their Prime Minister—that most able, remarkable and internationally respected woman—abducted in such a dastardly way.

He was thanked correctly. The Foreign Secretary saw no further need for diplomatic fencing. "Our police tell us," he said, "that earlier this year, your Embassy was visited by an Irishman wearing Arab clothes, and we have reason to believe that he may have collected weapons."

The Ambassador looked horrified.

"But, Foreign Secretary, you know that would be very serious. It would be abusing the privileges we enjoy in this country in common with the rest of the diplomatic community."

"Yes, but not for the first time," said Lord Carrington sharply. "I would remind you, Her Majesty's Government has had occasion to complain before."

His Excellency spread his hands. "I give you my assurance . . . "

"I'm not suggesting," the Foreign Secretary interrupted, "that you knew the purpose for which the weapons would be used. The abduction of a Prime Minister is a profoundly immoral act that strikes at the very heart of civilized government throughout the world. I am confident that your government would not be involved in anything like that."

The Ambassador relaxed. "Quite so. It has always been our—"

"I *am* suggesting, however," Lord Carrington added sternly, "that you may nevertheless have supplied the weapons." He brushed aside an attempted interruption, and continued: "We know that weapons have been obtained from your Embassy in the past, Ambassador."

"We have our enemies, as does Her Majesty's Government," the Iraqi said with smooth irrelevance.

The thinnest suggestion of a smile appeared at Lord Carrington's lips, at once sceptical and ironic.

"I don't doubt that is so," he said. "And we have made it clear on a number of occasions that we are not prepared for Arabs to settle their scores on the streets of London. But it would be even more intolerable were you to provide others with weapons for their own acts of terrorism."

Once more the hands were spread. "But, of course, Foreign Secretary. But I do assure you . . . "

"I think that is all, Ambassador. I have to warn you, however, that if this weapon is traced back to your Embassy the consequences will be very serious."

His Excellency the Iraqi Ambassador took his leave, bowing deeply and once more expressing his abhorrence for all acts of international terrorism.

Lord Carrington eyed his departing back sourly. Nothing had been gained. If this was really the work of the Provisional IRA—and the Commander of C.13 seemed convinced that it was—then their source of arms in this country remained as elusive as ever. And time was passing. For the Prime Minister's sake, and for the reputation of her government, it was essential that progress should be made, and quickly.

12

In the flat in Abbey Field a routine was being established that would become the pattern for many wearisome days to come. They rose early. Although they lived by artificial light, used sparingly, seldom more than one lamp at a time, Grady had decided that a semi-military schedule was to be followed. Maura went into the prisoner at seven o'clock. Sean stood outside the door, ready to join her at the first sign of trouble.

Mrs Thatcher was standing by the sealed window, a blanket round her shoulders. She shielded her eyes from the glare of the lamp as Maura entered.

"Am I to be kept permanently in the dark?" she asked quietly.

Maura smiled. In more ways than one, she thought.

"Come along, come along, we have our torch, dear, don't we?" she said briskly. "And matches and lamps are such nasty, dangerous things. And as for electricity, I'm afraid there isn't any."

"I understand." The older woman straightened her back. Her square-cut shift stuck out ridiculously, yet she did not look ridiculous. She retained a dignity and authority that was disturbing. "And it seems from your childish behaviour, young woman, that you're determined to play some sort of game with me. So be it."

"Game, dear? My goodness me, I'm much too busy for games." Maura clapped her hands together encouragingly. Patients, the reasoning went, shouldn't be allowed to get depressed. "Now then, dear. Breakfast! What about some porridge? Or a nice boiled egg and bread and butter? And tea or coffee?" She folded her arms. "There's no fresh milk, I'm afraid, but I'm sure we can make do with the tinned."

Mrs Thatcher eyed her shrewdly. "If the choice is genuine, then I would prefer tea and the egg. If not, then I will eat whatever I am given. You can tell that silly man in the army uniform, who is presumably your leader, that I intend to keep my strength up, no matter what."

Maura's face was already beginning to ache with smiling. "Isn't that nice? He *will* be pleased." She turned back to the door, then swung round, as if on an afterthought. "Oh yes, dear, and I brought *this* for you."

She held out the unbreakable metal mirror from her handbag. When it was not taken from her she tossed it on to the bed. Then she went out, locking the door behind her.

Sean saw her empty hands. "What about the bucket?"

Maura walked straight on past him. "I'm waiting till she asks."

At eight o'clock Maura took in the breakfast her prisoner had ordered. The tray was plastic, the cutlery and crockery also. The beaker of tea already had milk and sugar in it. Sean stood outside with the lamp, and she put the food down on the floor in the oblong of light from the open door. Mrs Thatcher was standing in the same position by the window, but Maura noticed the mirror had gone from the bed.

"I shall leave the door open," she said, "and Sean will stay out in the passage with the lamp so that we can see what we're doing. He has orders not to speak. We don't want another nasty scene like yesterday, do we?"

Mrs Thatcher didn't move. "I suppose you realize," she said, her voice soft but penetratingly cool, "that whether you kill me or not, you yourselves have not the smallest chance of getting out of this alive. You will never get what you want by murder—either of me or anybody else."

Maura pushed at the tray with her foot. "Tea's getting cold, dear," she said, and left immediately.

Grady, when he had finished his own breakfast, went to visit the prisoner. He took the lamp from Sean and sent him away. He'd had a restless night, staring blankly into the darkness, listening for cars, the stamp of boots on the outside staircase. There was no way the police could find them, none at all. But he lay and worried. His principal comfort was that the prisoner must be sleeping even worse.

He looked round the clean, bare room. "Any complaints?"

Mrs Thatcher had finished her breakfast and was sitting on the extreme edge of the mattress.

"Is that supposed to be a joke?" she asked coldly.

"Not at all. Now, conditions are not ideal, I know that. But people in your position need to be protected from themselves. I can only say that any reasonable complaint will be noted, and it may be acted upon."

"You don't imagine we're going to be here very long, do you? The British police, young man, are the finest in the world. You're living on borrowed time, every one of you."

Grady refrained from telling her that it was her time that was borrowed, and it was steadily running out. He'd read the literature. Courtesy was advised, but no contact. Above all, no argument: argument reinforced the sense of self.

"No complaints, then? Good." He picked up the breakfast tray and went out, closing and locking the door behind him.

At nine o'clock Maura took in a bowl of cold water, the carbolic soap, a face cloth and towel. She left them, went away, and collected them, used, half an hour later. Not a word was spoken. She noticed two of the prisoner's fingernails were broken. Perhaps she had been trying to work on the boarded window. That wouldn't get her anywhere.

The morning dragged. Maura spent much of it staring out through the spyhole in the wood at her own window. On the playing fields that Wednesday morning nothing moved. The sky was grey, the grass wintry. The trees were losing their leaves. Through them, in the far distance, she could see the rooftops of other garrison buildings. From the sitting room, the radio was very faintly audible. Liam had laid down firm instructions about the volume level. Music was punctuated by news broadcasts. Sean was in there with Liam and occasionally she heard their voices. She wondered what they were finding to talk about.

For lunch she opened a tin of ham, and served it with more bread and butter and tomatoes. Her prisoner's bucket was beginning to make the room smell.

"If you've issued demands," the Prime Minister told her, "I can assure you they won't be met. You're wasting your time." She smiled thinly. "And mine, which is far more valuable."

If the morning had been long, the afternoon was longer. The three of them sat round the radio. So far there had been no word from the terrorists, and the police search was intensifying. Several promising leads were being followed up.

Liam shrugged. "They've got to say something, the poor bastards." The dropped UZI, the flat, even the taxi when they eventually found it—none of it mattered. The poor sods hadn't a clue, couldn't have. And meanwhile, he was holding the whole bloody British Government to ransom. He smiled to himself.

Later Maura caught Sean having a cigarette in the toilet. He grinned at her sheepishly.

"Don't tell on me, darlin'."

She fanned the air. "I won't have to."

She used the toilet while Sean waited outside. Then she went back to the sitting room. For economy's sake it was the only room with a light in it. For excursions round the flat they used one of the flashlights. In the sitting room the gas heater was burning and the place was steamy, with moisture running down the peeling walls. Liam had set up the chess pieces on the table. He was the only one of them who played, and Farrell had supplied a book of problems. He was rationing himself to one a day. Maura picked up Saturday's copy of the local rag, the last day Farrell had been to the flat. She read: RAPIST STRIKES AGAIN, and flung it down.

Supper was at seven. It was to be their one hot meal of the day and, according to Liam's rota, Sean prepared it. He heated tinned stewed steak and peas, and burned the steak. There was tinned tapioca for pudding.

The bucket in the prisoner's room was near to overflowing.

"If we dirty the floor, dear," Maura said firmly, "we'll have to clean it ourselves."

Mrs Thatcher looked up from her food.

"I have no objection to emptying my own slops, if you will show me where."

Maura emptied the bucket herself. The Iron Lady was to see only her room and the corridor wall outside. And to be waited on in such matters was humiliating. But Maura knew that the victory this should have brought had somehow eluded her.

She talked it over with Liam.

"She should be asking many more questions: wanting to know where she is, what's happening outside . . ."

"And she's not?"

"Ah, she hardly speaks at all. When she does it's like some official announcement."

He smiled. "Got you beat, has she?"

"Of course not. It's early days yet. We knew she wouldn't be easy."

"At least if she's not speaking, it's an improvement on what we were afraid of."

"Sure, and isn't that the truth."

Maura nodded cheerfully, but she felt less confident. There was steel in her prisoner that would take a lot of breaking. Break it she would, though . . .

There was more at stake than the efficiency of the operation. Of course it was important to break the prisoner's will; to assert their own authority. That was why Liam had put her in charge. But it was also a battle, a private contest that for Michael's sake she was determined to win. To get the Brits out of the North—sure, wouldn't that be fine?—but it wasn't enough. Thanks to that woman in there Michael was dead and his murderer unpunished.

Maybe she should cut down on the food. They did that on the wards too, when the sister wasn't looking, and after a week or so the most troublesome patients became docile. And it wasn't, she realized, simply on account of Michael. Once she'd had a career, a life, a future. Now she had only this.

That evening Mr Whitelaw went on television again. By now, for the sake of convenience, a permanent outside broadcast unit had moved into Number 10, and the interview was recorded there, half an hour before transmission. The Deputy Prime Minister remained available, however, in case there was a last-minute development. There wasn't.

He told the public all that was being done by the police and the armed services, but made no mention of the "promising leads" earlier news bulletins had featured. Instead, demonstrating a typical and endearing frankness, he admitted that for the moment there was little else that the government could do. He then expressed his own conviction—one now shared, he said, by the authorities—that the murders and the abduction were the work of Irish terrorists.

"Mr Whitelaw," said the interviewer, "you have talked with terrorists in the past. Would you be prepared to do so again?"

It was a question he could have skated round, as Harold Wilson might have done, as being purely hypothetical. But Mr Whitelaw had expected it, and he thought it was fair.

"It's much too early to say," he answered. "We don't even know for certain who these people are, or what they want. Perhaps they should tell us. At least we would all then know where we are. But I can tell them this," he said, with sudden firmness, and looking straight into the camera, "whatever they want, they won't get it by violent means. They have murdered five people, and they will get nothing by murder. This government will never give in to terrorism."

Mr Whitelaw returned to his room to watch the transmission. He watched with especial care the last twenty-four seconds of his interview. He hoped the IRA would understand what he was trying to say.

Superintendent Whitaker, for once watching with his wife in the comfort of his own sitting room, sighed deeply. He, too, recognized the message for the IRA, but he had little hope that they would heed it. His children were in the next room, ostensibly doing their homework, banished there so that he could watch the news in peace, and seriously. Three-quarters of the transmission had been devoted to the one item, and its political and international implications. Whitaker closed his eyes. His sleepless night at the flat in Muswell Hill was catching up with him.

His wife leaned towards him on the sofa and put her hand gently on his knee. "Would you like to talk things over, Arthur?"

He shook his head. In all the long day there had been only one tiny advance made and that, on his own orders, was being kept strictly for police ears only. It wasn't often that he kept secrets from his wife. He trusted her discretion completely, and in the past her advice had been of immeasurable help to him. "Anything strange?" she'd say, wryly using the notorious Provo phrase for seeking news among themselves, and he'd smile sadly, and unburden his heart. But not tonight . . .

She nodded understandingly. "You'll beat them, my dear. You always have."

He grunted. It was a measure of her concern for him that she should try to make him believe something so blatantly untrue. Airey Neave's assassins were still at large, weren't they? And the men who planted that bomb in Euston station? Not to mention . . . He leaned back on the sofa, put an arm round his wife's shoulders. "Oh well, I'll tell you one thing, anyway, Edie. It doesn't make sense, and they may quite well have come from earlier tenants of the flat. But we've found fibres of British army serge all over the place. And that might point to an army connection."

13

Thursday afternoon, and the staff in the huge newsroom of the Press Association in Fleet Street were enjoying a rare slack period when the telephone rang on the desk of the duty editor. As he picked it up he heard the now familiar code of the Provisional IRA. He listened for a moment, and then, before he began to take down their statement, he shouted across the room: "The Provos—they've got Maggie."

Even as his pencil moved over the pad in front of him telex

machines were already transmitting the flash message to all news-rooms. Soon this was followed by the full wording of the Provision-als' statement. Immediately he had passed this over to his subs, the duty editor rang Scotland Yard and Downing Street.

The Prime Minister had been kidnapped by an active service unit of the Provisional Irish Republican Army. She was unharmed, and the Provisionals would be presenting their conditions for her release to the British Government within the next twenty-four hours. At that time they would also give some information on the Prime Minister's whereabouts.

By the time the statement had been torn off the teleprinters in the BBC's London TV newsroom at Television Centre in Wood Lane, the news had already been flashed on the screen. In Dublin a second member of the Provisionals' Army Council had simultaneously contacted the BBC's correspondent there, and within minutes— with the co-operation of Radio Telefis Eireann—he was interrupting British programmes with his own voiced despatch.

Mr Whitelaw received the news glumly. The only surprise in it was that the Provos were so confident the Prime Minister would not be found that they were prepared to make her government wait another twenty-four hours before revealing their demands. He immediately called together the small group of Cabinet Ministers permanently on hand during the emergency, and they reviewed the latest developments.

The picture wasn't promising. A full forty-eight hours had now passed since the kidnapping, and yet the police, in spite of the biggest search operation in their history, were no nearer finding the Prime Minister than they had been in the first ten minutes. She had simply disappeared off the face of the earth. Even the taxi in which she had been abducted was still missing.

The Police Commissioner was confident that Mrs Thatcher was still somewhere in London. Even though the terrorists would almost certainly have switched vehicles, he felt sure they could not have penetrated the ring of steel placed round the capital. Already their previous headquarters had been found. Locating their present hideout was only a matter of time. At that very moment vital new evidence was being analysed concerning their identities and charac-teristics. One of them, for example, either had a gastric ulcer or was severely dyspeptic, and a special alert had been issued to all dispensing chemists . . .

Mr Whitelaw thanked the Commissioner patiently. It was clear, however, to everyone in the Cabinet Room that the police were scraping the bottom of the barrel. "Ring of steel" might have a rousing sound to it, but they knew quite well that in practice it boiled down to infuriated traffic jams and harassed young policemen. And any self-respecting terrorist with stomach problems would have been certain to take his Milk of Magnesia with him.

Lord Carrington voiced the frustration they all felt. "So what it amounts to is that none of us has the faintest idea whether the Prime Minister is alive or dead, but assuming she's alive we don't even know where she's likely to be."

Muttered agreement greeted the Foreign Secretary's conclusion.

The Defence Secretary leaned forward. "So do we look for some initiative to pre-empt the Provos' demands? Or do we just sit here?"

Mr Whitelaw sighed. "We shall have to talk to them, of course. I've done it before. I can do it again . . . or Jim can," he added, turning to the Secretary of State for Northern Ireland. "As to pre-empting their demands, I think I can guess what those will be. Something to do with the Maze, or getting our troops out, or a united Ireland, or—heaven forbid—all three at once. It's old ground, and we've made our position clear. Any concessions now would look like weakness."

The Defence Minister laughed bitterly. "Let's call spades spades, Willie—it would *be* weakness."

"World opinion's on our side," Lord Carrington put in quickly. "Apart from all the messages that have been flowing in, I've been talking to Washington. There's a great revulsion there. And in Boston and New York, too, where the IRA gets a lot of support. I think this time they may find they've dug themselves into a hole they can't climb out of."

"Taking a hostage," said Jim Prior, "implies the ultimate threat of death. What shall we do then?"

There was a moment's painful silence. Mr Whitelaw broke it.

"We must pray it doesn't come to that. And these are early days. They'll want to talk . . . to bargain . . ."

"I was thinking of Denis," Mr Prior continued, "and Carol and Mark—"

"Of course they've been kept fully informed, and Carol and Mark have come home."

"But if Denis asks," the Northern Ireland Minister persisted, "asks if, in the end, the government is prepared to let her . . . be killed—?"

Mr Whitelaw looked down at the table, distressed. Then he raised his head.

"He won't ask. He's had plenty of chances already, and not a word. He's the Prime Minister's husband. He won't ask the question because he knows the answer."

A murmur of sympathy went round the room. Mr Whitelaw rose to his feet.

"It's agreed then. Until we receive the IRA's demands we do nothing. I only hope to heaven the police find her soon."

In the flat at Abbey Field the Provos' announcement, received over the radio, had caused a short-lived stir of excitement. Sean was all for telling the Iron Lady, but Grady forbade it.

"She must know nothing. Not even what time of day it is. I've told you before, O'Sullivan—read the reports from other hostage situations. Once you start hob-nobbing with the prisoner you're lost. And that prisoner in particular. She could persuade you black was white, that one could. Total isolation's the only answer."

He himself had made the mistake, on his morning inspection, of getting into conversation with his prisoner. She had given up making threats, and she asked no questions. Instead he found himself discussing the nature of reality. The very fact of the four of them in these darkened rooms, she said, was unreal because it was rooted in unreal ideas. And this unreality would increase as the days passed. They were all of them prisoners, and they even more than she, because they were prisoners of their own unreality.

He need not have answered. It was bloody laughable—this colourless scarecrow of a woman with hacked-off hair lecturing him on what was real and what was not. But her words struck a dangerous chord in his mind, so that he came near to blurting out the truth of her situation just to shut her up. It was Maura who saved him, arriving early with the prisoner's water, soap and towel.

Their excitement at the news on the radio soon faded. Sean returned to his whittling. He'd found a block of wood at the back of a cupboard and was hacking at it with his pocket knife. At first he'd said he was carving a horse's head. Then he claimed he was making a miniature gun. Grady watched sourly as wood chips flew about the room.

"You should clean the UZI."

"I cleaned it this morning."

"Then clean it again."

"Clean it yourself."

Grady stiffened. "What was that?"

Sean hesitated, then grinned innocently. "Sure, and 'twas only the wind that blew."

He got up, fetched the automatic rifle and began stripping it. "One day, me darlin'," he whispered, "one day I'll get to use you. We'll kill a good few Brits, you and me, one day, together."

Grady turned to Maura, who was reading a paperback with a noose and a skull on the cover. "Herself along there," he said, "what does she do?"

Maura looked up. "Do? Sits in the dark. How should I know what she does? What does it matter, anyway?"

"It matters because I'm responsible for her. We all are."

"She's in no danger of losing her mind yet, if that's what you mean."

"*Yet?*"

"Ever."

"You said yet."

"I meant ever." Maura looked from him to Sean, bent over the dismantled gun. Suddenly she laughed. "I do declare, Liam Grady, we should have brought a cat. Included it in the team."

"A cat? What for?"

"For you to kick, Liam. What else? Just for you to kick when you're feeling bloody-minded."

He looked back at her fiercely. "I'm not cruel," he said.

In fact they had a cat—or more of a cat than any of them wanted. It was a stray that haunted Abbey Field, and it had kept them awake in the night with its yowling.

That evening, well after dark, Farrell came. Maura heard his whistling first, then his footsteps, and her spirits lightened. All day the Iron Lady had not yielded an inch. She was cold, if the blankets she'd wrapped round herself were anything to go by, but she didn't complain. Clearly she had entered into a contest of wills, and Maura, who might have been said to hold all the cards, was curiously powerless. Time, however, was on her side. It was, she had heard, a great healer. But it was also a great destroyer.

Farrell let himself in with his own key. He was in civilian clothes and carried a well-filled plastic bag. They lit a lamp in the kitchen for him to unload it, leaving another in his honour on the sitting-room table. The shadows retreated. It was as if they were having a party.

"Nobody has a clue," he said. "Just you wait till they hear the ultimatum. The British Government are not going to let their bloody Prime Minister die, are they? We've got them at our mercy—there's nothing they can do."

It hadn't really felt like that, not until Farrell said it. Even Liam smiled. "I always knew that would be the way of it," he said quietly.

There was fresh bread in the bag, some apples, thin frying steak, and a bottle of milk. There was also a thick wad of the last two days' newspapers. And, at the bottom, a small box of chocolates for Maura.

Sean whistled. "How about that, girl? I do believe the sergeant fancies you."

She nearly hit him. Farrell came to her rescue. "Just one Blond Terrorist to another," he said lightly, laughing as he pointed at the papers. She thought he must have had the line prepared.

She accepted the chocolates, and handed them round. Liam didn't want one, so Sean took his, and another for himself.

"And if it's fancy presents you're thinking of, Sergeant, and you're not after bringing me something cuddly, then I could just do with one of them model kits. A sailing ship, maybe. And not wood—I've tried that and sure it's not worth the bother. The boss here had me down on my knees half the afternoon, picking up the pieces."

Farrell glanced at Liam, who nodded his agreement. "I'll bring one next time I come," Farrell said. "Maybe the day after tomorrow."

That was very soon, but Liam made no objection. Maura had suspected that their isolation was getting to him, and now she was certain. Farrell's arrival was like a breath of fresh air to them all.

He couldn't stay long, of course. And then it was time to get the ring. She picked up a lamp and went along the corridor. The Iron Lady was lying on her bed in the dark, wide awake. Maura held out her hand. "May I have your wedding ring, please?"

Mrs Thatcher smiled sardonically. "With or without the finger?"

But Maura too was tough, and she too could be sardonic. "I think your husband would rather receive it without the finger. Don't you?"

Momentarily Maura felt Mrs Thatcher's iron resolve was faltering, as her hands fussed nervously with the edge of the blanket. But the gaze that met hers was still cool, and almost contemptuous.

Maura waited. Finally her prisoner spoke. "I shall write a letter," she said firmly.

"I'm afraid not."

"Why is that?" She turned and sat up. Her eyes were moist, but she was in perfect control of herself. "I haven't any information I could possibly disclose, have I?"

"No letter."

"Do you not need to prove that I am alive? The ring by itself will hardly—"

"No letter."

"I see. You're afraid, aren't you? You react out of fear, young woman. I hope you realize that."

Maura closed her ears. "Your ring, please."

She knew she could always take it if she had to, and so did her prisoner. The ring was removed and calmly handed up to her. She took it and returned to the sitting room. She gave the ring to Farrell.

He looked keenly down at her. "What's the matter?"

"Nothing's the bloody matter." She indicated the ring with an impatient gesture. "Where are you going to post it from?"

Farrell accepted that she didn't want to tell him. "Don't worry. Nowhere near here. Not that it matters, but I'll take the car tomorrow morning, just in case."

She went with him to the door. Liam stayed behind but Sean insisted on going with them. They closed the sitting-room door and felt along the passage in the dark. Out on the balcony the night was pitch black, cold and damp, but the air blessedly free. She breathed deeply. Moisture gathered on her face.

Farrell found her shoulder in the dark. "See you Saturday night, then."

Sean laughed. "We're not going anywhere, and that's the truth."

Farrell hurried away down the stairs. Sean called softly after him not to forget the model. The *Cutty Sark*, maybe . . . Maura stood in the blackness of the night, leaning against the cold metal rail, feeling suddenly very alone and fearful.

At 10.30 the next night—Friday—a resident of Chester Court telephoned the nearest police station. For three nights running he had noticed a taxi parked in the basement garage. Its number plate was not the one shown on television and mentioned in all the newspapers, but he thought the police might care to have a look just the same.

Superintendent Whitaker's telephone rang just as he was getting into bed. All that day he had been waiting anxiously for the promised statement from the Provos. So had a great many other people, but Whitaker's interest was special. He was the man who was supposed to have the IRA in Britain sewn up, the name and address of every single suspect at his fingertips. It didn't matter that he had already pulled in all the more important ones because none of them had provided any information of the slightest relevance. They didn't know. But he was the man everybody—and especially the Home Secretary who had asked for their best terrorist expert—looked to. Yet, like everyone else, he was reduced to waiting upon the Provos' whim.

He had a line tapped into the Press Association, so that all a desk man had to do was throw a switch, and Whitaker could listen in and record the message at the same time. That no message came was puzzling. If the Provos made promises of that kind they usually kept them. The superintendent considered the possible explanations. Disagreement within the Army Council about the demands to be made? No, that would have been settled long ago. The Prime Minister still in transit, and the operation not yet complete? Possible, but he didn't believe it. Or perhaps, ironically, it was the activities of the Garda that were delaying things? In Ireland, the search was on also. Some Provos had been picked up, but all of them small fry. All the Army Council members had apparently disappeared. It could be it was this need for evasive action that was at the root of the trouble.

Or perhaps it was simply—and simple explanations were often the best—that the Provos were giving the British extra time to sweat. On the whole that was the explanation he preferred. He stared at the telephone ringing beside his bed. Perhaps this was it. His alarm clock showed twenty past eleven. Typical, he thought. But they'd timed it badly—another fifteen minutes and he'd have been asleep.

Whitaker picked up the receiver, listened briefly, relaxed, grunted, then replaced the receiver and wearily began to get dressed again.

"We've found the taxi," he said.

His wife looked across at him. "Can't it wait till morning?"

"Probably." He pulled on his shirt. "I can't, though."

The Provisional IRA's statement was delivered the next day—Saturday—in good time for the BBC to delay the start of *Grandstand* at

12.30 with a special newscast. Superintendent Whitaker, grey with weariness and frustration, was back in his office at Scotland Yard.

The statement read: *The British Prime Minister is unharmed and is being well looked after. She has now arrived at a secure hideout in Ireland. She will be released upon the fulfilment of the following demands: the complete withdrawal of all British troops from the Irish mainland; the release of all IRA prisoners from the Maze prison, Belfast; and a solemn undertaking from the British Government to begin negotiations with the Republic for the reunification of Ireland. The Prime Minister will be released only after the withdrawal of troops has been completed. Unless the withdrawal begins within the next forty-eight hours, the Prime Minister will be executed.*

Whitaker rested his head in his hands. The final sentence was a bluff. It gave no exact time. And besides, the Army Council weren't fools; they knew it would take longer than forty-eight hours to make the political arrangements for such a withdrawal, even if agreement in principle were immediately given. It's pure PR, he thought. They're fixing things so that when they extend the deadline they can appear to be magnanimous.

She has now arrived at a secure hideout in Ireland. North or South? He presumed they meant the South, since to them it was one island. But he didn't believe that either. Slipping through a hastily-erected police cordon was one thing; shipping someone out of the country was quite another . . . He checked himself wryly. He'd have to believe that, he realized. Anything else would be an admission of a failure of quite monumental proportions.

Still, for the moment, until he received positive orders to the contrary, he would continue on the assumption that the Prime Minister was somewhere in the British Isles — a view, not surprisingly, enthusiastically held by his opposite number in the Garda.

The taxi used in Mrs Thatcher's abduction had yielded little that was new. The same khaki fibres, the same three generous sets of fingerprints. That the fibres matched those in the flat at least denied the possibility that they might have come from a former tenant. But there was still no evidence as to how many of the terrorists had worn khaki, nor if they had worn it at any time during the actual attack. Splinters of familiar plywood had also been found in the taxi, linking it with the various visits to Epping Forest.

Whitaker was tempted to think the fibres irrelevant. Khaki was worn by any number of people for any number of reasons: hunters for example, and members of rifle clubs, often wore army surplus clothing. He found something basically unlikely in the idea of a serving member of the British Army getting himself caught up in an affair like this. It was more likely that the terrorists deliberately wore army uniform as a disguise; people didn't suspect men moving around in army kit.

Only one fact caused him to reserve his judgment. Tiny traces of paint that might have come from an army vehicle had been found on the pillar beside the bay next to the taxi in the underground garage. They were recent, but exactly how recent was hard to say. Analysis was proceeding. If it established their military source and if they were in fact in any way connected with the kidnap, then a whole new range of possibilities presented themselves. If the police had done their job, then a record would have been kept of all the vehicles leaving London that night. And if . . .

Whitaker sighed. There were too many ifs. He buzzed for Trew. The sergeant needed to know of the Provos' ultimatum. Besides, there was one far more positive piece of evidence, and Whitaker wanted to be sure it was being properly circulated.

In the present crisis, Parliament took the unusual step for peace time of sitting on a Saturday, and the Chamber of the Commons was crowded that afternoon for the Deputy Prime Minister's statement. Members were crushed together on the green leather benches, sitting on the steps between the aisles, grouped at the bottom of the Chamber by the bar of the House, and leaning over the rails of the upper galleries. Most of them had already heard the IRA's ultimatum on radio or television, and now they received it with an anger echoing that of Mr Whitelaw himself.

When he had finished reading the Provos' words, he went on with solemn determination: "There can be no question of the British Government withdrawing troops under a threat of this kind. I would point out, however, that it has been the policy of this government to reduce the number of troops serving in the province. And it will continue—"

He got no further. At this merest hint at what many took to be a compromise, the House erupted. Minutes elapsed before the Speaker could restore order. Mr Whitelaw waited patiently. Every word of his statement had been discussed and carefully considered with his colleagues and advisers. It was addressed not only to the House of Commons and the nation, but to the Provisional IRA as well. Finally he was allowed to proceed.

"It has been and will continue to be our policy to reduce the role of the Army. But this . . ." he rode out a fresh bout of disgruntled muttering ". . . but this is always dependent upon the level of violence. Our objective is to ensure that security becomes the whole responsibility of the Royal Ulster Constabulary and not the Army. I say this so that there should be no doubt in anyone's mind about the continuing policy of Her Majesty's Government. We have never, and we never will, give in to violence, or to the threat of violence."

He was loudly cheered. Afterwards question followed question from backbenchers on both sides of the House. Mr Whitelaw answered them frankly. Those that were critical of the role of the police he fielded as best he could.

When the Leader of the Opposition asked if any of the people now held under the Prevention of Terrorism Act had been able to give the authorities any help at all in discovering the whereabouts of the Prime Minister, Mr Whitelaw was able to imply momentous secrets by resorting to a time-honoured formula: "I would like to thank the Right Honourable Gentleman for the consideration he has shown at this difficult time, and I think he will know the nature of what is going on at present."

And the Right Honourable Gentleman, who did indeed know what was going on, and just how little, nodded discreetly and held his peace. The last thing anybody wanted was a witch hunt, with the Commissioner of Police as principal victim.

While Mr Whitelaw was making his statement to the Commons, Lord Carrington was seeing the Irish Ambassador at the Foreign Office.

The Irishman was wary. "I do not see how the Prime Minister could have been smuggled out of this country and into Ireland. I do not believe it."

"Neither do I," the Foreign Secretary said drily. "But the British public will believe she's there. They'll believe anything of the Irish," he added with the gentlest of ironic smiles.

The joke, bitter as it was, eased the atmosphere between them. The Ambassador sighed.

"Your government," he said, "will be criticized for allowing the Provos to escape, and mine will be criticized for letting them get in. We're neither of us in an enviable position . . ." He paused. "I don't have to tell you we are doing all we can. Our security services are in close touch with yours, there's a full exchange of information. But the Provos' Army Council has gone to ground, and we can't search every farmhouse and back room in Ireland."

Lord Carrington sat back. "It may come to that," he said regretfully. Then he stiffened. "We shall never give in, of course. The Prime Minister just has to be found."

Fifteen minutes later the Foreign Secretary was in the Cabinet Room for Mr Whitelaw's emergency meeting to consider the Provisionals' demands. The Deputy Prime Minister himself got there early, arriving in a characteristically breathless manner from his trying session in the House. He wanted a few advance words with the Secretary to the Cabinet, Sir Robert Armstrong. Sir Robert, an Old Etonian in his fifties, had been private secretary both to Edward Heath and Harold Wilson when each was Prime Minister, and had been Margaret Thatcher's own choice to run the Cabinet Office. It was his job not only to see to the ordering of Cabinet business, but also to prepare the elliptic minutes that emerged from the Cabinet meetings. He was a civil servant of formidable ability.

Mr Whitelaw was relieved to find his own judgment being confirmed on every point by Sir Robert, who also suggested that, whatever the pressure from the media, it would be unwise to give more interviews at this stage. It would look as though the government were responding to terrorists' demands. Silence, he believed, would be thought to come from strength. It was a tactic already used by the Provos, and now it could be turned against them.

Lord Carrington arrived before the others and found the Home Secretary standing reflectively looking into the gathering dark by the french windows that overlooked the garden of Number 10 and gave a view on to St James's Park. The Foreign Secretary gave an account of his meeting with the Irish Ambassador, adding a little impatiently: "We're not getting anywhere, Willie."

For the Cabinet meeting itself, Mr Whitelaw now sat in the Prime Minister's seat, an admission of the painful realities that did not go unnoticed. A copy of the Provisionals' ultimatum lay before every Cabinet member.

"We all know why I have called this meeting," Mr Whitelaw

began, "and in the absence of any further progress by the police, we've got to consider how we respond to this." He indicated the document before them. "In my judgment they have no intention of killing the Prime Minister at the end of forty-eight hours. That would simply throw away any chance of their demands being met. It's a negotiating ploy. That's also the view of the security services. This is a new kind of operation for the Provos, and they'll want it to succeed. So they'll extend the deadline. It seems to me, therefore, that our policy must be to play for time, and to obtain whatever extensions are necessary to give the police, either in this country or Ireland, an opportunity to find the terrorists and ... and also the Prime Minister."

The Lord Chancellor leaned forward to pour a glass of water. He had to stretch across the table for the cut-glass carafe. There were never enough of them to go round.

"You mentioned Ireland," he said. "My impression was that the Police Commissioner had already discarded that as a possibility."

Mr Whitelaw nodded. "It's a remote one, certainly. But in the absence of any firm evidence to the contrary, we can't ignore it. We—"

"This 'playing for time', as you call it—" Untypical as the interruption was, one Cabinet Minister could no longer hide his irritation. "You're not suggesting that we appear to negotiate, are you? Wouldn't that involve accepting the Provos on their own terms?"

Mr Whitelaw averted his gaze. "Any negotiations," he murmured, "would naturally not take place in the full glare of publicity."

"You mean we'd hush them up?" the other snorted. "That might work very well for us. But how about the Provos? They'd make sure the news was splashed across every paper in the country—the British Government giving in."

"Not at all." It was Lord Carrington who spoke now. "The IRA aren't naïve. Forcing us out into the open would gain them nothing. It would simply entrench the differences between them and us. They know they either negotiate in secret or not at all. Anyway, they've done it before."

There was a shifting of papers round the table. Sir Keith Joseph sat forward.

"They'll also know what we're up to," he said shrewdly. "String them along a moment too long and they could blow this whole thing sky-high."

Mr Whitelaw's slightly boyish look was etched with tiredness. "We shall tread a knife-edge. I know that. But I don't see we have any alternative."

The door opened and a messenger came in. All eyes in the room followed him as he circled the table and handed a folder to the Secretary of State for Northern Ireland. Jim Prior opened it, and his rubicund features deepened in hue as he read the slip of paper inside. He looked up.

"It's what we might have expected," he said. "They're putting on a show of strength. There's been a mortar attack on a police post near the border in County Armagh. At least two men of the Royal Ulster Constabulary have been killed, and others are injured. The mortars were clearly fired from the Republic."

There was a controlled explosion from Mr Whitelaw and despairing sounds from the other Ministers.

"I suppose it was bound to happen. What worries me now," said the Home Secretary, "is if the Ulster Defence Association or the Ulster Volunteer Force start to retaliate. Then we'll be plunged into another series of sectarian assassinations." In the tension of the moment he dropped the traditional Cabinet courtesy of addressing a Minister by his title. "Jim," he said, "you'd better talk to Ian Paisley. Get him to use his influence so we don't get the Protestants on the warpath. He's hardly famous for his moderation, but even he must see the last thing we want at this moment is a bloodbath up in the North."

In Abbey Field the Prime Minister's captors had listened to the six o'clock news. The Provos' ultimatum was repeated, there was a full report of the proceedings in Parliament with actuality of the Home Secretary's voice recorded in the Chamber of the Commons, there were interviews with senior police officers, the Irish Ambassador, and Northern Ireland politicians. Members of the government, however, were conspicuous by their absence.

Grady was triumphant. "They're running scared. They don't know what to do, so they're doing nothing."

Sean chewed his knuckles. He was feeling frustrated and, in the absence of anything better, was badly in need of a cigarette.

"But they should have said *something*," he muttered. "Maybe they're on to us. Maybe we should get out while we can."

"On to us?" Grady smiled ironically. "The day that happens we'll be knee-deep in troops, army helicopters, the lot. There'll be no getting out for us then, boyo, and don't you forget it."

Sean was silent. He seemed wretched, and Maura took pity on him. "They'll never get on to us. Not in a million years. And haven't the Brits got a lot to think about now? We knew it was going to take a long time. It's much too soon to start worrying."

"Worrying?" He straightened his back. "Who's worrying? If I'm going to get caught I'd like to get caught in the open, that's all. And take a few of the bastards with me." He got up from the table and moved to the shelf where the UZI rested. He touched its stubby barrel gently, almost caressingly. "And do for that bitch in there too," he whispered.

Hardly four full days had elapsed since they had entered the flat, and already the strain of their situation was beginning to tell. Maura felt restless. She could settle to nothing. In dealing with the Iron Lady she had abandoned her charade of nurse-like cheerfulness. When making her plans it had seemed undefeatable. She had seen it work on the wards time and time again, rebellious patients reduced to submissive nonentities. But Mrs Thatcher was neither sick nor senile, and in the face of her obstinate dignity Maura's performance was simply cheap. Now she got on with her duties with as few words as possible, and left the darkness and isolation to do the rest. And worried that she was failing in the one important task she had set herself.

Sean was like a caged animal. The tasks Grady set down for him were only scantily performed. During daylight hours he paced obsessively from one look-out point to the other, peering out at the unchanging prospect, muttering under his breath. He'd tried every book and magazine in the place, but he was no reader. He spent most time on *Men Only* and *Penthouse*, but they didn't help. They only made him feel worse. Saturday afternoon brought footballers to the playing fields, and ragged groups of spectators, but the sight of their freedom merely worsened his mood. In between his pacing he retired to the toilet—to smoke and to masturbate. Grady ignored the smell of the roll-ups.

Only Grady himself seemed at peace. He read, did exercises in the bedroom he shared with Sean, listened to the radio, studied his chess problems. For the rest he simply sat quietly and watched the others. His ulcer didn't trouble him, and he had the advantage over them of knowing precisely how long they were all going to be there. He refrained from criticizing them, thinking that his example would help to calm them. In fact it only made things worse.

Both Sean and Maura, in their different ways, were waiting desperately for Farrell's Saturday night visit. It was somehow going to make all the difference. And when it came it was, for both of them, a bitter disappointment. It could have been no other. The pervasive darkness, the terrible sense of anti-climax, the squalor of their confinement, Sean's craving for violent action, his sexual frustration, Maura's insecurity and need for love ... Farrell's presence alone was to have made up for all of these. It was too much to ask of any man.

When he came he brought food, the newspapers, and Sean's model. A joke or two. A breath of the outside world. Nothing more. So that they ended up resenting him—his easy ways, his freedom; and they waited impatiently for him to leave.

Only Grady, again, was unaffected. He was pacing himself. He knew that, barring discovery, they had twenty-four more days to go. No more than twenty-four, and no less. And he could keep them together that long, he thought, if he didn't ride them too hard. Months before he had suggested to Dublin that they should all share in his knowledge. He had been refused. In view of the personalities involved, he was told, uncertainty as to the outcome was recommended. He took the point. But he also knew that if anything were to break his hold over them, it would be just that uncertainty.

14

The weekend passed. On Sunday a secret envoy was despatched by the government with authority to open discreet negotiations. In view of the elusiveness of the Provisionals' Army Council a deep-cover British agent within the upper ranks of the IRA had to be used, but his loss of cover was, in the circumstances, considered justifiable. On Monday the Provos' forty-eight-hour deadline came and went, with no comment from either side.

On Tuesday afternoon, a week after the abduction, a small

package arrived Express Delivery for Denis Thatcher at Number 10. It was postmarked Dublin, and dated the previous day. When it had been checked for explosives and opened, it was found to contain the Prime Minister's wedding ring. Enclosed with the ring was a short letter, typed and unsigned. The British police were wasting their time with their continued persecution of the Irish community in Britain. Mrs Thatcher was in Ireland. She was in good health, and would be released from her captivity as soon as the Provisional IRA's demands had been met in full. In view of the British Government's clear lack of concern for her welfare the deadline had been extended. But if progress towards meeting these demands had not been made by eleven o'clock on Thursday night, she would be executed.

Within two hours a photostat of the letter was on Superintendent Whitaker's desk, while the original and the package went into the labs for detailed examination. He read the letter and tossed it to one side. It was worthless. If the Provos knew their job, and they did, the original and its packaging would be worthless too. Its Dublin origin was presumably meant to establish the Prime Minister's whereabouts, but it did nothing of the sort. There'd been plenty of time for the ring to be posted there from somewhere in Britain. And the letter was mere rhetoric. All any of it provided was proof, as if proof were needed, that the Provos did indeed hold the Prime Minister.

Whitaker turned his attention back to a piece of paper hardly more promising. It was a list, and it represented an extremely long shot indeed. But in an investigation totally devoid of firm leads, one was left with long shots or nothing. He looked up at Trew. The sergeant had brought in the letter photostat, and now he coughed apologetically.

"There's something else, sir. Essex CID have been on the jolly old blower. Superintendent Blackhurst's getting a lot of flak from the local press. They seem to think he should have come up with something on that old man's murder. It's four weeks now, and he'd appreciate it if he could make some sort of statement."

Whitaker frowned. "I'll call him later. But I'm afraid he'll have to stew. We've got enough egg on our faces without that." He tapped the paper in front of him. "And speaking of egg on our faces, who'd have thought there'd be so many? Thirty-seven, I make it. What the hell's the Army doing—running day trips into the capital for bored soldiers?"

"I suppose we'll have to follow up every single one of them, sir?"

"Of course we will." His eye ran down the page. "No—I lie. There's a motor cycle here. I doubt if even the IRA could conceal the Prime Minister on the back of one of those."

Trew smiled dutifully. "That still leaves thirty-six, sir."

"Thank you, Goodie, but I can count. I want every one of them followed up immediately. If one of them turns out promising, we'll go and take a look ourselves. You might care for a trip in the country, eh? Meanwhile, I must put together some sort of memo. It's all so vague—I hate to think what the Commissioner will make of it."

Trew sat down. He pulled the piece of paper towards him: it bore a list of all the army vehicles to have been checked leaving London on the afternoon and evening of the Prime Minister's abduction. Analysis of the paint scrapings from the pillar in the underground garage had established a military origin. Not that this on its own proved anything except that an army vehicle had at some time in the last few months been driven carelessly in or out. Taken with the khaki fibres, however, it did provide an interesting coincidence.

One of Willie Whitelaw's assets in government was his political instinct. It was an instinct derived, he would have been the first to admit, not from great intellectual capacity—though a common mistake among his political opponents was to underrate his intelligence—but from experience and human understanding. It was this understanding, his patience, and his instinct that had led him nearer to success in Northern Ireland than any other minister before or since. Now he'd had to trust his understanding and his instinct more than ever in talking to the Prime Minister's husband. But Denis Thatcher had made it easy for him. The Home Secretary came back from the conversation heartened and impressed. If one Englishman could display such courage and immediate grasp of the realities then there was hope for the whole nation.

Mr Whitelaw was met in the Cabinet Office by Number 10's Press Secretary. He brought with him a piece of Press Association tape, torn from the teleprinter. The Provisionals had issued a further statement, announcing that they had sent the Prime Minister's wedding ring to her husband, and established a second deadline for her execution.

"The boys are on the phone already. Can we confirm it?"

The Home Secretary nodded wearily. "Yes, Bernard, tell them the ring has been received, and the package was postmarked Dublin, yesterday. For any further information refer them to Scotland Yard."

Bernard Ingham had been Press Officer in too many Whitehall ministries not to know that a simple confirmation would not be enough. He had built his reputation for fair dealing with correspondents by knowing when they would be content with the bare facts and when they needed to know more.

"We're under great pressure, Home Secretary, to say something on the record in response to the Provos."

Mr Whitelaw worked his jaw thoughtfully. He could have wished too that the Press might have had an immediate grasp of the realities.

"We agreed," he said, "it was better at this stage not to be drawn."

"Yes, I know. But a full week's gone by now, and frankly, if we continue to say nothing it looks as if the government has nothing to say, doesn't know what to do."

"All right, Bernard. All right. What do you suggest?"

"You and Jim Prior must see the Press, and go on the box too. You must state the government's position very firmly, its public position, that is."

Mr Whitelaw noted the distinction but made no comment. "Later in the day, then," he said. "Draft some thoughts, Bernard. Meanwhile I'll speak to the Commissioner."

By the time Mr Whitelaw was ready to record an interview for BBC and independent television, he had learned in detail how all available police officers in the metropolis, and most other forces in the country, were working on what had been code-named Operation PM. So were units of the Special Air Services, the Army and the RAF, many of them combined in sweep-and-search operations. Every known supporter of terrorist organizations had been or was being interrogated, the Irish security services were giving full co-operation, and widespread searches were being made in the Republic. Interpol was giving every help. All the scientific resources of the Yard were being employed. The routine was thorough and unrelenting. But so far there was still no clue to the Prime Minister's whereabouts. But, to the Home Secretary's relief, an IRA bomb factory had been found in Hornsey. It did not matter that, according to the Police Commissioner, the factory almost certainly had nothing to do with what one newspaper had called the "Downing Street Massacre" and the kidnapping of the Prime Minister. It was a straw, not for a drowning man to clutch at, but from which a brick could be made.

Mr Whitelaw was interviewed in one of the drawing rooms at Number 10.

"We have been asked," he said, "why, if we value the Prime Minister's life, we have not responded to the demands made by the Provisional IRA. It is precisely because we value the Prime Minister's life and, indeed, the lives of political leaders throughout the world, that the British Government cannot respond in any way to terrorist threats. No Prime Minister's life would be safe if governments gave in to terrorism. If these people once thought that by their barbarous acts they could influence national policy, the future of civilized government itself would be in danger, not only in this country but throughout the world. I can tell you that no one holds to this conviction more strongly and with more determination than the Prime Minister herself. She has never been prepared to yield an inch in the face of terrorist threat. And she would not do so now. This government's policy is, and always has been, to root out terrorism wherever we find it. At this very moment the biggest police search in history is under way. We are confident that it will succeed."

He then announced the discovery of the Hornsey bomb factory. His interviewer leaned forward.

"Did this factory supply the weapons for the kidnap, Home Secretary?"

"I cannot say that." Mr Whitelaw had prepared his answer carefully. "It may have done. It may not have done. Two men are being questioned, but this particular investigation is still at a very early stage." He moved on smoothly. "I can only repeat that the way to ensure the Prime Minister's release is not to give in to threats, but by unremitting work to find her. That is going on round the clock. It will not fail."

After the recording, while he was relaxing, scotch in hand, with his interviewer, a note was handed to him. He read it, his face totally expressionless, then refolded it calmly and put it in his pocket.

It was his habit, with correspondents he could trust, occasionally to be less discreet than in his public statements. This evening, however, he possessed information he could share with no one outside the highest levels of government.

But he admitted to the correspondent that the two men detained in the raid on the Hornsey bomb factory were small fry, and almost certainly not involved in the Prime Minister's abduction. By the time the journalist got round to the matter that Mr Whitelaw guessed would be uppermost in his mind, he had his response ready.

"Between you and me, Willie, you're in contact with the Provos, aren't you?"

"Certainly not." The answer was firm. And, in the sense the question had been meant, truthful. "What makes you say that? Do you think we should be?"

"That's up to you, Willie. But they must know they're not going to get all they're asking for. They'll have fallback demands. I'd have thought there's plenty to talk about. And who better than you and Jim—the most skilful negotiators in the business?"

"I wouldn't be so sure of that, John. I mean," he added with a wry smile, "I wouldn't be so sure that they don't imagine they'll get what they want."

"And will they?"

The Home Secretary sighed, took a gulp at his scotch, and shrugged, but was not prepared to be drawn any further. In the face of friendly probing he fell back on reminiscences about June 1973 when he had managed, in Northern Ireland, to get an assembly elected and by several weeks of talking had persuaded Protestant and Catholic leaders to work together, and ultimately there had emerged the Council of Ireland concept and the Sunningdale Conference.

"You know as well as I do," he said, "that at some time there has got to be a closer relationship with the South. I thought once that it was on the way. How it's to be done now God only knows. Certainly not through a thing like this . . ."

Finally the correspondent left. He had to return to Television Centre to put together the Home Secretary's interview, plus the many other elements of the day's coverage, in a single report on the hunt for the Prime Minister. Only when he had gone did Mr Whitelaw take from his pocket the note he had been handed, and re-read it.

The government's secret envoy had returned empty-handed. He had been allowed to meet IRA leaders, and had clearly been permitted to return unharmed only because the Provisionals wanted the British Government to be left in no doubt about their determination. The message was unequivocal: there was to be no discreet negotiation. The Provisional IRA had issued their ultimatum and they were sticking to it. They appeared to be going for all or nothing.

After his Saturday visit Sergeant Farrell stayed away from the Abbey Field flat for several days. He told himself this was only common sense. No matter how small, an element of risk always existed. On

Tuesday he restarted his evening snooker games with his sergeant friend. And Wednesday night he had to run a regular Territorial Army instruction course. Grady's lot would be doing fine. They had plenty of food and fuel. And they were quite safe.

In fact he stayed away because he wanted to. The place disturbed him. It was like a cave, a dungeon inhabited by freaks. He had avoided all contact with the Iron Lady. Though he would never have admitted it, this was self-preservation. If things should ever go badly wrong, then those she couldn't positively identify had a better chance of survival. But this avoidance was also at the root of his unease. He didn't want to know what they were doing to her, and yet the thought of it haunted him. On his last visit he hadn't wanted to look them in the face.

He himself had killed four people. He knew that and could live with it. In war these things happened. But if he was a murderer, then what were they?

There'd been a time, not so very long ago, when he'd felt drawn to Maura. Emotionally, as well as sexually. She had a vulnerability that roused the protectiveness in him . . . It was thinking of this that decided him finally to return again on Thursday night. In spite of everything, she needed him.

In preparation for his visit he went out shopping on Thursday morning. As he re-entered the Sergeants' Mess one of his fellow NCOs stopped him. "You're wanted, mate. Company office."

He rested his carrier bag on the step. "Will do."

"You're for it, I'd say. All that gash stuff you've been flogging."

"What stuff's that?"

"Very nice. But you can save the injured innocence bit for the CID. Spotted him a mile off. Toffee-nosed sod, and dressed to kill. Flashing his warrant card like it was American Express."

Farrell eyed him thoughtfully, thanked him for the tip, then went on into his room. He was crossing the barrack square when the Company clerk finally found him. He marched at once, very stiff and military, to the Company Office. His CO was waiting for him.

"Ah, Sergeant, *there* you are."

Farrell answered the implied criticism. "An off-duty morning, sir. Just slipped out of barracks."

"Quite so. One of my most reliable men. I was just telling Detective Sergeant Trew here." The CO indicated the immaculate young man seated respectfully behind him and to one side.

"Detective Sergeant Trew is from the London police. He is conducting enquiries into the disappearance of the Prime Minister and he would like to ask you some questions. I—"

"Me, sir? I hope he's not suggesting I might have . . ."

"I have to tell you," the CO ground on sternly, "that you do not have to answer these questions. Unless you have something to hide, however, you would be strongly advised to do so. I myself shall be present throughout the interrogation."

The young Detective Sergeant coughed apologetically. "Interrogation's a pretty strong word, sir, I think . . . Just one or two things, Sergeant. I'm sure you don't mind." He smiled agreeably up at Farrell. "You may sit down if you wish."

Farrell stared straight ahead. "I'd rather stand."

"Anything you say. I'll try not to keep you." The Detective Sergeant opened his notebook, turned a few pages. "Your commanding officer has been very helpful. The reason for your trip to London, that sort of thing, all perfectly straightforward. I may say that we're checking up on an awful lot of chaps like you. Our main hope is that you may have seen something."

"Seen something?" *An awful lot of chaps like you* . . . the man was like every upper-class twit subaltern Farrell had ever known. "What sort of something?"

"After all, Sergeant, you were almost certainly on the road at the same time as the kidnappers."

"Judging from the jams, so were half a million others."

Farrell was aware of his own reputation. The CO would have thought it odd if he'd suddenly been all smiles.

The Detective Sergeant nodded. "Fair enough. All the same, a military man, a trained observer . . ."

He let the sentence dangle in the air. Farrell didn't believe a word of it. They were on to something. He felt utterly calm. Whatever it was, they'd get nothing from him.

"There wasn't much to see. Only the arse of the car in front."

"I was afraid you'd say that. Still, it's perfectly understandable." The young man stared at his notebook. "Now, as to your movements while you were still in London . . . It's helpful to establish these things. Sort of negative evidence. After all, if you didn't see anything then there probably wasn't anything to see."

"I didn't see the Prime Minister being carried across the bloody street, if that's what you mean."

Farrell's CO shifted uncomfortably at the swear word. The policeman smiled imperturbably. "I see that you left the Albany Street barracks at around 1.25, yet it was nearly five before you were checked at one of our road blocks. Now, your movements during that time could be very helpful."

Farrell hesitated. He looked at his CO. "There was nothing to get back here for that day, sir. I always consider my time's my own, so long as I'm here for morning duty."

The CO gestured impatiently. "Just answer the Detective Sergeant's questions."

"Yes, sir. I'd have spent the time in the Hampstead area, sir. There's . . . there's a young lady I sometimes meet, sir. She's a nurse at the Royal Free. Works nights mostly."

The policeman clicked his ballpoint pen. "Her name and address?"

Farrell turned to him slowly. "I could give that to you, but it wouldn't do you much good. I rang her bell, but she didn't answer. I thought, either she's out or she isn't up yet. And if she wasn't up she wouldn't thank me for waking her. So I cleared off and had a cup of coffee instead." He paused. "Anyway, I thought it was my movements you were after, not my love life."

Once again his CO came near to interrupting. But the Detective Sergeant wasn't troubled. Farrell thought, give it to 'em rough. They'll be far more suspicious if you snivel.

"A cup of coffee, Sergeant? For three hours?"

Farrell agreed equably. "More or less . . . There was this bloke in the caff with a transistor. I was just pushing off when the news came through. So I hung around a bit, to see what happened."

The young policeman considered. Then he snapped his book shut and stood up. "Many thanks for your help, Sergeant. And yours, sir." He turned to Farrell's CO. "I'm sorry we have to ask all these questions, but that's police work for you."

The CO didn't answer. He said, "That will do, Sergeant Farrell."

Farrell came smartly to attention, saluted, and turned about. At the door he paused. "I wouldn't want you to think, sir . . . I mean, if I'd seen anything suspicious I'd have come forward days ago. A couple of my mates died in Belfast, sir. For what it's worth, I hate the bloody IRA."

His CO had the grace to be embarrassed. Not so Detective Sergeant Trew. "One more thing, Sergeant. The Land Rover you used—if it's not too much trouble, could I have a look at it?"

Farrell glanced at the CO, who shrugged his agreement. They'll be asking for my fingerprints next, he thought. And a fat lot of good *that* would do them. He led the way to the huge corrugated iron shed that was the transport pool, reflecting that he had been wise to return the vehicle for a service and cleaning. Inside the door he waited while the policeman looked up the registered number in his book and checked the vehicle thoroughly, inside and out. Farrell had no idea what he was looking for. Strands of the Iron Lady's hair? He must know that army vehicles were hosed out for inspection—even if Farrell hadn't personally cleaned up the back of his vehicle on the night of the snatch there'd be not a trace of her left by now.

The Detective Sergeant seemed satisfied. Then, on their way out of the shed, they bumped into the Motor Transport sergeant. They paused to pass the time of day. The policeman complimented him on the smart condition of his trucks. Farrell shifted his feet, trying to hide his impatience.

"I expect you have your own spray shop," Detective Sergeant Trew remarked.

The MT sergeant nodded. "We got some pretty good drivers, though. It's the training, see. Haven't had a touch-up job in . . . oh, in months."

The policeman was impressed. They moved on across the square, leaving the MT sergeant scratching his head behind them. Bloody civvies, poking their noses into *his* MT shed.

At the Guard Room they stopped. The Detective Sergeant held out his hand. "No hard feelings I hope, Sergeant Farrell. You were right, of course—there's more in this than just your movements. A lot of army vehicles left London that afternoon. It sounds pretty jolly daft I know, but one of them *might* have been carrying the Prime Minister. Anyway, we've got to check. You do understand?"

Farrell nodded minimally. It sounded like a prepared speech, one that the copper had already gone through more times than he cared to remember. They parted, Farrell to report back to his CO. There'd be more questions, he felt sure, but none he couldn't deal with. Afterwards he'd have to pick his moment, nip back to the MT shed with a screw-driver and switch number plates again. He'd thought all along that the trick would be a waste of time, but he liked to be certain. What counted was an eye for detail, and he flattered himself that he had one.

Suddenly, on his way back across the square, he stopped dead. Sweat prickled his scalp. Grady had been in the front of the Land Rover with him. What if the copper had asked him about Grady? A hitch-hiker? Just how many thin ones like that would the copper have swallowed? He walked on slowly. They'd been saved by the merest chance: too few policemen, too hard pressed to note more than a car's driver and number plate. He wondered grimly what similar good luck would be needed before the operation was safely over.

Terry O'Donovan was known both to the security services in the North and to the Garda. Moreover, being the younger brother of James O'Donovan, a member of the Provisional Army Council, he was in a position to know the hideout of the Iron Lady. Furthermore, in an organization that prided itself on its sexual propriety, he was a practising gay. In the face, however, of the clampdown by the British police—"the continuing persecution of the Irish population in Britain" as the Provos had proclaimed it—Terry O'Donovan was the best man the Army Council had available. So he was to demonstrate the Provisional IRA's limitless resources. He was going to play the role of the big lie.

He had arrived in Britain two days after Operation 10's Downing Street snatch, and by remaining on his own and moving constantly, he had stayed at liberty ever since. His contact with existing IRA cells had been limited to one brief visit to the Hornsey safe house some three days before it was discovered, for explosives and bomb-making equipment. Last night, Wednesday, he had stayed at a small private hotel in Kensington. Tonight he was booked in at a shabby Greek-Cypriot establishment near Paddington.

O'Donovan was a skilled bomb-maker. To him, it was a job that had to be done. He didn't think much about it otherwise. His father had been shot to death at his front door in Belfast by UVF men, and his mother terrified out of her mind. For him, working for the Cause was almost a physical necessity.

His target that night in London was Lockets restaurant in Marsham Street. No more than ten minutes' walk from the House of Commons and a favourite rendezvous for MPs and Westminster journalists, it had been bombed during a mainland campaign some years before, but anti-terrorist precautions had long since been relaxed. O'Donovan's instructions were that the explosion was to be timed for eleven o'clock that Thursday night—the latest deadline for the Prime Minister's release—and that there was to be no loss of life.

He went about his task methodically, casing the chosen target and constructing the simplest bomb he knew: no more than half a pound of plastic explosive, detonated by an electric contact made by the rotation of the minute hand of a cheap watch. There were other timing devices, but few that offered the same precision with such small financial outlay. Its only drawback was that it provided a time-lag of, at the outside, one hour. But for the operation O'Donovan had in mind half that time would have been sufficient.

Outside the restaurant there was a dark blue awning and a small potted tree. Early in the evening, there was often a waiter near the glass door, but by ten o'clock the small foyer was usually empty. Just inside the door there was a bar which gave a reasonable view of the street, but customers mostly moved further along into the lounge.

At 10.30 that night O'Donovan, wearing a smart dark suit and raincoat and carrying a briefcase, got out of his taxi at Broad Sanctuary. A chilling drizzle of rain was falling. With scarcely a glance at the towering structure of Westminster Abbey, he turned briskly into Great Smith Street and on into Marsham Street. Two policemen were about fifty yards ahead of him walking in the same direction. Since the Downing Street operation the whole Westminster area was patrolled at regular intervals. He slowed, keeping the policemen in sight.

By the time O'Donovan reached the blue awning, and ducked under it, the policemen were a long way ahead. He stood there for a moment, looking about him. On the other side of the road was the block of flats from which Airey Neave had made his last journey in his car to the House of Commons. O'Donovan brushed the fine mist of raindrops off his shoulders, a typical London businessman debating whether he should continue to walk, or wait there and look for a taxi instead. He glanced at his watch. The time was twenty to eleven. The studded metal doors were open. He propped his briefcase against one of them and opened it. A waiter passing in the foyer came towards him, but he shook his head and pointed down the street, keeping his face lowered and in shadow from the internal lights. He closed his briefcase and turned away, resting it on the corner of the tub containing the small tree as he lit a cigarette. He held one hand out beyond the edge of the awning, palm upwards, to test the rain. Then he shrugged, retrieved his briefcase and hurried away towards Whitehall.

On the soil of the tub he had left a small package covered in coarse, earth-coloured sacking over thick waterproof plastic.

Now for the first time he began to feel cold, as the rain trickled down his face and tangled his hair. He went directly to one of the telephone boxes in Parliament Street, between the Treasury building and the bus stops. The time was almost ten to eleven. He dialled Lockets restaurant, got the engaged signal, drummed his fingers, dialled again. When the number answered he spoke slowly and clearly.

At eleven o'clock precisely the bomb exploded, blowing in the front of the restaurant and destroying the blue awning. By that time the restaurant had been cleared, and nobody was hurt. O'Donovan was on a bus travelling north up Whitehall. Shortly afterwards the woman sitting next to him pointed out of the window at a police car coming fast in the opposite direction, its siren blaring.

"I knew it was a bomb," she said, "I just knew it was."

O'Donovan had taken a newspaper from his briefcase. He looked up from it.

"A bomb?" he said. "Where? I didn't hear anything."

The Provisional IRA issued a statement on the Marsham Street explosion in time for the BBC's early morning news bulletin. It was telephoned in the usual way to the Press Association, and its text was before the Home Secretary when he sat down to breakfast.

It read: *The Provisional IRA accepts full responsibility for the explosion in Marsham Street last night. Adequate warning was given, and no one was injured. This action has been taken to demonstrate that the Provisional IRA still has the capacity to launch a full-scale bombing campaign on the British mainland. This need not happen, however, if the British Government respond to our demands. It also marks our most recent deadline for the execution of the Prime Minister. She is, however, alive and well. Although the British Government has failed to reply to our demands, we understand the reasons for this and have no wish to be unreasonable. We are, therefore, extending the deadline for a full week. This represents the British Government's last chance to respond in a positive and helpful manner. Failing this, we shall have no alternative but to execute the Prime Minister. Finally, the British Government must*

not suppose that the additional time we have allowed increases the
possibility of the Prime Minister being found. Her Irish hideout
remains secure.

Mr Whitelaw's experience of Northern Ireland in general and the Provisional IRA in particular led him to see a number of encouraging signs in this statement. To begin with the government had mercifully been right in assuming that the Prime Minister's life was not in immediate danger. Secondly, the Provos were sufficiently mindful of public opinion to underline their serious purpose without endangering life. Thirdly, the statement spoke of the British Government responding to their demands in a "positive and helpful manner"; it no longer mentioned the immediate fulfilment of those demands. And fourthly, there was the uncharacteristic sentence expressing understanding and saying, incongruously, that they had "no wish to be unreasonable". This suggested for the first time the possibility of negotiation. Perhaps they were climbing down and, if so, it might be possible to renew secret contacts. But not yet.

This was the interpretation that Mr Whitelaw gave to his colleagues at the meeting he had called for 9.30 in the Cabinet Room. To save repeatedly summoning a full Cabinet, it had been agreed that the present emergency should be dealt with by a special committee. This comprised the Home Secretary, the Lord Chancellor, the Foreign Secretary, the Chancellor of the Exchequer, the Defence Secretary, the Lord President of the Council, who was also the Leader of the Commons, and the Northern Ireland Secretary.

The Ministers agreed that the Provos' insistence that the Prime Minister was in Ireland probably indicated that she was in fact on the British mainland. Their intention would be to achieve a relaxation of the British search operation.

"So," said the Chancellor of the Exchequer in his customarily quiet and unruffled tone, "we continue to play for time, and we make no public response to this latest offering?"

"Now more than ever, I think," said Mr Whitelaw. He sorted through his papers. "There were two more Catholics murdered in Belfast last night, almost certainly by UDA killer squads. If we appear to give an inch it will make things even worse."

Everyone round the table knew that, contrary to popular opinion, the Protestant Ulster Defence Association had probably killed more civilians than any other paramilitary organization in the North, including the IRA. They had stepped up their attacks since the Mountbatten murder, and the UVF—the Ulster Volunteer Force, a separate organization—had recently intensified its own offensive. Jim Prior sighed. "I've seen Paisley," he said. "I think he understands the situation. Contact will be made with the UDA commander. Tyrie's a difficult man, but he might respond."

"You'd better go on the box," Mr Whitelaw told him. "Just in Northern Ireland, Jim. Appeal for calm and so on. And stress that any sectarian activity now, any attempt to take revenge, can only endanger the Prime Minister's life. The Provos should see that as a good sign. It'll give them hope, and that's what we need if we're going to play for time."

"I could advance the withdrawal of the next battalion," said the Defence Secretary, John Nott. "If you think it would help."

"So what would that leave?"

"Nearly twelve thousand men. It wouldn't matter very much to us. Terrorist activity is, in fact, down in the province. And there's still seven and a half thousand members of the Ulster Defence Regiment, even though they're mostly part time. It might just encourage the Provos to hold their hands."

Ultimately the ministerial committee decided that it should be announced informally, by the Press Secretary at Number 10 in answer to questions, that a battalion of British troops was being withdrawn from Belfast in a week's time. It would be emphasized that the decision had been taken some time ago, and the government saw no reason to alter it. Neither did they see any reason to advance the date. On the whole, the Ministers thought they would get away with it. And the Provos could read between the lines.

It was cold in the flat in Abbey Field. Cold and damp. The gas heater Farrell had supplied did a good job in the sitting room, but the rest of the place was like an ice house. It had not been helped by the fact that, many days back, Grady had realized that somehow they had to get fresh air into the flat. The atmosphere had become intolerably stale, especially in the prisoner's room. So at night, a section of the boarding in the kitchen had been carefully cut away, to be replaced during the day time. This also meant leaving the door of the prisoner's room open. During that time a guard had to be mounted in the corridor. It had unquestionably added to the tension that was building up. But they had to have air.

Maura provided her prisoner with more blankets. She had been confined to that one room, mostly in the dark, for nine days. What she did with her time Maura had no idea. On Thursday morning, briefly, there had been sounds of violent activity, but when Maura went in to her the Prime Minister was standing quietly by the window. Her nails were broken, however, and although she kept her head turned steadfastly away, Maura had seen smears of dirt, as if from tears, down her face.

She said quietly: "You won't get the boards off the windows that way, you know. Only spoil your fingers."

The Prime Minister ignored her.

On another occasion, Maura's curiosity got the better of her. Ignoring Grady's strict instructions, she asked her prisoner: "What do you do all day?"

In the light from the open door and the torch, Maura saw the clear blue eyes looking back at her. With the merest hint of a smile, the Prime Minister said: "There isn't a lot I can do, is there?" After a pause, she added: "You're providing me, young lady, with a lot of time to think. It's not that boring, you know—not when you know how to do it. You might even discover things about yourself. You should try it. I can recommend it. And I probably have a lot more problems to solve than you do."

Maura shrugged. She knew it was a gesture of defeat in the face of the puzzling self-possession of her prisoner. The rough blankets, the darkness, the cold, the coarse carbolic soap, the primitive sanitation, her chopped-off hair—she suffered it all without complaint and with dignity. Only once had she made a spontaneous request, for a new torch battery, and that in a calm, take-it-or-leave-it fashion.

Maura had provided the battery. "You needn't economize. There's plenty more where that came from."

Later, when it was time to empty the slop bucket, she'd taken in a book as well. She expected no gratitude and she received none. And the book, a murder mystery, appeared to remain unread.

None of this was what Maura had been prepared for. Ranting, even physical violence—anything save this tranquil, self-possessed withdrawal. It wasn't natural. She knew something of what sensory deprivation could do, and it worried her. That evening she talked it over with Liam.

He chewed his lip. "You think now she might be going crazy?"

"Wouldn't you be?"

"That's—"

"I know *I* am."

For the first time in days Sean grinned. He crossed his eyes and made slobbering noises. It obviously cheered him to hear of their prisoner's sufferings. Maura hunched her shoulders. There was a play she'd heard of, by a Frenchman, all about hell, which was the ceaseless company of two other people.

She watched Liam control his irritation. "That's got nothing to do with it," he said sharply. "We aren't the Iron Lady. You're not going soft, are you? Would you like me to take over?"

"Or me?" said Sean enthusiastically.

They both ignored him.

"Is it soft not to want a lunatic on our hands?" Maura asked.

Liam thought about it. "That confidence of hers—do you think it's helping her? Or do you think it's broken?"

Maura reviewed the last few days in her head. "I think . . . I hope it's helping her."

"I shouldn't worry." Liam leaned forward and patted her arm. "Some people have certainty. It's a great gift. Churchill had it. The hunger strikers had it." He smiled quietly. "So did Hitler."

The joke was lost on Sean. The gesture wasn't. Maura saw his grin fade abruptly, his gaze fixed on Liam's hand on her arm. She eased herself away. Too late. Sean got up, knocking over his chair.

"I'm going out for a walk," he announced through clenched teeth.

Liam was very still. "If you do, you're not coming back."

"What d'you mean? You can't—"

"If you do a thing like that we don't need you. You're more trouble than you're worth. Just see how you manage, on your own out there. Where's your discipline?"

Sean took a step forward. "It's all right for you. Maybe a quick feel now and then is all you need. But I've been living like a monk now for too bloody long."

"You should have thought of that before you accepted the job."

"For Christ's sake, where's the harm? A couple of hours, boss— it's not much." His tone had changed. He was wheedling now. Maura relaxed. For the moment the crisis was over. "Now, where's the danger, boss? You've seen me picture in the paper—that artist's bloody impression. Sure, and me own mother wouldn't know me from that."

Liam appeared to hesitate. Sean spread his hands. "You think I'll get boozed and shoot off me mouth? Look—a quid in my pocket is all I ask. And it won't go on the drink, I promise."

Maura shuddered. What sort of sex could you buy for a quid, she wondered.

Liam frowned. "I'll think about it."

"But, boss—"

"I told you. I'll think about it."

And in spite of persistent appeals, that was all Sean could get. Maura understood Liam's problem. His hold on Sean had become precarious. If he could just string him along . . .

The next evening, Friday, Farrell came. They'd expected him sooner, but he gave no real explanation. He seemed preoccupied, and he stayed for scarcely five minutes. Maura was glad to see him go. He'd had the easy end of the operation right from the beginning and it got on her nerves. She could see it irritated Sean too—the sight of the man going freely out into town. *He* didn't have to live like a bloody monk.

The papers he brought were full of the London bomb blast, and the battalion of troops that was being pulled out of Northern Ireland. They'd heard it all on the radio already, but somehow reading it and seeing the pictures made it all seem more real. Another few days maybe and they could all go home.

In his office in Scotland Yard that Friday Superintendent Whitaker studied the Bomb Squad's findings, and the reports of the previous day's interviews at army barracks in different parts of the country. They'd obviously been difficult interviews, insulting to the soldiers who had to be questioned. He was glad he didn't have to do them himself. But the ever conscientious Trew had essayed into Essex, and had had a right bastard up in Colchester, but who could blame the man? If a bloke had served in Belfast he wouldn't take kindly to being accused of working for the IRA.

No, if the terrorists had used an army vehicle—and that was far from sure—then it would almost certainly have been a fake, just like the army uniforms they'd worn. And even if the fake were identified, now, nearly a fortnight after the event, it would only leave the police with something else to look for—something the terrorists would hardly have left parked obligingly outside their hideout.

The Bomb Squad's report suggested that the materials for the Marsham Street bomb had come from the Hornsey cache. Which further suggested that there were similar bombs at large in London, together with at least one man willing and able to plant them. Someone had indeed been seen outside the restaurant shortly before the explosion, but the witness, a waiter, could give no description other than that he was well dressed, carried a briefcase, and walked in a manner that was . . . well, not completely masculine. Which, Whitaker mused, included just about half the male population of the West End.

He filled his pipe lugubriously. Now, to add to all his other problems, he had to find a queer bomber. The adjective was chosen advisedly. There was nothing in the world that would ever make him describe a man who distributed lethal explosives as "gay". He sighed. As far as finding the Prime Minister was concerned, the blank walls were closing in again. Meanwhile, the government was understandably getting anxious, and the Press critical. He and Trew would continue to follow up army leads whenever they could make the time, but he no longer believed in them. Unless he got lucky only one chance remained—and that, in many ways, was the longest shot of all.

15

Another weekend came and went. In the flat at Abbey Field things were better. This was partly because the routine had begun to take hold, blurring the edges, merging one tedious day into the one before and the one after. But it was also because, on Sunday night, Grady had allowed O'Sullivan a couple of hours out in town. O'Sullivan had wanted to go in uniform, just for the hell of stamping about like a bloody Brit, but Grady insisted he wear the civvies Farrell had provided. Neither of them had worn uniform after the first night. It would have seemed an affront to everything they stood for.

Grady let O'Sullivan go for a number of reasons. The first of these, he admitted to himself, was that relationships were becoming so tense that he didn't dare stop him. There were times when wise leadership entailed letting go, and this was one of them. Of the twenty-eight days, seventeen still remained, and O'Sullivan could be kept on a tight rein for so long and no longer.

To Maura he offered other justifications. O'Sullivan was like a child. To show him you trusted him was the best way of making sure he was trustworthy. There was a risk, of course, but a very small one: O'Sullivan's own sense of self-preservation would see to that. And as to the advantages—Grady gestured widely to include the absence of Radio One's incessant pop; the freedom from the tensions of a model kit that refused to become more than a heap of sticky parts; the simple lack of O'Sullivan's baleful presence—weren't they worth a tiny risk or two?

And they were. O'Sullivan was aggressively larger than life, and the flat was like a suit several times too small for him. In his absence the others could breathe. Grady could give Maura a chess lesson uninterrupted by jealous, sarcastic comments. And Maura could wash out their prisoner's spare shift in the kitchen without O'Sullivan trying to get her in a corner for a cuddle. So when he returned, safely and in the best of spirits, it was as if all three of them had had a holiday and could look at each other with fresh eyes. The outing, and Grady's nagging anxiety, had been worth it.

This feeling of ease lasted through Monday and Tuesday. For Sean and Maura the news on the radio continued to be encouraging. Ian Paisley even gave an interview in which he pleaded for moderation, which was a climb-down if ever there was one.

On the Wednesday, as the latest deadline approached, tension mounted. They both knew that the previous deadlines had been merely window-dressing. But Thursday would mark their hostage's fifteenth day in captivity. The Provos had called it the British Government's last chance, and this time Maura really believed concessions would be made. Probably not the full deal yet, but definite signs that the British were cracking. Wednesday night, therefore, she felt restless and, for the first time, impatient.

She had just returned to the living room from giving their prisoner her supper. The food was holding out well. It had been her turn to cook, and she'd made two tins of salmon and eggs and dried mashed potato into salmon fishcakes, with baked beans, and tinned peaches to follow. Her plan to cut down on Mrs Thatcher's food had only survived the first day: the woman's privations had seemed bad enough without that.

She was in the living room with Sean. Liam was washing up in the kitchen. Suddenly, from the back of the building—which looked on to the grassed drying area and the entrance into Abbey Field—she heard a car draw up. There was a brief pause, then its door opened. She sat paralysed. She heard running footsteps. They stopped abruptly. There was a scuffle, then a woman's scream, sharply cut off. Maura leapt to her feet, stumbled out along the passage. Inside the closed front door she paused.

The sounds of struggling were unmistakable. A gasp, a soft obscenity, and then the woman again. "No . . . no, *please* . . ."

And now the man: "Shut up, or I'll break your bloody neck."

Maura reached down to the key in the door. Newspaper reports of the Colchester rapist flashed before her eyes. Her hand was clumsy. As she struggled with the lock another hand closed over hers. She started back. Liam stood over her in the dim light from the half-open door behind them. "Are you crazy?" he hissed.

Below them, in the courtyard, the scuffling increased. She heard the sickening crack of bone against bone. Suddenly there was silence. Then a thin wailing that seemed to go on and on. And the man again: "You're wasting your time, darling. Nobody'll hear you."

Maura kicked out in the shadows, but Liam held her fast. "I know it's tough. But there's too much at stake. I'm sorry."

By now Sean had joined them. She could imagine his leering face as the sounds of rape came up unmistakably from the grass below. She tried to get away, to hide, but the two men blocked her.

"No," Liam whispered. "This is our responsibility. We're in this together, all of us."

She sagged, leaned weakly back against the wall. He was right. But she hated him for it. She would always hate him for it.

The girl below them was silent now. The other sounds continued, quickening. Maura raised her hands to her ears, then checked. What were mere sounds against the outrage the other woman was suffering? She felt it now herself, and shuddered.

Sean chuckled softly. "Ah, the little darlin's a martyr for old Ireland, so she is."

Maura struck at him wildly. Liam pinioned her arms. "O'Sullivan—you'd make any decent man ashamed."

But O'Sullivan stayed. They all stayed, listening, each of them alone with their thoughts. Maura's were of murder.

Finally it was over. Shoes scraped. The man, whining now: "I didn't want to do it. If only you'd . . . Honest, pet, I didn't want to do it."

Maura came near to vomiting. Footsteps retreated. The car door opened, closed, and the car drove away. The girl, weeping now very softly, got to her feet. Then she too went away.

They returned to the sitting room. Maura was trembling violently. She avoided looking at either man. She felt profoundly unclean. She remembered their prisoner. Her room was at the front of the building, overlooking the playing fields. With her door tightly closed, she couldn't have heard anything.

Maura sat down at the table, rested her head on her arms. Liam made her a cup of instant coffee. But his mind was on other things. "You realize we'll probably have the police here in the morning," he said thoughtfully. "I must get down the moment it's light enough and make sure everything's all right."

By Thursday noon there had still been no formal response from the British Government. The Home Secretary and other Ministers remained confident that as yet the Prime Minister was in no real danger. The day would come, however, presumably when the Provisionals were satisfied that no further progress could be made. Exactly when that might be was difficult to judge. Mr Whitelaw had consulted the Commander of Special Branch, Superintendent Whitaker, the Commander of C.13, MI5, and the agent who had returned empty-handed from Dublin—indeed, anyone and everyone who might be in a position to assess the Provos' current thinking. The general opinion—and everybody was painfully aware of the stakes involved—was that the Provos would hang on for as long as possible, six weeks being the period most often mentioned. Which meant also that the Provisionals must be totally confident that the Prime Minister would not be found. In these circumstances they had everything to lose by murdering her, and nothing to gain. Nothing that is—and Mr Whitelaw shuddered at the thought—except credibility should they ever take a second hostage.

That afternoon he faced a restive House of Commons. The eleven o'clock deadline was in everybody's minds and MPs, in common with the Press and the nation at large, were troubled at the lack of progress, even angry that the government, the security services, the police and the armed forces could all be led such a dance by a single small group of terrorists.

One right-wing Conservative even suggested that the time had come to tell the Irish plainly that they were not welcome in this country. It brought a brisk and tart response from Willie Whitelaw.

"My Honourable Friend's remarks are not helpful at this time," he said, and the Opposition, as well as a number of Tories, roared their approval. Then came the question which he guessed was inevitable but which he'd been hoping to avoid, and it came from one of his own backbenchers.

"Can my Right Honourable Friend assure the House that there is no question of negotiating with these murderers?"

The Home Secretary's eyebrows rose and he looked briefly upwards in a gesture of supreme patience and understanding. The expression was not lost upon the Opposition front bench.

"It has never been the policy of any government in this country," he said, "to give in to terrorism, and it is not the policy of the present government. But both Labour governments and Conservative governments have at times found it necessary, in the national interest, to make contact with representatives of the Provisional IRA, and I am not prepared to say that will never happen again."

An uneasy murmuring broke out. The better-informed Members, however, recalled that in July 1972 Mr Whitelaw himself had called IRA leaders to a secret meeting in the Cheyne Walk home of one of his ministers, Paul Channon. Six Irishmen had come: Sean Mac-Stiofain, David O'Connell, Martin McGuinness, Seamus Twomey, Ivor Bell and Gerry Adams. It's true the Irish had made demands that the government obviously could not accept, and finally, for a number of reasons, the whole initiative had led to nothing. But a measure of personal trust had been established between the Irish and Mr Whitelaw which had helped him later, at the Sunningdale Conference, to come nearer than anyone else to restoring peace and some kind of stable government in the North. Parliament which had trusted him before must do so again.

As the murmuring subsided, Mr Whitelaw continued: "All I ask is that the House should not seek to tie my hands. The government must be left, at its discretion, to decide what action is best at any time in the interests both of political stability and the Prime Minister's safety."

Mr Whitelaw's statement, predictably elaborated, made headlines like: WILLIE TO TALK TO IRA? and PROVOS FOR LONDON TALKS? and even DO NOT TIE MY HANDS, SAYS WILLIE. Members of the Emergency Committee were not displeased. The fact would be denied, but the Provisional IRA would nevertheless see in it the signs they needed. More time had been bought at little if any cost.

But for Terry O'Donovan nothing had changed. Another deadline had come round and he had his job to do. Last time he'd done the nobs; this time it had been decided he should stir up the common people. And for the common people, the common touch: he dressed himself in tight jeans and a short leather jacket, and he carried a plastic carrier bag with the green insignia of John Lewis.

He'd spent the week in sleazy hotels round Chiswick and Richmond. When he reached the West End he found it teeming with police. Obviously he wasn't the only person to have remembered the eleven o'clock deadline. He wasn't deterred. Not even the fuzz had eyes everywhere, and anyway, in his present outfit there was nothing to link him with the smart city gent of a week before.

The target was to be Oxford Circus underground station—platform 2 of the Central line. Afterwards, he'd ring London Transport on 222 1234 from one of the public telephones up in the big central concourse. He bought a ticket for Notting Hill Gate from a machine, fed it through the automatic turnstile, and went on down the escalator. The time was 10.30 and the bomb in his carrier bag would explode at eleven.

Once on the platform he positioned himself by a litter basket attached to the wall. The next train was a long time coming, and the platform filled up around him. He glanced at his watch. 10.40. What the hell were all these people doing down here when they ought to be at home in bed? A minute later the train rattled in, and under cover of the confusion he slipped his carrier bag into the litter bin. He crumpled it down so that it looked like rubbish. Then he joined the people who had left the train and went up with them on the escalator.

The black ticket collector called after him: "Hey, mister—you haven't used this ticket."

O'Donovan cursed under his breath. Nine times out of ten they didn't even look at the bloody things.

"I know. I bought it just now. I was going to Holland Park. I changed my mind. It's a free country, isn't it?"

The collector stared at the ticket. "But you've only just bought it."

"That's what I said, didn't I? I've changed my mind."

The ticket collector scratched his chin. O'Donovan nearly panicked.

"For God's sake—I've paid the bloody money. I'm not asking

for it back. I'm just not going anywhere. London Transport should be cheering."

He turned on his heel and walked firmly away. The ticket collector let him go. O'Donovan circled the concourse. There were a series of open, partitioned telephone booths near a photograph-yourself machine. He chose an end one because the two nearest booths to it were also vacant. He stood close in, so that he wouldn't be heard, and started to dial, his coin ready. Someone tapped him on the shoulder.

"Excuse me, Peachblossom."

O'Donovan ignored the interruption, concentrated on the ringing tone.

The tap on his shoulder was repeated, more insistently. O'Donovan depressed the receiver rest, and swung round furiously.

"Why don't you leave me alone?" he hissed. "There are empty bloody phone booths all over the bloody place."

The man in the shabby raincoat smiled apologetically.

"It's not your phone I'm after, Peachblossom."

Another man had drifted over now and they stood one each side of the partitions.

"Sorry to bother you, Peachblossom, but—" At that moment alarm bells rang harshly, their din resounding in the enclosed space. Suddenly the two men were no longer smiling.

"Joke time over, you bleedin' poncey Provo git," the first one shouted over the strident urgency of the bells. "How long have we got? Tell me! Or I'll bash your pretty face in."

Two hours later Superintendent Whitaker was on the telephone to his counterpart in the Garda. The two men had a long association, and usually Whitaker would have had to endure friendly ribbing about his artistic efforts. He'd had a painting holiday with Edie in Ireland once, organized by the local force, and it had been a disaster. The weather had been terrible, his pictures worse. He'd stuck to portraits ever after.

But tonight both men would rather have been in bed and asleep. Whitaker came straight to the point.

"I've got Terry O'Donovan here, Tim. I was wondering if you knew something."

"Would that be Terry O'Donovan the bomber, Art? Or Terry O'Donovan the folk guitar feller?"

"He doesn't seem to have his guitar with him, Tim."

"Ah. Then it'll be Terry O'Donovan the bomber. I know a lot about him."

"I thought you might."

"Nasty piece of work. Clock timers, radio control, you name it. If you've caught him red-handed I love you. We've never managed to pin a blamed thing on him . . . Oh, and there's something else. He's younger brother to the O'Donovan on the Army Council."

Whitaker tensed. "You're sure of that? Sorry—silly question. How close are they?"

"Two peas in a pod, Art. Brother's the thinking one. Terry's the man of action—but he's no fool either. He's queer too—though that means damn all these days. Except that without his brother I doubt if the Provos would have given him the time of day."

"They'd have been right, too. It was his style, if you know what I mean, that first put us on to him. Talk about police harassment —we've been picking on queers with handbags or whatever all night."

The Irishman laughed. "Good luck to you . . . Anyway, what's happening over there? Are your people really going to negotiate?"

"Over my dead body, Tim. Still, there's no harm in the Provos hoping. Well, thanks, Tim, thanks a lot. Looks like I've got a busy night ahead of me."

It was five in the morning before Whitaker took a break. With Sergeant Trew's help, he had insisted on doing the interrogation himself. Now, stirring at a sweet cup of coffee, he felt and looked a crumpled wreck. Trew was as dapper as ever.

"I'll swear he knows, guv."

"Of course he knows. He's far too pleased with himself. And besides—with that brother of his he couldn't *not* know."

"Then where do we go from here, sir?"

"Short of boiling oil, Goodie, I've no idea."

Trew sipped his coffee thoughtfully. "It's pretty jolly important, sir. I mean, the right word from O'Donovan and we could wrap this thing up."

"Not worthy of your brain, Goodie. If that's all you've got to tell me, save your breath for your coffee."

They both fell moodily silent. The clock on the wall above them clicked on another thirty seconds closer to dawn. Trew crossed his legs, stared down at his gleaming Oxford brogues. The silence lengthened. The sergeant made a little tentative coughing noise.

"We could call in one of the top CID chaps. They're . . . vicious deadly at the old questioning sometimes."

Whitaker was exhausted. "No," he shouted. "I've told you, Goodie, this one's mine. Superintendent bloody Whitaker, Special Branch. I'm supposed to be the Yard's best man. That's what Whitelaw asked for—remember? I've got to get that little bastard—"

"Even if it means the Prime Minister's life?"

Whitaker let out an enormous sigh, rested his head in his hands.

"Get O'Donovan sent back to his cell, will you? We'll take a nap. Come at it fresh in the morning."

"It *is* the morning, sir."

"Don't argue, Goodie. Just do it."

In the corner of the room there were two truckle beds. Whitaker fell on one of them fully clothed. In less than a minute he was fast asleep.

The BBC's early morning radio news bulletins carried yet another statement from the Provisional IRA. Although the Army Council would certainly have known of the failure of the previous night's bomb attack, they understandably made no mention of it.

Yet a third deadline has come and gone without any meaningful response from the British Government. We would point out that conceding the withdrawal of another battalion of British troops from Northern Ireland still leaves an occupying army of nearly twelve thousand. Our requirement remains the same. All troops must be withdrawn. Only then can negotiations begin towards a united Ireland. Time is running out. But because the British Government has taken a first step, we are prepared to extend the deadline. This should not be taken as a sign of weakness but of responsible behaviour. By Tuesday week, exactly four weeks will have elapsed since we took the British Prime Minister prisoner. If our demands have not been met in full by that date we shall assume that the British Government's imperialist ambitions have overridden all other considerations and we shall act accordingly. At three o'clock on the afternoon of that day the British Prime Minister will be executed.

Margaret Thatcher, at a Conservative Party Conference, not too long back, had the party faithful rise clapping and cheering to their feet when she referred to the Right Honourable William Whitelaw as "a marvellous deputy"—and that in spite of the fact that he was known to many as the chief "wet". He stood now with his back to the bookcases in the Cabinet Room—cases filled with the gifts of Cabinet Ministers since Ramsay MacDonald started the collection in 1931—and sadly wondered what was going to be "marvellous" about his present stewardship. The six other members of the Emergency Committee arrived, and they all took their places at the table, copies of the Provisional IRA's latest statement in front of them.

"I think we can take it," Mr Whitelaw said slowly, "that this time they mean what they say. The whole tone of the thing is different. Crude polemics . . . blatant propaganda. It's the end of the road."

There were nods and an uneasy clearing of throats.

"So," he said, "we've got to meet them. I don't see any alternative. Does anyone? I wish I could say that last night's capture of Terry O'Donovan had brought the police any nearer to finding the Prime Minister, but I'm afraid it hasn't. All the investigations have, so far, not yielded a clue to the Prime Minister's whereabouts. So we just have to talk. The question is: how much leeway will the Commons give us?"

The Leader of the House, Francis Pym, had no doubt: "A lot of them won't like it—oddly enough more on our side of the House."

"And if we set up talks," said the Lord Chancellor, "what can we realistically offer?"

"We could agree to withdraw more troops," put in the Defence Secretary, "in exchange for a guarantee to stop the violence and the killing."

"But damn it," Mr Whitelaw said despairingly, "half the killing is done by the Protestants, and we'll be expected to stop that too."

Jim Prior, the Northern Ireland Secretary, had been reflecting that, when he had taken on the job, he had said that he was throwing all his weight, all his life, behind "trying to get this thing right". Now it looked more impossible than ever. He tried to see the faintest hope.

"At least," he said, "the UDA's quiet at the moment. The threat to the Prime Minister's life is more or less keeping them in line. But one hint that we're talking to the Provos, and it'll be hard to stop them. But I see no alternative to talking."

"If we could get a guaranteed ceasefire from the IRA," Lord Carrington suggested, "the UDA would find themselves out on a limb. But would that matter to them?"

"Where do we have this meeting?" asked the Defence Secretary.
"It'll have to be here, on our own ground." Mr Whitelaw was definite. "We can't be seen to be going to them. They'll have to get themselves to Belfast—safe passage and all that. Then you can organize the RAF to fly them over."

The Lord Chancellor steepled his fingers. "Let's not rush it, though. What's a reasonable time in which to set up a meeting? A week at least, maybe longer . . . I think we can take it that they'll hold back if they see definite signs of movement. And meanwhile the police . . ." he tailed off, shrugged.

The Foreign Secretary did not oppose the idea; indeed he couldn't see any alternative either.

"But it's ironic, isn't it?" he said, his lips moving into a barely perceptible but characteristic smile. "If the BBC goes to some secret rendezvous and seeks an interview with an IRA man, we expect them to turn him over to the police. Yet we shall have these people in London, and we shall even promise them a safe passage. But to do anything else would get the Prime Minister killed at once."

"They're going to expect a lot more than cakes and tea," said Jim Prior. "There will have to be realistic negotiations. Troop reductions we're planning anyway. What else can we offer? Talks, and more talks, and the Council of Ireland in some new disguise. That won't be enough. But any hint of a closer link with the South at the present time would bring the UDA out on to the streets. Then if the RUC can't hold the situation, we have to put the Army in again. It's a vicious circle."

A silence followed. The Lord Chancellor spoke again.

"Let us not get confused about our objectives," he said. In the past he had argued that, but for mistakes in the nineteenth century, the "Irish problem" need not have occurred, and now he saw the ultimate solution as probably some sort of federal system. He continued: "However desirable and necessary—and of course it is both—that there should be a proper settlement in Ireland, with some kind of relationship with the South, that is not our immediate objective. It is to get the Prime Minister released. In this our best hope is still for the police to find her. But for that to happen more time is obviously needed. If we can achieve that by contact with the Provisionals, even having them over here, embarrassing though that will be, then well and good. But I suggest that we make haste slowly. And as to what we say to them when they finally get here . . ." He smiled coldly. "I'm put in mind of the scriptural precept, apt in politics and elsewhere: 'Sufficient unto the day is the evil thereof'."

"Liam . . . Liam, d'you think the Army Council really means it this time?"

Grady looked up from his book. He'd been aware of Maura in the room for some minutes, staring at him, willing him to notice her. O'Sullivan, he knew, was in the toilet, smoking up a storm.

He took his time answering. Finally he said, "What makes you think that?"

"Don't mess me about, Liam. Everything makes me think it. Hang about much longer and we'll have the whole world laughing at us."

"My dear girl—"

"Don't 'dear girl' me. What about the provisions? Farrell takes his orders from you—and you're running them down, aren't you? The way things are going, in a week or so's time we'll be left with rice and tinned soup."

Grady closed his book with a snap. Ever since Wednesday night's unfortunate incident he'd been worried. Not about the police. A couple of coppers down there on Thursday morning, half an hour spent looking for trouser buttons, had been all they'd run to. No, it was Maura who worried him, stirred up his ulcer. He feared she was cracking. She had even suggested bringing that bloody cat in for a bit of companionship. For another thing, she was spending more time with the Iron Lady. She said it was simply to get away from O'Sullivan, but he had his doubts. Sometimes women turned to their own kind, and if that was happening now he was in trouble.

It was Saturday. Only ten days to go. Somehow he had to keep them all together. Frankly, he was disappointed. He'd always expected O'Sullivan to be a pain in the neck, but not Maura.

He looked up at her. "Do in Herself? Is that what you're thinking?"

"We always knew we might have to." Her jaw was firm. "I only want to know when, that's all."

"Sure, and won't it be in *The Times*, girl? In her eightieth year, Kathleen O'Hara, peacefully, in her sleep, no flowers by request?"

Maura nodded. "I know that's what was arranged. And we do it two days after. But arrangements can be altered . . ."

"And how could that have happened? Haven't we all been out of touch from the beginning—and wasn't that the plan? And, I'm asking you, Maura, what would be the point of it? Why, Herself is our trump card. Do her in and we're back where we started."

"If you're sure—"

"Of course I'm sure. Look, Maura, I give you my word. You hear the news, don't you? We're winning, all the way. The poor bastards haven't got a clue, and we've got them at our mercy—the whole bloody British nation. Another few days and the Chief himself will be lording it in Downing Street, telling those mealy-mouthed bastards what's what." He paused. He didn't want to overplay his hand but ... "So let's have no more talk of doing in Herself. She'll live to a grand old age so she will."

And Maura believed him. He'd known she would. In the end people always believed what they wanted to. But just to make sure, when Farrell came in again on Saturday night Grady gave him, in her hearing, orders for a stack of provisions they'd never need. He was throwing good American money down the drain, but that couldn't be helped. Keeping his team together, and happy, was far more important.

Later, and out of her hearing, while she was in the kitchen heating some of the fresh milk Farrell had brought for his stomach, Grady gave the sergeant a second, less domestic list of requirements. Four sturdy metal corner brackets, screws, a screwdriver, a roll of broad adhesive tape, an aerosol of hair lacquer. Also a length of nylon rope, a soldering iron, some solder, and a cheap watch. Farrell had narrowed his eyes at these, but he'd made no comment.

Grady had to admit that, apart from the business of the gun, he was pleased with the sergeant's performance. He did his job and didn't mess around. For a time Grady had been afraid a personal involvement might be in the wind: that box of chocolates, glances he had intercepted between Farrell and Maura. But if there had ever been anything in it, there wasn't now. They hardly spoke to each other. Farrell stayed as long as was necessary, not a moment longer. The previous week he had appeared anxious, laughing too easily, as if there was something on his mind. But that, too, had passed, and the sergeant was his usual bloody-minded self again.

The local papers Farrell brought were full of the rape. A master at keeping his own counsel, he didn't ask about that either. O'Sullivan, however, had to enlighten him. Maura, back from the kitchen, sat quietly and calmly throughout the whole story. Grady put down his empty glass, and cut in on the lurid details as soon as he could.

"It was . . . unfortunate," he said.

Maura repeated the word after him, under her breath: "Unfortunate . . . unfortunate . . ." staring fixedly at the floor.

It was Farrell who eased the moment, turning smoothly to the national press. "This bomber," he said. "Who is this O'Donovan, anyway? Doesn't look like he's much good."

Grady had known Terry O'Donovan, had despised the man and admired his skill. And had learned a lot from him. But he didn't say so.

"Any agent can have bad luck," he said coldly. "I seem to remember we didn't have exactly plain sailing all the way."

That started O'Sullivan reminiscing about the snatch. Apart from the more recent rape, it was his favourite subject. Farrell left soon after, and the three of them settled back into the armed truce that was all Grady could now hope for. Or, indeed, needed. Liking each other was beside the point.

"I wonder, Maura, if you would care to tell me why you hate me."

The Prime Minister's gaze was steady and cool.

"I don't hate you."

"I think you do. Not just for what I stand for. I think you hate me personally."

Maura had taken a chair into the prisoner's room. She was sitting on it with the gas light on the floor beside her. The Iron Lady sat back on her mattress, leaning against the wall. It was Monday now, but the twenty days that had elapsed since her hair had been hacked off had done little to help it. Her face, too, although freshly scrubbed, had not been improved by her imprisonment. Although the complexion remained clear, the features were pitifully pale and haggard. Yet of the two of them, it was she who seemed the stronger and, at this moment, almost relaxed.

Maura hesitated. "All right," she said, "so I do hate you. If you must know, I . . . I hate you for what you did to my brother." Painfully she sketched in the story. No matter how many times it was told, it still hurt. When it was done she added scornfully, "Oh, I don't expect you to remember. Just another name, just another bloody murder statistic. Anyway, it's nearly two years ago now, and—"

"But I do remember. Michael. Michael Lynch . . . he was mentally retarded, wasn't he?"

Maura froze. That was the part she never told. Some things were too painful. She took refuge in anger.

"No, he wasn't. That's too bloody clinical. He was a half-wit. He shouldn't have been out on his own. He was a bloody idiot, that's what he was."

For a long time the room was quiet. If her prisoner had said one word, one single word of explanation, of sympathy, of apology even, Maura thought she would have struck her, hit out at her and gone on hitting. But finally, "Yes," was all the Iron Lady said in a very soft voice. "Yes . . . I do understand why you hate me."

Maura got up then without a word and went away. Even the shrewd inhumanity of Liam was preferable to that woman's understanding. And as for Sean—she had discovered she could live with Sean. Once you accepted that the basic human ability to feel for others was missing from his make-up you could get on with him very well. He didn't know what he did. Liam, on the other hand, knew very well.

On her visit to see the Iron Lady the next day, Tuesday, Maura kept the conversation impersonal. Once she wouldn't have talked at all, but now conversation of some kind was somehow imperative. They talked of Ireland, and Maura even allowed herself to be lectured. The older woman knew her history. The Lowland Protestant Scots planted in the North in their thousands by King James, taking land on which Irish people had lived for a thousand years. Then Cromwell, and William, Catholic land and property confiscated, the Old Irish landowners, even the Old English, driven out, two long centuries of suppression and exploitation. All this she conceded. The terrible famines of Victorian times, while absentee landlords bled the countryside dry. Then the First World War, the Troubles, and finally partition—the Protestant majority hived off in the North, and given responsibility for the Catholic minorities in their midst. And the result of that yet more years of Catholic suppression, and rights denied to them that were enjoyed by Protestants.

Mrs Thatcher denied none of this—the past mistakes of innumerable governments of every political colour. But it was the present, she said, that she and her government were trying to deal with. Today Protestant Ulstermen were determined not to become a religious minority in a united Ireland. Repeatedly they had voted for the right to remain part of the United Kingdom, and their leaders had made it clear they were ready, if necessary, to fight for that right. To suggest that they simply feared the repression they had previously meted out to others was beside the point. Even if the British Government wanted to force reunification upon them, such a course was impossible, both constitutionally, and for practical reasons. And politics, she told Maura, was the science of the possible.

"Frankly, Maura, I find it hard to understand the IRA's reasoning, just as I find it hard to understand what you think you can possibly gain by holding me here. Violence can never achieve your ends. If you really want the co-operation of the North, then surely you should be wooing Ulstermen, not terrorizing them. Nothing makes a people dig in its toes quite so much as the threat of violence."

At first Maura had listened. But it was as if her prisoner's long days of silence were a dam that had suddenly been breached. She didn't rant. She spoke fluently and quietly, almost as if she were thinking aloud. But by the end Maura was simply letting the flow of words wash over her. To her the basic premise was wrong. It made no sense. She was Irish, and for many Irish people the reunification of their country transcended politics or reason. It was natural and inevitable, like a beautiful flower just waiting for the right combination of sun and rain to make it burst open.

Now, addressed directly, she started. "Woo them, is it? Sure, and it's easy to see you've never tried wooing a British soldier with a gun in his hand."

"So that's it? That's why I'm here—to get the British soldiers out? Soldiers your Catholic community was the first to welcome when we had to put them in."

Maura didn't answer. Suddenly it seemed that all the talk had been no more than a roundabout way of questioning her.

"Well, if that's why you've got me here," the Prime Minister continued quietly, "you are indeed wasting your time. Do you imagine for a moment that—?"

Maura picked up the lamp and stood, cutting the Iron Lady short. She felt betrayed. For the past few days she had come here to share her loneliness, because they were both women, and both prisoners. Prisoners, finally, of men, in a man's world. But now she saw that the Iron Lady was no prisoner at all. Whatever might happen to her, she had her escape. She had, as Liam had said, her certainty.

Maura left the room, taking the lamp with her, closing the door and locking it firmly. Liam looked up as she joined him, made space for her at the table. There was a jig-saw puzzle spread out on it, nearly completed. Farrell had brought it for Sean last Sunday, but it was Liam who had patiently fitted it together.

He eyed her speculatively. "What does Herself think about rape, then?"

"I haven't asked her."

"Come on, Maura. All the time you've been spending in there— you expect me to believe that?"

"It's true." And it was. The subject had been too immediate, and too ugly.

"I tell you one thing, girl—she'd never hang a man for it. She'd hang him for killing a copper, she's said so. But never for rape."

Maura knew what he was doing. He didn't like her sitting with the prisoner, and he was trying to drive a wedge between them. But the wedge was already there, of gleaming steel, a million miles wide. She picked up one of the few spare pieces of jig-saw left.

"I would, though," she said softly. "I'd hang him high and watch him dangle."

16

On the twenty-second day of the Prime Minister's incarceration—a Wednesday in the middle of November—and just five days after the Emergency Committee's decision to talk to the Provisional IRA, an arrangement was tentatively agreed. Two Irishmen were to be collected by helicopter at a secret rendezvous on the Republican side of the border, flown to Aldergrove airport, Belfast, and thence by the RAF to Brize Norton in Oxfordshire. There an army helicopter would be standing by to ferry them to Battersea heliport, where they would be met by car and taken to Cowley Street, just behind Westminster Abbey, to the home of a Cabinet Minister not involved in the planned negotiations.

Arrangements of this complexity, involving as they did delicate contacts between agents on both sides, needed a few days to be set up. The day finally agreed was the following Saturday, just three days before the deadline. Any further delay would have made clear just how calculatedly the British Government was dragging its feet. It had been decided that no official announcement would be made about the projected meeting until after it had taken place, and then only with the agreement of both sides.

As Mr Whitelaw had expected, representatives of the Provisional IRA as such would not be coming; the job of negotiation was to be handled by the Provisional Sinn Fein, the political—and legitimate—wing of the movement . . . The visitors, therefore, were to be Rory O'Brady and Gerry Adams, the president and vice-president of Provisional Sinn Fein. Adams had been a member of the delegation that met Mr Whitelaw in 1972 and, at that time, he had been an officer in Belfast's IRA command. He was an uncompromising man of strongly left-wing views, and the Home Secretary had little hope of stringing him along with anything less than very real and extensive concessions. As he had no intention of making these, he proposed, at the last minute, to demand proofs that the Prime Minister was still alive before he was prepared to discuss any terms at all. With any luck that would bring about a further delay.

But then, late on Friday, and surprisingly from the Irish end, the arrangements were abruptly cancelled. The Irish contact had noted that, in a memorandum, the British had named the Sinn Fein representatives. That wouldn't do. No named people would go to London; they had to go anonymously. Secretly relieved at the postponement, Mr Whitelaw protested vehemently. As the two men were to be guaranteed safe conduct, and no official record was to be made of the conversations, surely the fact that their identities were known was of no consequence?

But the Irish contact was predictably adamant. All arrangements would be suspended until he had received written assurances from the Secretary of State for total anonymity. Mr Whitelaw was delighted, but was careful not to show it. He countered with his request for evidence of the Prime Minister's well-being. It was only reasonable to ask for proof that she was still alive before entering discussions about her release. He reckoned that should hold off the meeting until Wednesday at least, and so force another deadline. Surely the police would be able to come up with something by then?

If the Home Secretary and Deputy Prime Minister was beginning to show real signs of impatience at the lack of police progress in finding Mrs Thatcher, then so was the Commissioner of the Metropolitan

Police. Not for nothing had he earned the nickname The Hammer, and from his wood-panelled office on the eighth floor of the tower block of New Scotland Yard, his impatience shuddered its way through the Anti-Terrorist Squad, the CID and Special Branch, and landed with a flutter of stiff memoranda on Superintendent Whitaker's desk. Whitaker accepted them in the spirit in which they had been intended—rumbles from above, strictly for the record in case the worst happened. He and the Commander of C.13 were doing all they could, and the Commissioner knew it.

Terry O'Donovan was now being held in Brixton prison on remand, while he awaited trial. Whatever inside knowledge he might possess he had taken with him. For a time Whitaker had even suspected him of being the mysterious fourth man. Not the gunman on foot who had killed the policeman—the wounded CID man's identification ruled that out—but perhaps the taller of the two blond terrorists. But the date Immigration gave him was incontrovertible. O'Donovan had arrived in England two days after the kidnap.

So the mystery man remained elusive. All the reports Whitaker had requested on army transport bound that night for destinations beyond the immediate vicinity of London had now come in, and all were negative. No vehicles with their paint-work damaged. No significant mileage discrepancies. He wasn't surprised. The only lead he had had, and it had never been a promising one. More than ever it looked as though, if they had used an "army" vehicle, it was a fake, and had yet to be found.

That Saturday he took the morning off and went to see Denis Thatcher, the Prime Minister's husband. As always, the man had shunned publicity. But Whitaker could imagine what he must be going through. The superintendent felt personally responsible, that he owed Denis Thatcher an explanation. It was also just conceivable that he might be able to help.

Whitaker had telephoned the previous afternoon, and Mr Thatcher was waiting for him in the morning room of the flat above the official quarters at Number 10. His bespectacled face was haggard, its normally benign expression drawn and weary, but he remained as calm and courteous as ever. Although he had been kept fully informed and had received regular bulletins, Whitaker detailed to him every stage of the investigation so far. He listened seriously, asking a number of extremely pertinent questions.

Finally Whitaker was done. "So you see, sir, we nearly caught them at the beginning," he confessed. "Only missed them by an hour or so. But since then, we've frankly got nowhere. Nowhere at all."

Mr Thatcher frowned. "It's nearly four weeks now, Superintendent. I find it incredible that four people, five including Margaret, should vanish so completely. They must have some sort of contact with the outside world. Food, for instance—they must eat, mustn't they?"

"As I see it, sir, that's the fourth man's job. He's servicing them, as it were."

"Wouldn't he be seen? I mean, presumably they're somewhere very isolated—a cottage, an old farmhouse. A stranger buying food, surely—?"

"I agree, sir. In fact, that's our best hope now. But the fourth man is the one terrorist we know nothing about at all. But every police station in the country has drawn up a list of possible places. They are all being checked. It's a monumental job. And the hideout might be in the middle of a city. Anonymous places, cities."

"So time's the answer." Mr Thatcher smiled greyly. "And Willie's doing a good job, gaining us that. You're . . . you're still sure that my wife is . . . in this country?"

"Everything points to it. And especially the difficulty of getting her out in the first place. Then again, the lack of contact. If the Prime Minister were really in Ireland, and her captors as confident as they pretend to be, we'd have been sent pictures, tape recordings . . ."

Mr Thatcher sighed, looked down at his hands. "Superintendent Whitaker . . . you have the most experience in these matters. You won't want to answer this, but I'd appreciate honesty. Do you believe my wife is still alive?"

It was a question Whitaker had been prepared for.

"No doubt of that at all. As long as they're asking for negotiations they're expecting success. And success will mean keeping their end of the bargain and returning Mrs Thatcher unharmed."

"And . . . how do you think they're treating her?"

"The same applies, sir. If they're planning on releasing her, they won't want her coming back with evidence of IRA brutality. They'll be treating her very well." In this Whitaker hoped he sounded more confident than he felt. "And that's something, sir, that perhaps you can help me with. Mrs Thatcher—would she be a good prisoner? I mean, would she do as she were told? Or would she fight them all the way?"

Mr Thatcher considered, smiled wanly. "Given the chance, she would argue with them, try to convince them they were wrong. But if she saw that resistance was quite useless, then she'd save her energy for other matters."

"What sort of other matters?"

"Escape? Personal survival? I don't know . . ." He turned away. "I keep thinking of that Dutch businessman—Herrema. Nineteen seventy five, wasn't it? God, it doesn't seem that long ago." Whitaker remembered well enough that knife-edge of a seventeen-day siege at Monasterevin, about forty miles south-west of Dublin. At least then they knew where Tiede Herrema was. He wished he could say the same for the Prime Minister. But Denis Thatcher was continuing almost reflectively: "What that poor devil must have gone through —that's what I think about. And now it's Margaret. But I'll tell you one thing, Superintendent. She will never break. And she'll escape if the smallest chance is offered. She won't be giving her captors an easy time of it wherever they are."

"Thank you, sir." Whitaker sat back. "It's what I expected, of course. But I'm glad to hear it all the same."

He was glad for the Prime Minister's sake, but he was glad for his own as well. It introduced another factor in the police's favour. A difficult prisoner put her captors under constant pressure—pressure from her, and pressure among themselves. And the days shut away in their hideout were adding up. They'd come out like lambs, he thought—just as eventually they had done at Monasterevin. If he could only find them.

On Sunday morning a police Ford van containing two tracker dogs and their handlers turned in at the entrance to the disused army quarters in Abbey Field. They drove between Blocks B and E and parked in front of Block D. Attracted by the sound of the engine, Grady watched their arrival through a hole in the boarding over one of the back windows. He sent O'Sullivan and Maura immediately to silence the Iron Lady. "And when you've done that," he told O'Sullivan, "bring the UZI."

Down on the tarmacadam the dogs piled out of the van, their tails waving. They scouted around, sniffing through the grass in the centre. Grady thought back. He'd been down there on the morning after the rape, but never since, and that was a full ten days ago. And the other two coppers had poked around a few hours later. Farrell hadn't been near the place for a week. Unless the dogs knew exactly what they were looking for, they'd have a hard time of it.

The handlers took them down the block. They passed out of Grady's line of sight, their tails still waving slowly, uninterestedly. Grady was prepared if necessary for a bloody shoot-out. There was a possibility the men weren't armed. If so, then it would be better to take them out quickly, before they could use their radios, then the dogs. In that event, they'd have to get out immediately, and he would use the Browning automatic on the Iron Lady. If they were armed, and it was a proper shoot-out, then they'd have the whole place swarming with police, army and SAS in minutes. Then he'd have only one priority—to get the Iron Lady. As it happened, he would never know what it was that saved him from discovery on that grey Sunday morning.

The handlers had their orders: to search the derelict married quarters in Abbey Field. It was an unwelcome Sunday chore, and discussion occurred between the two men as to whether they need go upstairs and along each first-floor balcony. One pointed out that that was what the dogs were for: if anyone had recently climbed the stairs the dogs would know it. The other, glancing at his watch, agreed with him.

Possibly the dogs did detect Farrell or Grady's scent upon the D Block staircase. What is certain, however, is that they detected, and with considerable enthusiasm in spite of their training, the Abbey Field cat. She crouched at the top of the stairs, glaring evilly down at them, her tail the size of a sturdy cucumber.

Grady, hunched in the flat's dark corridor, heard their excitement. Just behind him, O'Sullivan checked the magazine of the UZI and the spare magazine in his pocket. Maura, Grady's Browning in her hand, stood over the gagged and bound figure of their prisoner. She stared down at her in the harsh gas light and knew, as the other woman knew, that if she had to she'd shoot.

If the dogs had ever caught the cat they'd have torn her to pieces. But their handlers, being kindly men, dragged them away, to nose out the staircases of A, B, C and E Blocks instead. The whole place was totally derelict and, but for the marks on the grass where the rapist had been, not a sign that anyone had been near the place for months. It was a bloody daft idea anyway—as if anyone would hide out in the middle of a garrison town. But everything was being checked, from remote country cottages to disused railway stations.

The sounds of police activity faded. After ten minutes or so the coppers returned. Grady, peering through his peep-hole, saw them put their dogs back into the van, climb in themselves, and drive away. Slowly he unwrapped a bismuth tablet and chewed it. Perhaps the police had been reacting to a tip-off, but he thought not. If they had, they would have come in force, not just two dog-handlers. It was more likely a routine inspection. Either way, the hideout was still secure. Only two more days remained. They were going to make it.

That evening Sean went out on the town again. The group's euphoria after their narrow escape had quickly faded, leaving them restless and irritable. It had not been helped by the Iron Lady who, guessing at the cause of the crisis, quietly insisted, immediately Grady had ungagged her, that they hadn't a chance of remaining undetected much longer. They had no conception of the vast resources available to the authorities, or of the high technology, the sophisticated listening devices, that could be used. The first they would know of anything, she told them confidently, was when the SAS stormed in and efficiently despatched them.

"Shut up," Grady had rasped at her. "That's all crap. No one has a clue where you are. That's obvious from the radio."

"You don't imagine, young man, they'd tell you, do you?"

Indeed, it was the radio which somehow added to their irritation. For once, it hardly mentioned them. Rioting youths in Birmingham the previous night occupied most of the bulletin in *The World This Weekend* at one o'clock. The Prime Minister's kidnapping was well down the running order—just a reference to massive police enquiries and arrests being expected in the near future.

By four in the afternoon Sean felt he was going crazy. The flat was like a nightmare. The cold weather now restricted the three of them entirely to the living room, and the gas heater. He was running short of fag papers. Maura had muddled up the jig-saw and was doing it again. Liam seemed content simply to sit. Sean knew that if he had to stare at those same four walls just one hour longer he'd start breaking things.

He said so to Liam. His hands were shaking, and he didn't try to hide them.

"Just a walk round the block, boss. Sure, and I swear I'll not go any further."

"Where's your discipline, O'Sullivan? We knew it was going to be tough. The Chief gave you the chance to get out at the beginning. You've got to have the guts to finish it."

Sean stood there trembling. For a moment Grady thought he'd gone too far, and that Sean was going to hit him. He saw the effort at control.

Sean managed it by bursting out, "Look—it's not the fucking women. It's . . . it's just this bloody place. It's breaking me up, I tell you."

Liam stared at him coldly, not answering. Sean felt the eyes of both of them on him now, silently accusing.

"For Christ's sake—I've been out before. You can trust me, can't you? Can't you?"

Liam looked away, sighed wearily. "All right. Once it's completely dark. Round the block, no more than that. You understand?"

Grady reasoned that this should last O'Sullivan for the remaining two days. It was worth it.

Sean, for his part, understood all right. He understood that once he was out of the place he was his own master.

Seven o'clock found him sitting in one of Colchester's back-street pubs, a pint of draught Guinness on the bar by his elbow. He hadn't told Liam, but he still had money in his pocket from the old man's wallet, and he planned to stay till eight or so, when the tarts came in. By then he'd have a comfortable buzz on. Nothing wild: he hadn't been like that in years. He'd just be feeling very happy, that's all.

It gave him an immense feeling of power, sitting at the bar, feet up on the rail, joking with the barman, and knowing all the time he was one of the most wanted men in Britain, with the ability to bring the whole country to its knees. Slowly the place filled up round him, bloody Brits in their Marks and Spencer's sports jackets, with not a thought in their heads except where the next drink was coming from. And there he was . . . sweet Jesus, he'd like to see their faces if they only knew.

He was into his fourth pint when he happened to glance up and catch sight of a man watching him from the far end of the bar. Their eyes met, lingered, moved slowly apart. In the back of his mind a warning bell rang. Words from his training came to him: the Brits dislike eye contact. Usually they look away instantly. If a man doesn't, either he's pretending he wasn't watching you or he's a pick-up.

Sean struggled to clear his thoughts. Obviously the man, something of a bruiser, wearing a heavy dark blue sweater under a grubby open anorak, wasn't a pick-up. Therefore . . . Sean looked towards the door marked "Gents". He'd already been out there: the toilet itself, filthy and stinking, was across a small back yard, with a way out on to the road. That would prove it. If he went out there again, and he really was being watched, the man would have to follow him.

He lowered himself from the stool and moved away unsteadily towards the door, taking his drink with him. Once outside the unsteadiness left him. The yard was dark, lit only by light slanting in from the street and a dim sign over the toilet entrance. He made sure the toilet was empty, then quickly flattened himself against the wall beside the pub door and waited.

Almost immediately the man came out. He didn't go at once into the toilet but ran to the yard entrance and looked sharply up and down the street. Then, satisfied, he returned and entered the toilet. There was a muttered oath. Sean caught him as he came out again, fast.

"Looking for something, friend?"

"I—"

Sean hit him. The blow should have gone in low, doubling the other man up and leaving him wide open. Instead, the side of his hand came down unerringly, like an iron bar, on Sean's wrist, deflecting it. In another second his other hand would have come up for Sean's throat. But the Irishman had been in a fight or two himself. He recovered his balance, stepped sideways, and was back out of reach. With a lightning movement he switched his glass tankard to his right hand and smashed it against the wall, retaining a grip on its handle. He advanced into the toilet's narrow entrance. "Right, mate," he whispered.

The other man retreated. He might have done a course in unarmed combat but now, in that restricted space, he seemed mesmerized by the threat of the tankard's handle, its jagged shards of razor-sharp glass glinting in the dim overhead light.

Sean lunged at him playfully, and continued to advance.

The man's foot came up, kicking for the Irishman's right elbow. Sean was ready for it, but only just. For a bruiser, the man was surprisingly fast. Sean's hand, which should have caught his ankle and thrown him up and back, found only air. But the man was against the back wall of the toilet now, and desperate. Abandoning all science he launched himself, head down, fists flailing. Sean let him come. He'd played long enough. The man's head hit his belly, bored sickeningly in. Sean grunted. Bent forward. Slashed—with the jagged tankard at the man's neck.

He stepped quickly back. The blood that gouted didn't touch him. It pumped, fast and bright, on cracked tiles and stained porcelain. The man fell forward on his face. He didn't move.

When the blood had stopped Sean turned him carefully over. His throat was cut in a jagged line from windpipe to ear, and he was quite dead. Prompted by sheer habit, Sean fastidiously removed his wallet from his anorak pocket. Then he wiped his fingers clean on the man's blue jersey and moved away, under the light. The wallet contained four pound notes. It also contained the warrant card of a Detective Constable David Wilson. And, carried loose in the front pocket, a glossy three-by-five colour photograph.

Up to that moment Sean had acted entirely out of a life-time's conditioning. Now, suddenly, as he stared down at the photograph, the enormity of the night's events came home to him. He had killed a copper. He didn't have to guess at Liam's reaction. More than that, he had killed a copper who carried in his wallet an excellent colour photograph of Sean O'Sullivan, dressed in a blue boiler suit, at the wheel of a taxi, staring out, with half of another figure—the back and one arm—up the left-hand side. The picture was crooked, but mirror sharp.

As in a speeded-up newsreel, past events flickered across the screen of Sean's memory. The Iron Lady being dragged from the car. The policeman emerging out of the smoke at a run. The harsh stutter of Farrell's automatic. The policeman falling. The fan of the bullets moving on. Screams. A tourist going down, and then another. And in the grasp of one of them—the newsreel slowing now, moving in, stopping—a small, expensive-looking camera.

The bastards. They'd had a picture of him all along. That artist's impression had been so much bullshit.

He glanced over his shoulder. Now, too late, he was thinking clearly. He'd been out of the pub for maybe three minutes. He could be interrupted at any moment. Quickly he removed the money, wiped the wallet carefully on his sleeve, then flung it, photograph and all, on the ground beside the body. Then he backed away and went quietly out into the street. A couple was passing, but they were absorbed in each other and didn't even glance in his direction. He walked to the corner, took a right, and then a left. The bitter November wind gusted round his legs. He went on, still not hurrying.

After nearly a mile he stopped by the high corrugated iron wall of a building site. He was still carrying the handle of the broken beer mug. He wiped it meticulously on his handkerchief, then tossed it over the wall. From the sound, it fell on loose earth on the other side. But it was clean now, and he'd touched nothing else. Plenty of things in the pub itself, of course, but so had fifty other people. He'd have to take a chance on that. The thing was, there must be no connection between the dead copper and himself. Just a man found dead, and robbed, in a pub toilet. The police must not, must not, *must not*, ever get the idea that Sean O'Sullivan had been near the place. If they did they'd put two and two together, and then—

Christ. The door out. The pub door out to the toilet. Apart from the copper, and the man who would find him, he'd been the last one to use it. His flesh crept. The knob—his prints would be all over it . . . Then he relaxed. The door had opened outwards on a spring. He'd been playing drunk, with his glass in his hand, and he'd simply leaned against it. Luck was on his side. He was all right. All of them, Liam, Maura, even Farrell, they were all right.

He walked on. He never even heard the siren of the police car that was called to the Brewer's Arms some ten minutes later. When he finally got back to the flat there was no use pretending he'd kept his promise and just gone round the block. He'd been away for nearly three hours, and there was drink on his breath. So he confessed to a pub, not the one he had been in, and Liam bawled him out, and he replied resentfully that he'd only had a couple, and he hadn't fallen down dead drunk or got himself caught in a punch-up, so where was the harm?

The truth he kept to himself. And by the morning it seemed more like a dream, a waking nightmare, something that could never really have happened. So that when Farrell arrived that night and brought with him a copy of the Colchester *Evening Gazette* full of the brutal murder of a young police officer, it required no acting ability whatsoever for him to meet Liam's suspicions with an air of the most total innocence. He *was* innocent. He didn't go round murdering police officers for no good reason. Someone else had done it. They must have.

17

At the meeting of Ministers that Monday morning—the day before the deadline—it was decided immediately to announce the withdrawal of another thousand British soldiers from Northern Ireland. This, it was thought, would sweeten the pill of the further delay in the talks that Mr Whitelaw's latest demand had been designed to produce. The withdrawal would still leave nearly eleven thousand troops there, which the Defence Secretary said would be sufficient. The Commons wouldn't like it, but to be told later that talks had already taken place would displease them even more.

The Commons did not like it. The row it produced delayed the start of the second-reading debate on yet another Housing Bill by more than an hour. An Ulster Unionist MP succeeded in tabling a private notice question to the Secretary of State for Defence, asking if he would make a statement to the House to explain the reason why the government should withdraw troops at a time when terrorists of the Provisional IRA were still holding the Prime Minister hostage.

The Defence Secretary, John Nott, remained his precise and equable self but adopted his sternest manner. He told the packed green benches that there was no connection between the government's decision and the fact that terrorists were holding the Prime Minister. He rode through storms of protest, some of it from his own backbenches, to point out that the level of violence in Northern Ireland had declined and was continuing to decline. These men simply were not needed. They could be of much greater use elsewhere. The government had important responsibilities to NATO, and these troops could perform a much more useful service in Europe than in Ulster.

The Ulster Unionist was bristling on his feet as soon as the Defence Secretary sat down.

"Even if what the Secretary of State says is true, doesn't he think this is a singularly inept time to pull out troops? Doesn't he think the

Provisional IRA will see it as an act of weakness? Isn't the Secretary of State giving in to the terrorists?"

The House broke into a conflict of sounds. There were cries of approval for the questioner from other Ulster Unionists and from some backbench Tories, and roars of "no" from loyal government supporters. That was the word the Defence Secretary used with a stern determination when he returned resolutely to the despatch box.

"No. There is no further need for these troops in Northern Ireland. They have other defence commitments to carry out to our allies. Moreover, I must tell the House that I hope, in the near future, that I shall be able to withdraw more troops from the province. As the Royal Ulster Constabulary assume the full policing role, as they have virtually done now, and if the level of violence continues to decline, the need for army personnel will also decline."

Another Ulsterman was on his feet.

"Can't the Defence Secretary understand that loyal subjects of the Queen in Ulster are outraged at the foul acts of terrorism that have murdered innocent people in this country and led to the abduction of the Prime Minister? Let me tell the Right Honourable Gentleman that Ulster Protestants can scarcely control their anger; that it would not be surprising if some of them sought revenge out of loyalty to the United Kingdom. This is the potentially explosive situation in which he chooses to pull out British soldiers. Is he mad?"

The MP had spoken against a murmuring rising almost to a roar as he mentioned revenge. The Defence Secretary got to his feet again and firmly gripped the sides of the despatch box, as his voice rose sternly but calmly above the hubbub.

"The Honourable Member does not help when he talks of revenge," he said. "I have to tell him that such remarks are irresponsible in the extreme." The rising "hear, hears" told him that, even if it was worried and doubtful, most of the House was with him. "Such words can only inflame an already dangerous situation. And any retaliatory acts by Protestant extremists would directly endanger the life of the Prime Minister."

The towering, burly figure of Ian Paisley rose from the backbenches.

"Will the Right Honourable Gentleman," he thundered, "give this House an assurance that there have been no talks of any kind with the terrorists of the Provisional IRA who are holding the British Prime Minister a prisoner?"

The Defence Secretary hesitated, glanced at Mr Whitelaw on the bench beside him. There were cries of "Answer . . . answer . . ." Mr Whitelaw nodded.

The Defence Secretary continued: "I can give the Honourable Gentleman the assurance for which he asks. There have been no talks with the IRA."

Before the Speaker had even called him for the customary supplementary question, Mr Paisley had lumbered to his feet: "And will there be none? And will there be none?"

"My Right Honourable Friend," the Minister began, "has repeatedly told this House the government will never give in to terrorist threats. But he has quite reasonably asked that the House should not seek to tie his hands . . ."

The House erupted. The Defence Secretary and the Deputy Prime Minister sat side by side on the government front bench patiently waiting for the noise to subside. Mr Whitelaw rolled his eyes to the ceiling and then glanced with weary patience at the Speaker. They exchanged nods. When most of the tumult had died, Mr Whitelaw got to his feet.

"If I might help the House, Mr Speaker," he began. "From time to time in the past governments of both parties have found it necessary to talk with the Provisional IRA. The Honourable Member knows that as well as I do. No government could ever commit itself—especially when the life of the Prime Minister is at stake—not to talk to these people. But I repeat," he shouted, "we shall never give in to terrorists."

The sitting continued stormily. At the end of the questioning, Mr Paisley sought, under Standing Order No. 9, an immediate emergency debate. His request was refused by the Speaker, and at last, as Members became seized by the need for at least the appearance of Parliamentary unity in dealing with the crisis, the noise subsided, and the House was able to move on, with a certain sense of unreality, to the business of the day.

When the Home Secretary eventually returned to Downing Street, he found that another communication had been received from the Provisional IRA. The Cabinet Secretary had it waiting for him, and in the loneliness of the Cabinet Room Mr Whitelaw studied the document.

In view of the British Government's blatant delaying tactics in the

commencement of serious negotiations, the Provisional IRA wishes
to make its position clear. On certain demands there is no room for
compromise. These are as follows:

That Her Majesty's Government undertakes to withdraw all
British troops from Northern Irish soil. The withdrawal to be
phased over a period, and to be completed within two years.

That the British Government acknowledges the right of the whole
people of Ireland, acting and voting as a single country, to determine
the future of Ireland. Towards this end it will begin immediate
negotiations with the Government of the Republic to achieve the
reunification of Ireland on a free vote of all its people.

That the political status of all members of the IRA held in prisons
in Northern Ireland be recognized, and that there will be an amnesty
for all such political prisoners.

That, in return for these concessions, the Provisional IRA will
enforce a permanent ceasefire, and the end of all violent actions, and
further undertake that there shall be no discrimination of any kind
against members of the Protestant community in the North.

Finally, to save further misunderstanding, the Provisional IRA
demand an immediate response as to whether the above conditions
are acceptable. These are a starting point. No further negotiations
are possible without them.

Mr Whitelaw put the paper down on the long Cabinet table. It was
impossible. He could never accept such terms: the Cabinet would
never accept them, and neither would Parliament. The first conces-
sion alone would cause immediate assassinations by extremist
Protestant groups, and the Provos would inevitably retaliate. It
would mean civil war. Yet the Provos were twisting his arm. He
wondered if civil war was what they wanted.

Wearily he rang for the Cabinet Secretary. This meant a meeting of
the full Cabinet. The Provos were demanding an immediate reply.
They knew well enough that the demands must prove totally
unacceptable to the British Government, but that they would need
detailed Cabinet discussion nevertheless. And the latest deadline was
less than twenty-four hours away. Yet the Provos had not repeated
their threat to execute the Prime Minister. So presumably they were
willing, as they had been on other occasions, to extend the deadline
further. Nothing else bore thinking about.

Tuesday morning—the twenty-eighth day of the Prime Minister's imprisonment—was one of those damply chilling but dry, grey November days; and on that day routine police work turned a peculiarly brutal and pointless murder into a matter of vital national importance.

The victim was a plainclothes police officer savagely done to death in the gents of a Colchester public house. In common with virtually every other policeman in the country, he had carried with him a colour photograph of one of the men wanted for questioning in connection with the abduction of the Prime Minister. The picture had been obtained from the camera of one of the foreign tourists shot down at the time of the kidnap. Its existence had never been made public. An inadequate artist's impression had been issued instead. The intention had been to lull the subject into a false sense of security. Whatever disadvantages there might have been in this, senior officers in charge of the case thought they were outweighed by the possible advantages.

Now, on Tuesday morning, routine examination of the photograph carried in the dead man's wallet revealed the recent prints of a thumb and two fingers not his own. Routine checking with Scotland Yard's data bank established that these prints were identical with those found on the steering wheel of the taxi used in the Prime Minister's abduction. The man, it seemed, had placed his own fingerprints upon his own picture.

Superintendent Whitaker received this information in his Scotland Yard office about half an hour after midday. He acted promptly. His instinct told him that for Colchester to crop up twice in the case was too much of a coincidence. Briefly, he discussed again with Sergeant Trew the visit to Colchester barracks, exchanged views with his own Special Branch Commander and then with the Commander of the Anti-Terrorist Squad, who had shared with him much of the burden of the last month's investigations. Then, with all the authority of the man whom the Home Secretary had asked to be in charge of the case, Arthur Whitaker gave instructions that Sergeant Patrick Farrell of the Royal Corps of Signals, Permanent Staff Instructor to the Territorial Army, and at present stationed at Colchester, should be found and kept under close observation. Once located by the police he wasn't to be allowed out of their sight. This he argued was better, at this stage, than inventing a reason for detaining the man. If he was involved—and by now Whitaker's hunch suggested he was—then there was also the chance that he might lead them to the others and to the Prime Minister. Immediate interrogation, and he'd probably clam up like O'Donovan. In any event, Whitaker did not consider the Provos' latest deadline, due to expire in a few hours, especially significant. With the government continuing to pull out troops, and secret contacts being made, he believed the IRA had nothing to lose by keeping the Prime Minister alive, and everything to gain. Moreover, he was determined—in the interests of the Prime Minister's own safety, apart from his own personal predilections—that the discovery of the terrorists' hideout should be handled calmly and systematically.

At two o'clock he set out for Colchester with Sergeant Trew in a fast car.

About the same time, Sergeant Farrell took the Land Rover that he was allocated as a PSI to the Territorials and gave himself a little drive round the lanes of Constable country. It had been Grady's instructions that he wasn't to remain in camp but was to be mobile until he called to collect them at 3.30. The previous night Grady had finally let him in on the Provisional Army Council's plan. Sean and Maura, he explained, did not know of it, but they were moving out the following afternoon, and they were not taking the Iron Lady with them.

When Farrell drove to Abbey Field he parked immediately below D Block. The wall hid the vehicle from the access road, but even if it were noticed he reckoned an army Land Rover was not going to arouse curiosity. He went upstairs. He felt excited, a little afraid, and strangely unreal, like an actor in a play.

The time was exactly 3.30. The deadline had already passed, but Grady couldn't help that. Once they were well away from Colchester he needed darkness if their escape was to be even remotely possible.

At breakfast that morning he'd announced his intention, or those parts of it he calculated would satisfy Maura in her present edgy state.

"We're getting out," he said. "The Brits have got the wind up. They're withdrawing troops as fast as they can. They'll be a laughing stock if they go back on it now—especially since they've pretended all along that the withdrawals have got nothing to do with us. So we're getting out. This is entirely my responsibility. But I reckon we're running out of luck. Always leave a way out—remember? And the police roaming round here on Sunday—they just about saw the last of our nine lives. Next time they'll make a proper job of it. And now with that CID man dead, they'll be swarming all over the place in no time."

The death of the copper was, for him, an unexpected bonus. He didn't believe for a moment that O'Sullivan had had nothing to do with it, and neither, he guessed, did Maura. The fact that police were not thick on the ground already suggested that somehow the oaf had got away with it. But it was a good point in the present argument.

Maura wasn't completely convinced. He hadn't thought she would be. From where she stood it must look like a retreat just when total victory was within their grasp. But she wanted out probably more than any of them. So, as he'd expected, she stifled her doubts. The responsibility, anyway, was his. He was the leader.

Since breakfast he'd kept them busy. He'd carefully explained the stages of their getaway. First of all there was the chair. He set Sean to screwing it to the floor of the living room with the brackets Farrell had provided. For Maura there was the wig for her to do her best with—remembering that all their lives might depend on just how good that best would be. Then there was his own visit to the Iron Lady.

He handed her a pad of writing paper and a ballpoint pen.

"I want you to write to William Whitelaw," he said. "I want you to instruct him to tell the Cabinet to accede to all our demands. They're dragging their feet. But they will listen to you."

Mrs Thatcher looked up at him. He'd grown used to her appearance by now, so that he scarcely saw it. But the directness of her gaze still troubled him.

"And what are those demands?" she commanded.

"Does it matter?"

She smiled quietly. "I suppose not. At least you're frank about it."

"Do you know how long you've been here?" he asked.

"Twenty-eight days. Four weeks exactly. Today is Tuesday."

He shouldn't have been surprised, but he was. He looked round in the bright lamplight for marks on the wall, something to number the passing of the days. There were none. She must have recorded them mentally, perhaps counting the breakfasts, committing them to memory. The discipline astonished him.

"I shall ask you once again. Will you write that letter?"

"It would make no difference. My colleagues know my views. The government would never agree."

"Then why not write it?"

"I cannot, and will not, give in to terrorism. Nor will my government."

He bowed stiffly. "Thank you, Prime Minister."

Outside the room he clicked off the small cassette recorder in his pocket. The Army Council would like that. It was the stuff of true martyrdom.

By the time Farrell arrived they were almost ready. Maura retired to her bedroom. She'd lost weight in the last four weeks, which made the Prime Minister's blouse and expensive coat and skirt an even looser fit. They weren't in a very good state either due to rough handling and the long ride in the back of the Land Rover. But nobody would expect her to be bandbox fresh after four weeks of captivity.

Maura looked at herself in the mirror. Her face was all wrong. But the wig wasn't bad and, if the police ever did catch up with them, it should be enough to make the coppers think she was Mrs Thatcher. And that would hold them at bay. But it was only a last resort. With any luck at all they'd make it to the rendezvous, the boat would take them off, and the pretence of still having the Iron Lady with them as a hostage would never be needed.

She helped Sean take their prisoner through to the sitting room and tie her securely down to the chair.

"You won't be here for long," she told her. "Only a few more hours, till we're safely away. Then the authorities will be told where you are."

The Prime Minister didn't answer. She stared up coldly. Maura knew she didn't believe her.

Colchester central police station had set up a special operations room devoted to the murder of Detective Constable David Wilson. Now it also had the task of discovering the Prime Minister. Sergeant Patrick Farrell had disappeared. He wasn't in his own office, and his Land Rover was missing. He might be anywhere.

The very mention of a Land Rover made Whitaker feel uneasy. The terrible possibility occurred to him that the events of four weeks ago might be repeating themselves. Supposing the terrorists had smelt danger. After all, one of their number had killed a man. Last time he had got to their base too late. This time, he felt he was just a step ahead of them. All roads in the vicinity of the town were being watched.

Maps were spread out, covering a fifty-mile radius, marked with isolated houses, derelict buildings, barns, anywhere that might be a hideout. They had all been checked already. Now they had to be checked again. There were hundreds of them.

He paced the room, dodging police clerks hurrying to and fro with messages, filling the place with pungent tobacco smoke. Although by rank he was the junior, his special commission from the Home Secretary meant that Whitaker shared the responsibility for the whole operation with the local Detective Chief Superintendent and the Commander of the Anti-Terrorist Squad, C.13. He was satisfied that everything possible was being done. The Army was on the spot, helicopters were up, the SAS were standing by, and additional police were being drafted in from neighbouring counties. Within an hour or so their coverage of the area would reach saturation point. But what if the birds had already flown? The thought nagged at him.

Sergeant Trew sat quietly in the midst of all the frantic activity. He was not a man to show the shame he felt at his failure to spot Sergeant Farrell as a villain. Neither did he make excuses. He knew, however, that he had a lot to make up for.

The next time Superintendent Whitaker passed within reasonable earshot, Trew spoke to him.

"I feel a bit spare here, sir. At least if we were out in a car we'd be doing something. And there'd always be the radio, in case you were needed."

Whitaker checked in mid-stride. And for the first time that day he smiled.

The Prime Minister's chair was secured to the floor in the middle of the room. They checked the ropes tying her, then pushed the table and the other chairs back against the wall, well out of reach. They hadn't gagged her. With the place shut up and boarded up, she was unlikely to be heard however much she screamed ... She was wearing only her shift and, at Maura's suggestion, they left her both the gas heater and the lamp. Outside the day was bitter. As far as Sean was concerned their prisoner could freeze to death, but he didn't argue. He was so glad to be getting out that he'd have agreed to anything.

Grady was down in the Land Rover making last-minute arrangements with Farrell. As Maura and Sean went down to them a helicopter clattered by. Maura looked up curiously, but it was out of sight behind the long roofs of the married quarters and its sound quickly faded. A good thing too, she thought suddenly; even the most bored helicopter pilot might have come back for a second look if he imagined he'd seen Mrs Thatcher climbing into a Land Rover.

Grady got down. "I'll just have one last look round," he said.

The chill damp of the November day was already sputtering into a drizzle, and greying over into dusk. Maura took off the wig and waited for him by the shelter of the wall. She wanted him in the Land Rover ahead of her. The person in the middle had the gear lever to contend with, and the skirt she was wearing was narrow. Sean was already in the back of the vehicle. Grady had decided that, without the wig, it was safe for her to travel in the front with him and Farrell. There, if her disguise were needed, she'd be where she could be seen.

Grady was upstairs a long time. She wondered what had gone wrong, if she'd forgotten something. But when he finally appeared he seemed satisfied. He checked his army uniform, then got into the Land Rover without a word and she squeezed up beside him.

Farrell drove out into the access road.

"And so we say farewell to romantic Abbey Field," he drawled. Then he glanced across at her. "I bet you never thought it would end like this."

She hadn't. She had always expected it to be more dramatic. A triumphant safe conduct, television cameras, crowds, something like that. But there was an edge to Farrell's question she didn't like.

"End like what?" she asked.

It was Grady who answered her.

"I reckon the sergeant was looking for death or glory," he said smoothly.

Farrell kept his eyes on the road. Suddenly the thinness of Grady's story came home to her. If they were going to a rendezvous, how had it been arranged?

"End like what?" she repeated angrily.

They were waiting at the entrance to the main road. Nobody spoke. Finally, as he pulled out into the line of traffic, Farrell said, "What the hell? She's got to know sometime, hasn't she?"

"Know what? Know what, for God's sake?"

Farrell leaned forward, turned on the sidelights. "Shall I tell her, Grady, or will you?"

"You bastard," Grady seethed between his teeth. "You were always out to make trouble—right from the start. Thought it should have been your bloody show." He turned to Maura. "I wanted to save your feelings, love. Fact is, there never was a chance the Brits would give in. All their troops out of Ireland, reunification? Don't make me laugh. They'd stall and they'd stall. And then, sooner or later, they'd find us."

"So?" She was trying desperately to understand. "So why the kidnap? Why did we go to all this trouble?"

"Public relations. We gave them every chance, didn't we? The whole world could see it. Four full weeks, just to come to the negotiating table. And what happened? Exactly what we knew would happen—bloody damn all. We set them deadlines and they ignored the lot. They had to. They couldn't be seen to negotiate with the likes of us. But nobody can say we didn't warn them. Four weeks, Maura. And not a bloody thing. So it's on their own heads, so it is."

Of all he had said only four words stuck in her mind. They were like an accusation.

"On their own heads, Liam? What's on their own heads?"

"Clever girl like you, Maura—I'm surprised you haven't worked that out. I've taped a bomb to Herself's chair. Not a big one, but enough. She's got an hour. Now that's decent, that's fair."

Maura took a deep breath, steadied herself, but made no reply. There weren't any words—no words adequate for the sense of personal betrayal she felt. She'd trusted him. But for all her trust she had been told nothing. Neither Liam nor anyone had trusted her.

They were travelling slowly, the traffic heavy around them. The drizzle had now settled in, and the windscreen wipers swung lazily.

"This whole escape, then? The lonely cove, the boat waiting. It was planned all along?"

"All along, Maura. She had to die. Now I really am surprised you never saw that."

She never had. She still didn't. She had believed in their purpose, and he'd betrayed her.

"But why?" she asked. "What good will it do?"

"For us Provos, all the good in the world. We're fair, we're reasonable, we keep our word. And now we're going to be the victims of the biggest Proddie backlash in the North you've ever seen. The UDA, the UVF and the Ulster Freedom Fighters—why they'll all be out on the streets. And can't you just hear that man Tyrie? And he'll drive the Ulster Catholics right into our arms. The Irish-Americans too. They won't like Herself's execution, but they'll like the Protestant killings that follow even less. By the time all this dies down, Maura, in maybe three or four months, or more, we'll—"

She could stand no more. It was no longer just the Iron Lady—he was talking of the deaths of hundreds. And for what? So that Ireland might be free? So that her brother Michael might be avenged? No. No, it was so that men like Liam and Sean and Farrell could have a licence to maim and to kill . . .

She fumbled with the door catch. Grady saw too late what she was doing and tried to stop her. The door swung open and she fell. Instinctively Grady reached for the UZI and pointed it after her. Farrell struck at his arm, and already she was gone, left behind, out of sight. The two men struggled as Grady tried to bring the UZI round to send a burst of fire after her. Farrell pulled fiercely at Grady's arm. The Land Rover lurched wildly, mounted the pavement. The car behind them blasted its horn.

Maura was on her elbows and knees in the gutter. She had fallen hard, smashing one wrist, and the hand hung limply. She stared at it, the pain amazing her. She got to her feet. The rain was now falling quite heavily. The street was lined with tidy semi-detached houses. She never had discovered exactly where they were going. Away to her right the Land Rover had left the line of traffic and was careering along the grass-bordered pavement. It struck a pillar box and then a garden wall. Veering back, it mounted a small bank surrounding an ornamental tree and turned over. Its engine roared and its rear wheels continued to spin. Cars in the roadway skidded to a halt.

Maura staggered across the pavement. Her leg was bleeding badly. As she went up the garden path to the nearest house the Land Rover exploded into flame. Petrol spread across the grass, flaring as it went. Motorists who had got out of their cars retreated in panic. Suddenly, close overhead, was the deafening clatter of a helicopter.

By the time Maura reached the front door of the house it had already been opened. A man in his shirt sleeves stared at her. In spite of the pain, she drew herself stiffly upright. She knew, as a nurse, that if you wanted something done in a hurry, then you had to remain calm and speak slowly and clearly.

"May I use your telephone, please?" she said. "If we're not quick there is going to be the most terrible accident."

217

The man, looking past her, thought she was crazy. The accident had already happened.

Whitaker and Trew received the all-cars message as they were cruising in the residential streets between the Maldon Road and the London Road, looking for a Land Rover, about two miles from Abbey Field. With siren shrilling, blue lamp flashing and headlights full up, plus the skill and local knowledge of the driver, they arrived at D Block scarcely four minutes later. Another patrol car was ahead of them. They raced up the stairs and into a flat stinking of stale humanity. They passed a kitchen piled with bulging plastic rubbish bags.

In the small room lit with a glaring gas lamp, they found a woman, for all her humiliations, still unmistakably the Prime Minister. They checked themselves in the doorway. Mrs Thatcher was tied securely to a wood-and-canvas garden chair, which was screwed to the floor. A tall, uniformed policeman, his face deathly pale, was staring at her. There were smudges round her eyes, but she looked astonishingly calm.

"Ah. Thank goodness you've come. Someone in authority at last. I keep telling this young man the thing stopped ticking at least ten minutes ago. He doesn't seem to believe me."

With the sound of the gas lamp, Whitaker wondered she could have heard anything. The constable stiffened at the sight of the superintendent's warrant card.

"Constable Dawson, sir. The bomb squad's on its way, sir. Didn't want to risk the Prime Minister's—"

Trew pushed past him, Whitaker at his shoulder. The sergeant trod very softly as he approached the Prime Minister, then squatted down beside her. Whitaker motioned the uniformed constable out of the room and down the stairs. Then he rejoined Trew. The Prime Minister sat quite still, watching them.

The bomb was attached to a chair leg. It consisted of a fist-size lump of *plastique*, with its detonator wired to a torch battery via a cheap watch. The glass of the watch had been removed and an insulated terminal taped to its face. When the watch's minute hand came round to touch this terminal the circuit would be completed and the bomb would explode.

The hand still had a good ten minutes to go. Whitaker listened and watched attentively. The Prime Minister appeared to be right. The thing seemed to have stopped. Not, he reflected, that a woman in her position would be likely to be wrong in such a matter.

The bomb was simple. Every single one of its parts was visible. Whether, if the watch had not stopped, the minute hand would have reached the terminal before he got there, Whitaker would never know. The thought was not one to make him pleased with his conduct of the case.

Trew reached out and delicately eased the terminal away from the face. When it was clear he gave a sharp jerk, ripping its soldered end off the battery. It was now impossible for the bomb to detonate. And Whitaker found it no longer of the slightest consequence whether he was pleased with himself or not.

From outside, down in the yard, there were sounds of other cars arriving, doors slamming. Trew got out his silver-bladed pocket knife and cut the tape holding the watch to the *plastique*. He shook the watch and it started ticking again. He sat back on his heels and grinned foolishly up at Whitaker.

"Should we send it back to the makers, sir?"

The Prime Minister was not amused.

"When you've finished playing games, young man, I'd be grateful if you'd untie me."